Political Strategies
for Industrial Order

JOHN ZYSMAN

Political Strategies for Industrial Order

State, Market, and Industry in France

UNIVERSITY OF CALIFORNIA PRESS
Berkeley
Los Angeles
London

University of California Press
Berkeley and Los Angeles, California
University of California Press, Ltd.
London, England
Copyright © 1977 by
The Regents of the University of California
ISBN 0-520-02889-9
Library of Congress Catalog Card Number: 74-22976
Printed in the United States of America

Contents

Contents

Preface

When I was a graduate student it struck me that constantly evolving technology was a basic feature of industrial society. So for my dissertation I set forth to study the impact of technology on social organization. As I proceeded it became evident that technology is not some autonomous process pushing social relations along, but that technical innovation is one solution to certain problems. In our western market economies one might, in fact, consider innovation as a strategic response of the firm to its economic and political environment. Yet, once we view innovation as a strategic choice of an organization or individual, then clearly other strategies and other choices that do not involve technological development are possible. If product innovation is a response to market competition, an alternative is political action to control the market and limit competition. While Danish farmers in the 19th century responded to the flood of cheap American grain with the agricultural innovation of dairy and pig farming, feeding cheap imported grain to cows and pigs and then selling those animals as products, the German landowners answered with tariff walls that allowed them to preserve their social organization. Large-scale, plantation-style farming that underlay their political and social authority was incompatible with the Danish innovation of dairy farming. In that case an innovation that meant unwanted social changes was simply suppressed politically.

Technological possibilities involve costs, and those who would benefit from change must bear those costs or impose them on others. Political conflict over which opportunities will be taken and which will bear the costs, then, channels the direction of technological evolution and the character of the social response. Because most technological innovation, as distinct from scientific discovery, occurs within firms, my study rapidly became an examination of the politics of industrial activity, and more precisely of the relations between business and the state. Furthermore, since the market for electronic goods (electronics provided a focus for much of the research) is international, I was forced to consider the place of a national industry in the international economy and the role of the nation-state as the mediator between domestic and international markets. My efforts, then, expanded as the project moved from graduate paper to dissertation to book. Three themes are developed in the book: the links between technological change and social development: the relations between political and economic activity, specifically the organizational and economic consequences of particular relations between business and the state; and the role of the nation-state in mediating the position of the national economy in a global economic order.

The research for this book required the active encouragement, cooperation, and support of a multitude of individuals and institutions in France and the United States. Without the assistance of nearly all of them, it would have been difficult if not impossible to complete this project. Executives and civil servants alike gave generously of their time. They are simply too numerous to mention individually. However, I owe a particular debt to Mr. Olivier de Nervaux and Mr. Jacques Sevin of the Delegation Generale à la Recherche Scientifique et Technique who both encouraged my research and helped arrange a view from within the French system. Clearly the interpretation of the materials and conversation that formed this research are my own as are any errors of commission or omission. In all likelihood many who have assisted me so generously will vigorously take exception to my conclusions.

A project without material support remains a dream. Six different organizations supported this research during one phase or another. They are the Council for European Studies, the National Institute for Mental Health Doctoral Fellowship Program, the Delegation Generale à la Recherche Scientifique et Technique, the Carnegie Endowment for International Peace, the National Science Foundation, and the Institute of International Studies in Berkeley. I can only hope some part of their expectations is fulfilled.

Preparing a manuscript requires the personal support and assistance of many. Peter Gourevitch's always insightful remarks helped me select the lines along which to change a dissertation into a book. David Laitin, Ezra Suleiman, Jan Turĉan, and Suzanne Berger read the manuscript and pointed out the weaknesses that still remained. Christine Schofer helped edit the manuscript and prepare the footnotes. Bojana Ristich at the Institute of International Studies, who managed the typing and preparation of the manuscript, was patient and understanding throughout what is a long and tedious process, and Nadine Zelinski helped with the typing.

I owe a particular debt to Grant Barnes and Gene Tanke of the University of California Press. Grant took the risk that I would be able to transform a promising dissertation into a book. Gene copy-edited the manuscript, helping me in no small way to write about society in English. It was a real pleasure to work with them, a pleasure of which I'm sure few authors can boast.

A book which begins as a dissertation owes a particular set of debts, for one learns not only the answer to a question, but what a question is, how it can be asked, and what constitutes an answer. Professors Eugene Skolnikoff and Harvey Sapolsky gave willingly of their time and assistance. Jan and Maja Turĉan helped me to understand that national differences are not simply ones of detail, but of underlying equilibrium, logic, and dynamic. They helped me learn, as well, how to penetrate the veil of another culture, and what some of those costs can be. To Suzanne Berger I owe a debt that has been accumulating over the years. She began helping me understand the subtle process of asking and answering questions long before graduate school, let alone before a dissertation or book were issues at all. From the conception of this work her encouragement and assistance was essential, and her patience with my gropings allowed me to identify what it was I was studying. I only hope this work is some reward for those efforts.

I

Culture Competition and Organization: Two Hypotheses

1
Industrial Politics and Economic Activity

In the 1960's the French state attempted to secure the future of a national electronics industry, which was considered essential to the nation but was threatened by intense international competition. The success of that effort rested ultimately on the ability of French firms to compete at home and abroad. These firms, however, were burdened with organizational structures and business practices suited to an earlier era, with a more stable and protected environment, and ill-equipped to compete in a science-based, innovation-centered industry such as electronics. Traditional practice in French industry was squarely at odds with the organizational structures and procedures required for the competitive development and production of the technologies these firms sold. The value which these firms put on the industrial efficiency required for market competition determined their response to technology's constraints on effective organization, and efficiency was not prized by those who could find shelter from competition under the state's protective umbrella. Moreover, once the privileged were under the umbrella, the ongoing tasks of dealing with the state further supported traditional practices. It is hardly surprising that in France, where the state has long insulated firms from the market while promoting industries considered important to government goals, the politics of protection and subsidy would be as important to the organization and behavior of the firm as the logic of markets, competition, and efficiency.

State intervention in the electronics industry was prompted by strategic as well as economic purposes. Because electronics forms an integral part of most large-scale technological systems, be they military or civilian, the state was prepared to subsidize heavily firms manufacturing critical

3

products. Yet despite massive subsidies, it could not effectively protect the national market. Consequently, the analysis of this industry, particularly when contrasted with other industries where similar policies proved more successful, suggests the limits on a government's ability to shape the growth of a domestic industry that forms an integral part of an international marketplace. The story of French electronics—both the relations of the state to the industry and the internal transformation of the firms—must in fact be considered as part of the postwar effort of the French state to promote economic growth and carve out a protected reserve for French firms in the wilderness of international competition.

Before recent and rapid growth, and even in spite of it, France has been characterized as a society resistant to change, its economy stagnant and its political life stalemated. Until the sudden burst of postwar economic growth led the British and Japanese, among others, to review French policy practices in the hope that some could be borrowed, most analysts looked for explanations of the stagnation. Yet, as Peter Gourevitch succinctly notes, it is a long way from Richelieu to the present, and quite evidently France does change, often quite rapidly. The issue, at any rate, would seem to be why supposed obstacles proved frail or were overcome, and whether the present configuration of political possibility and economic opportunity is stable and can continue. Certainly, no single economic or technical explanation will suffice to explain either the recent pace of French growth or its stops and starts in the past, as Kindleberger convincingly demonstrates.[1] For example, arguments that a lack of coal has slowed French growth can easily be reversed to contend that the discovery of coal was slow because growth was inadequate.[2] Similarly, inadequate capital formation or the export of capital, two other causes often cited for lagging French development, could just as easily result from a hesitancy to seize available ones. For those who attribute growth to entrepreneurial initiative, the family firm in France and the social values it embodies is offered as the villain of the piece.[3] Supposedly irrational fears that bank financing would endanger family control were thought to have restricted investments to a firm's internally generated funds. Yet this examination of electronics firms suggests that financing the expansion of a small company by bank credits in France today, if it is possible at all, does pose real difficulties and dangers that would not be encountered in the United States. Medium and long-term credits are inordinately difficult to obtain, and rolling over short-term credits for long-term needs is quite risky. If bank refinancing is ever denied, the firm is in immediate danger, and the month-to-month struggle to continue credit which often ensues inevitably gives the banks the opportunity to influence if not to supervise business expansion. Thus hesitancy to accept outside finance can be viewed as a rational reaction to the structure of French banking and financial markets, and cannot so simply be attributed to social attitudes and values.

Nonetheless, whether or not the family firm initially inhibited growth, it certainly did not prevent rapid industrialization once it was underway. In electronics, small firms were finally shoved aside or muscled into mergers. One must ask, therefore, why more aggressive entrepreneurs in the nineteenth century did not emerge to make their fortune and push aside the timid. One explanation, of course, would be that the liberal social values of the bourgeoisie were so engrained in all members that none would risk the dangers of aggressive business tactics. Certainly, social pressures against "predatory" actions—active, expansive policies that threatened other businessmen—have been reported, and the virtues of market competition were certainly never widely espoused. Yet, for example, a new breed of British entrepreneurs recently arose in both banking and industry using tactics that were anathema to the "statesmen" of English business. The newcomers' rapid success, however, forced the more traditional to change their ways.[4] Similarly, amongst the ambitious sons of the bourgeoisie there must certainly have been some who would have been willing to bear the opprobrium of their peers for the material rewards of an expanding business.

Perhaps such a strategy of business conquest was not possible, or at least not so simple, and those already entrenched in the market possessed powerful instruments for discouraging new competitors. For example, small shopkeepers in France have fought the rise of supermarkets with an ever-changing array of weapons. At one time, differential taxes that penalized large turnovers handicapped supermarkets and department stores, and even now the state's acquiescence in the ongoing tax fraud of small shops, which dramatically understate their receipts for tax purposes, is vital to the survival of these operations. Not so long ago, small shopkeepers organized their suppliers to deny produce to large competitors, a practice overturned by the government. More recently, they have won the right to restrict supermarket construction with legislation requiring the approval of local commercial interests before building permits can be granted, although the supermarkets have often built whether granted the permits or not. Building without permits, though, requires the tacit toleration of these violations by the Finance Ministry charged with enforcing them, and without a government commitment to rapid growth these sanctions could have proved fatal to the supermarkets. As it is, the shopkeepers have not been swept aside by potentially more efficient supermarkets.[5]

In the stock market, to select a more modern arena, the mere threat of sanction appears to affect share prices. For example, Granick describes a recent case of a firm girding for active expansion by internal rationalization and aggressive takeovers that forced newly acquired companies to fit a mold defined by the parent company.[6] In America such actions would be likely to result in rising stock values, reflecting anticipation of the increased profits of more efficient and aggressive operation; but in France the stock value plummeted, suggesting that investors feared that existing firms possessed instruments to discipline such upstarts. Cartels, which became a widespread and permanent part of French business life after 1900, could be seen as formal instruments of discipline, though they were by no means entirely successful when left to their own devices. One might argue, in fact, that cartels in France, as in Germany and later in Japan, were effective when market allocations could be enforced by some grant of authority from the state.[7] The exclusion of foreign competition was an essential prerequisite for the cartelization of business in France, and perhaps in any country. Government action on tariffs, though, required a political alliance on tariff matters with agricultural interests.[8] It would appear, then, that the social restraints on economic growth required and received political support, and would cease to be restraints without such support.

Thus, one can argue that the political deal which established the Third Republic and preserved the social balance of the time must be part of any explanation of the pattern and character of France's economic growth in the last half of the nineteenth century. That deal, so brilliantly dissected by Stanley Hoffmann,[9] made the bourgeoisie and the peasantry the twin pillars of the new regime and preserved the interests of both at the price of more rapid growth. "The celebrated freezing of the capitalist spirit, which may have kept France behind in the world race, had at least domestic advantages from the viewpoint of the all important equilibrium . . . the timidity of entrepreneurial drives was a prerequisite for the conciliation of the interests of the groups included in the consensus."[10] A sudden industrial thrust, then, required the destruction of the particular alliances that characterized the Third Republic. One must therefore account for the political shift that made economic growth possible, not simply describe and analyze the patterns of economic change itself. La Croissance française argues convincingly that improved capital stock, consisting both of innovation and investment in existing but previously unused technologies, account for the pace of postwar growth,[11] a position supported by Kindleberger's analysis of the first years of that period.[12] Why, though, were businessmen suddenly willing or able to make capital investments they had previously shunned? Kindleberger, himself an economist, contends that there is in fact no economic explanation, no shift in factor prices or market opportunities which can account for the change in the behavior of the firms, but rather that a shift in the attitudes and purposes of the state bureaucrats who managed economic recovery, along with the allies they found or created in the business community, altered economic behavior.[13] Stephen Cohen, making the same case, depicts the Planning Commission as an instrument of adult education used by state planners to alter the intentions and perspectives of the business community.[14] The state went further in industries such as electronics and steel, actively intervening in product, price, and merger decisions to influence the industry's organization. Importantly, these planning activities amounted in fact to part of a new relation of the state to the business community and the society at large. The state which had traditionally "expressed, protected, and guaranteed social order"[15] came increasingly to dominate and direct the society. Again, according to Stanley Hoffmann, "what changed French society was a completely new recourse to and considerable extension of a pre-existing machinery as well as society's old habit of dependence on the State. *When the watchdog became a greyhound those who had been holding the leash had to learn to run.*"[16] (My italics.)

Growing power for the bureaucracy has gone hand in hand with industrialization these last years, but fashioning the state machinery into an instrument for active intervention was a political and not a technical problem. The independence and power of the bureacracy during the Gaullist years has simultaneously been reinforced by and has provoked changes in the fashion by which political power is obtained. A career begun inside the bureaucracy could be transplanted onto political soil if the Gaullist party would provide a local constituency. This brought corresponding declines in the power of the local notables, and the habitual avenues for influencing state policy withered.[17] It remains to be seen, of course, whether this practice will endure under Giscard, whose own party is in fact composed of local notables, but who must confront the Gaullist UDR as the largest party in his parliamentary coalition.

Although the executive branch and the bureaucracy won an important measure of independence from the Assemblée Nationale and could pursue a course that the parliament would never have chosen, the continuing weight of peasants, small shopkeepers, and small businessmen in the nation's political and economic life has staked out definite limits on the course industrialization can take. These long-enduring holdovers from a rural and partially industrial France do not have the power to block the current pace of industrialization, but they can affect the terms on which it occurs. The government does not have the power to uproot traditional France by direct assault, but neither does it have the intent, for such action would destroy an important social bulwark against challenges from the left.

The domestic efforts to advance the industrial and modern sectors while preserving politically significant but economically marginal groups are paralleled by policies in the international arena. The agricultural arrangements of the Common Market, the prerequisite for French membership, have served to subsidize the French peasantry, and one might speculate whether the government commitment to industrial growth would have been possible otherwise. The government would have had to support the peasants with resources drawn directly or indirectly from other sectors of the economy, and that most likely would have held back growth. Meanwhile the state has created elaborate programs to establish and protect advanced industries such as electronics. French efforts to make the terms of interdependence favor France had mixed results. The open international economy of the postwar years now appears to be as much a result of American political hegemony as of "natural" economic forces,[18] and French policies may have greater success if the Western world splits into rival trading blocs—certainly not an impossible outcome of current difficulties.

One must wonder, though, whether the conditions that allowed for rapid growth during these last years are not ending. Part of French growth unquestionably derives from a transfer of resources from agriculture to industry;[19] and the resulting population migration has reduced the agricultural population as a percent of the nation while increased industrial production has diminished the percentage contribution of the rural areas to the total national product. Yet these events may have occurred without altering the structure of the agricultural sectors, although the pattern of ownership and farm size have evolved to reflect the techniques used for production. Thus, until now the drain was for the most part on the unemployed or underemployed members of the agricultural community with the result that fewer people were dividing the rural income. Some argue that further transfers from agriculture to industry would require critical changes in rural life, which would be actively, and most probably successfully, resisted.[20] Whether immigrant labor can, in fact, substitute and allow industrialization to continue without thereby creating politically unacceptable demands on the peasants, or whether it will, in turn, generate other problems, is at least unclear.

Similarly, in the industrial sectors, the state has forced the financial merger of many small firms into larger enterprises which are often too unwieldy to manage without a corresponding rationalization of the structure of production. The change in structure and control has unquestionably altered the relations of industry to the state, but there is scant evidence that these mergers have increased productivity. H. Aujac, the director of the BIPE (Bureau d'Information et Prevision Economique) contends in fact that the new organizations' structures will prove a handicap to the firm and an obstacle to continued growth.[21] In electronics, for example, the state's activities, dictated by its strategy of intervention, have encouraged and maintained these bureaucratic rigidities.

Thus, there is at least the possibility that the postwar boom will end, making the period not the starting point of a new pattern of industrialization, but only another phase in the off-again, on-again growth of the past. If so, one might argue that the stop-and-start character of French development has occurred because the compromises required to overcome entrenched groups and allow growth at one moment have resulted in new problems that have finally stymied expansion. That the solutions to problems at any one moment may pose difficulties for the resolution of subsequent issues is, of course, not unique to France, but the continuing presence of peasants, small shopkeepers, and small businessmen may result in compromises that pose serious obstacles to further growth. An aggressive state may, in fact, be able to force continued growth, or the new generation of competitive businessmen may maintain expansion. Yet, clearly, neither is an inevitable or even obvious outcome.

The pace and character of a nation's industrialization, or the development of a particular sector such as electronics, are, then, problems for political as well as economic analysis. Success for a firm will often rest as much on political manipulation of the business environment as on production, marketing, and financial control. In the electronics example presented here, industrial efficiency and political efficacy proved to be alternative and seemingly incompatible strategies. Political activity and economic behavior are, then, inextricably entangled, and while they may often be usefully distinguished and considered separately, they ought not to be conceived as distinct and sovereign realms.

Yet, if this be the case, how does the analyst proceed to examine a problem such as the development of the electronics industry and the firms in it? The political scientist, for the most part, views the businessman as a lobbyist seeking to influence the content of government policy. This political analysis, though, seldom emerges from a consideration of business problems and the tactics for resolving them, and thus does not consider the place of politics in a businessman's overall strategy. The economist, on the other hand, focuses almost exclusively on the businessman as an economic actor seeking to maximize profits by varying his output or the mix of factor inputs and production technologies. The theoretical framework of neo-classical economics tends to push aside considerations of power and social behavior. The firm is seen as a single decision-maker pursuing a clearly defined goal single-mindedly, rationally, with perfect informaiton, and free from outside interference, rather than as a complex organization whose actions may be shaped as much by its organization and political needs as by its economic options.

Power slips into the analysis only when market control by oligopolies or monopolies is considered, and even here the focus remains almost exclusively on the firms that comprise the oligopoly, potential new entrants, and the relationships between them. Market position and the technical characteristics of production and distribution are seen as the determinants of the power of control the behavior of the industry, and not as the product of power and politics in the larger community.

However, in a historical situation, rather than in pure theory, the position of the firm in an industry—or even of the entire industry in the economy—cannot be separated from its political position in the community. Economic power and the right to exercise it must be defended in the political realm, and political power may win economic advantages that are otherwise unreachable. The critical theoretical point is that the economic choices of the firm will reflect its political as well as its economic position. The analytic approaches of the political scientist and the economist may be valuable for the particular range of problems they choose to attack; the difficulty is that many important questions fall into the chasm between them.

In fact, the economy consists of a set of institutions—those directly affecting the production and distribution of goods—jockeying with one another for power and economic advantage to achieve a variety of different purposes. The choices open to these actors are at the same time constrained by political and economic limitations and possibilities. The institutions that comprise such a political economy and provide the focus for this analysis are the state, the firm, organized producer associations, the banks, and organized labor.* Together they constitute the economy's institutional structure, and the strategies, choices, and

*The state consists of both legislative and administrative elements, the making and implementation of rules, although the central theme in this study will be the relations between business and the state bureaucracy. The state, of course, is not a unitary actor, and one can only speak cautiously of *state* policy for this or *state* actions for that because, quite obviously, various branches are often not simply fighting for contradictory policies inside the administration, but actively pursuing contradictory goals in the society. Business is encountered most simply as individual companies pursuing profits either as their most important goals or as a prerequisite for other ends; but equally important in this framework are organized producer associations, which act both as interest groups trying to influence state policy as well as formal cartels that organize the market for one or several products. Alongside the business, but analytically distinct from them, are the banks. In many countries, most notably Germany, they have acted as initiators and organizers of industrial activities, not simply as the passive financial servitors of business. Finally we have organized labor, both as bargaining agent in the plant and industry and behavior of any of these actors must be considered against an enduring pattern of constraints and opportunities created by these structured relations. Structure, in this sense of the term, means more than the economic issue of the number and size of firms, or the conditions of competition that prevail in any industry. It points to the pattern of control and influence that exists amongst the various institutions, the pattern that determines such matters as entrepreneurial initiation of new business activity, the reorganization of sectors in difficulty, and the organization of day-to-day business activities on the one hand, and remuneration, conditions of work, and the political power of labor on the other. It points as well to the instruments of formal organizational relationships, the legal possibility of restraint, and the actual control of critical resources that serve these institutions in maintaining or seeking to change any particular pattern of power and control.

The question is who controls *which* decisions and directs particular actions; and this is, ultimately an empirical, not a theoretical, question. The firm in a capitalist economy may theoretically and formally control investment or wage decisions, but part of that control may in fact lie with trade associations, the state, or the unions. Access to capital markets for the French steel industry, for example, has often directly depended on agreement within the trade association, not on negotiations between individual banks and particular companies.[22] Thus, just as the structure of a single organization, with its particular distribution of tasks and responsibilities and its set of rules and procedures, sets the strategies which any group or individuals within the organization can adopt to achieve any aim, so the institutional structure of the economy implies an enduring division of labor and a set of rules of play. At any given

---

as political institution attempting to affect the terms and conditions under which human labor can be used as a factor of production. Quite intentionally, this analysis excludes consumer or environmental groups, which although organized, lie outside the actual system of production and distribution and attempt for one or another end to influence the actions of the actors in the political economy. One might distinguish between two subsystems, one a labor relations subsystem such as that described by John Dunlop (*Industrial Relations Systems*, New York, Hold, 1958), and the other a business-relations system. The justification would be that the labor-relations systems was concerned with the price of labor and the conditions of work, while the business system focuses on the organization of production and distribution. However, the growing concern of labor organization with the policies of the firm and the formal institutionalization of such concerns with formal representation of labor on boards of directors, as in Germany, makes any such general division unwise, though for any particular issue only several of the institutions may be considered.

moment, it is structure which sets the terms in which problems are formulated, says who will be involved in the choices, and dictates the instruments available to carry out the decisions.

The structures themselves are initially established during the process of industrialization, with the particular national route to industrialization establishing a nationally specific pattern of relationships. The confrontation between the demands of industrialization at a specific historical moment and the existing organization of politics and the state bureaucracy is most important in defining the strategies open to the several actors within the economy. Thus, for example, German industrialization —occurring as it did in the age of steel with heavy capital requirements[23] and amidst already intense international competition that could be met only by rapid transformation—seemed to require a preponderant role for banks and the state in the early phases of industrialization. British industry, conversely, emerged more slowly and at an earlier and less capital-demanding point, and thus could remain at arm's length from both the banks and the government. More concretely, the modern German banking system arose, in a sense, to finance the rise of industry, whereas in England the system emerged to provide financial services to commercial merchants. In France, where a modern state with a centrally controlled bureaucracy existed before industrialization, and where industrialization occurred later than in Britain but earlier than in Germany, the state and the banks developed powerful but not predominant roles in economic life. The bourgeoisie managed to preserve through political action a place for small family-controlled firms.

These initial patterns, though, are not immutable, and the dominance of one institution may decline, and the relations between others may change. The conditions for such changes in structure appear to involve subjective shifts in what institutions conceive of their possibilities, obligations, and strategies, and more objective changes in the pressure placed on them and the resources needed to respond. One might hypothesize that changes in the patterns of relationships—changes in the structure—occur most often at moments of crisis, moments of sudden jumps in pressure, rapid declines or increases in resources and the like, which require speedy adjustment of one kind or another.

Let us take, as an example, the reconstruction after World War II, which had very different consequences in the several European countries. In France, where the state had been caretaker of society, government control of the allocation of domestic credit and Marshall Plan funds permitted the bureaucracy to stake out a new role as architect of the renovation. Later in the 1960s, crises in particular industries allowed the state to direct their reorganization. In Germany, where industry with direct and indirect assistance from the state had long been cartelized, the state was discredited by Weimar impotence and Nazi war disaster. At the same time, the Allies' goal of using the occupation forces to reduce the power of the German state suited the American ideological commitment to a "free market." The vacuum created by the removal of the German state from a massive position in economic life was filled, it appears, by the major banks, and the focus of industry-wide relationships shifted from the state to the banks.

Relationships, though, may also evolve without crisis, either as the result of ongoing maneuvering between several institutions for advantage which can then be defended, or as a result of the internal evolution of the institutions themselves. For example, in France in the early nineteenth century, the struggle between the banks and the state administration over domination of activity in industrial sectors and control of infrastructure investment is clearly depicted by Levy-Leboyer.[24] In a different vein, but certainly just as important, technological evolution and economic development will affect the institutional structure by creating new problems and by changing the number, resources, and organization of the industrial actors.

This struggle is, in the most basic sense, a political one, being a fight about the exercise of power in the economic system, and thus ultimately about the division of economic rewards. Nonetheless, the players in this game cannot strike just any imaginable deal. The possible bargains or arrangements are limited by the broader political community of which they are a part—constrained, that is, by the activities of groups not directly involved in the choices—as well as by the limits of technological and economic feasibility.[25] In fact, one possible tactic in the maneuvering amongst the primary actors in the economy is certainly the threat to broaden the scope of the conflict, and to seek support in the larger political community for particular positions or for a change in the rules. Alternatively, mass political movements may arise in reaction to industrial activities, forcing changes in industrial structure and behavior.[26]

Even the development of a single industry and the organization of the firms in it, our subject here, must be considered as another episode in the continuing course of industrialization in a particular country, and must therefore be analyzed in terms of business-state structures in that country. The particular aspects of institutional structures, of the relations between institutions, or of national political and economic history to be considered in any case, will be determined by the problem being analyzed.

The character of the French electronics industry and the difficulties it faced thus set the focus of this essay. Unlike the steel industry, the fate of powerful old families and entrenched capital interests were not important elements in the electronics industry's evolution. Nor did the electronics industry's difficulties endanger the jobs of concentrations of workers, thus engaging the unions and left-wing parties, as has been the case in the collapse of the Concorde project. The development of the electronics industry did not directly touch the interests of broad social or political groups. Those groups which it did affect either had no political instruments sufficient to influence policy, as was the case of the small firms, or they had powerful allies inside the state bureaucracy. In fact, it often appeared that elements within the state, within particular Ministries and Grands Corps, reached out into the industry and into the management struggles in particular firms to advance their own purposes. Policy-making for electronics, then, became a fight within the bureaucracy and among particular industrial interests, somewhat apart from the general arena of politics. Consequently, this book will emphasize the struggle within the state administration, the patterns of administrative relations between state and business, and organizational developments in the firm.

Part I of the essay will proceed by developing two hypotheses about the responses of French electronics firms to the conflicting pressures from the state and their technologies. Chapter 2 focuses on the conflict between the organizational constraints of technological efficiency and traditional practice in French firms. Chapter 3 considers the effect of the firms' political relations with the state on their organizational behavior and the development of the industry. Part II will consider what happens to the organization of the firms (Chapter 4), and the policy dilemmas the state faced in influencing this industry (Chapter 5). Part III will offer a general interpretation of the results of this case. Chapter 6 will analyze the organizational behavior of the firm as a product of its internal dynamics and external relations, and will also consider the impact of firm organization on economic behavior. The final chapter will examine the role of the French state in industrial life, and the relation between its domestic and its international strategies.

2

Technological Evolution and French Organization

A series of inventions and innovations transformed the manufacture of cotton in eighteenth-century England and initiated an even broader sequence of technical change that was to become the industrial revolution. Since then, technological advance has become a fundamental feature of modern industrial societies and in itself a powerful agent of change, prompting the transformation of traditional institutions and the creation of modern ones. Machines, though, have never evolved or diffused according to some internal logic of their own; but rather their development has been inspired by the twin motivations, power for the state and profit for the entrepreneur. In England, where the industrial process began, it was a social innovation, the free marketplace, that rewarded and encouraged technological development by permitting the pursuit of private profit to regulate production. In France the roots of industrialism were directly political. Seeking to extend its own power and authority, the state inspired and supported the establishment of industries.

Those who would profit from the technologies, however, must accept the constraints and the costs, or impose them on others. Technology's imperatives, the requirements of the tasks of production and the use of the different products and processes, constrain the behavior of the individuals and institutions that employ the technologies. Political power to make and enforce social rules is often required to impose these constraints and the costs that accompany the use of a technology. Technological development, then, is not simply a technical matter of efficiency, but a political question: what goals are to be pursued in a society, and how the costs and benefits of that development are to be distributed.

15

The analysis of technological evolution, then, offers a valuable perspective on the continuing development of industrial societies. Not only is technology an important element in all advanced countries, but it can be defined independently of a particular national context. While technology does not impose particular forms of social organization, the tasks of making and using machines and their products do define certain constraints which must be respected. Comparing the variety of social solutions to a single technical problem can illuminate both the continuing development of industrial societies and the sources of divergence among them. In a technical sense, constructing an automobile is much the same task in both Sweden and America. However, Swedish and Italian automakers have begun experimenting with small-group assembly of complete automobiles as an alternative to the assembly line, an intentional effort to allow the worker to become a producer of cars, not simply a source of human labor. This represents a sharp break with the Taylorian notions of efficiency that were prevalent in the first half of the century. Rising absenteeism rates, perhaps a result of rising worker income, have forced management to experiment with new solutions to the continuing problem of automobile assembly. Why, though, did such an innovation occur in Sweden and Italy, and not in the United States or France? Similarly, the organization of Dassault Aircraft Company in France and Boeing in the United States represent alternatives, albeit equally successful ones, to the technological problem of developing new aircraft.

The constancy of the technological problem can provide us with comparable evidence from different societies, different solutions to a similar problem. Comparing other phenomena, such as voting behavior, for example, has certain pitfalls. Because the political game and the potential for influence are different in France and America, a vote does not mean the same thing in the two countries. Should differences in voting rates, therefore, be attributed to a public sense of the political efficacy of voting, or to the different meaning of the vote itself? The very notion of the vote is inextricably tied to the context in which it is found. Because the meaning of an institution is defined by its context, it is difficult to compare it with a similar institution elsewhere. Comparative analysis, therefore, often involves comparing the similar elements in parallel systems, not the different responses of each system to the same parameter. In contrast, technology represents a more nearly neutral, though not entirely pure, prism in which we can refract and compare the elements of several industrial societies. The emergence of electronics technologies and of science-based industries in general, one part of the ongoing course of industrialization, poses sharply new organizational problems for the firm. Setting out the difficulties these new requirements have posed for French firms will allow us to consider the process of change in French industry and, more broadly, to examine those conditions which allow institutions to accept new technologies and those conditions which force change.

The two faces of technology—the opportunities created for profit and power, and the constraints imposed on organization and behavior— allow us to understand technological evolution as a process of social and political development. Those who would benefit from the opportunities offered by the technologies must accept the constraints and often impose them on others. Thus, for technological *possibilities* to induce social change, the *opportunities* must be perceived and then pursued and the ensuing constraints understood and enforced. To take a historical example: the emergence of a capacity to design and build new textile machinery did not make factories inevitable.[1] The factories were created by entrepreneurs who, in pursuit of profit from lower costs of production, induced or compelled laborers to become factory workers. On the continent the rural "putting-out" system of textile production (which distributed individual production tasks into peasant homes) continued after it had all but vanished in England. The differing factor prices made the opportunity of the factory less valuable, while the political importance of docile rural labor made the potential costs of imposing the constraints of factory discipline too high.[2] Competition between firms and between states pushed the evolution of machines precisely because because it raised the value of the opportunities implicit in technological possibilities.

Even when the opportunities are appreciated, though, understanding the constraints may not be simple. The constraints on the organization of production may be directly linked to particular technological advances, as the idea of assembly-line production was tied to the notion of interchangeable parts, but other constraints may only become evident from tensions, inefficiencies, and outright failures in production. Even then, work tensions and production failures or inefficiencies may not be perceived as the result of the firm's organization. Tensions may be blamed on the violation of rules or the bad will of others; competitive weakness may be attributed to inadequate tariff protection or some other state action; and outright failures may be blamed on willful negligence or the incompetence of one group or another. Even a slow and cautious evolution, to be successful, requires some implicit predictions about the relations between organizational structures and behavior. One can only wonder what changes would have occurred in the French electronics industry without the pressure of the American firms—not simply the pressure of their economic competition, but the example of the organization of American firms must have been a constant suggestion that organizational change might affect market performance.

Even after the problem is understood, however, the constraints must still be accepted or imposed on the organizations. In the French firms studied here, the leadership imposed changes that probably never would have evolved internally, even though the new procedures were often welcomed and accepted once they were established. Because the power to order these changes had been institutionalized in the form of management prerogatives, and because the management did not overstep the bounds of law and custom in making the changes, the issue of power does not appear in bold relief in this study. However, the element of compulsions applied on behalf of particular interests cannot be ignored. The impositions were hardly noxious in this case, but that has certainly not always been true. *Although technological imperatives may be abstractly defined as the most efficient way of carrying out some production task, they appear in social life as rules men accept or impose on others in order to achieve some particular objective.*

Since technological evolution represents opportunities for some groups and constraints and costs that must be imposed on others, it is immediately the subject of political debate and conflict. Imposing the constraints may require political authority and outright force, and even more significantly, political action may be an alternative to adjusting to the requirements of a technology. In different settings therefore, a particular technological development may result in a variety of outcomes. For example, small firms faced with the development of production techniques that favor large-scale producers may be able to resist the pressures for merger and industry concentration by winning tariff protection against foreign producers and then dividing the market between themselves. A cartelized and protected industry simply has less need to respond to technological developments than a thoroughly competitive industry.

Technological innovation and political action, in fact, may represent alternative reactions to a particular economic situation. High agricultural tariffs in Germany, for example, resulted from the efforts of the Junkers to preserve a way of life which rested on large-scale grain production in the face of a flood of cheap American produce on the world market.[3] Danish peasants in the same situation responded with what amounted to a technological innovation in their farming practices. They turned to pig farming, importing cheap grain and exporting expensive meat. However, in Germany the social organization of pig farming was a threat to the large landowners, and they chose political action to protect themselves from the economic problem rather than adopting the farming innovations required to adapt to the market. As in the case of the French electronics firms, isolation of the national market not only protected the producers but also permitted them to maintain the existing authority arrangements. The important difference, of course, is that the support of particular social arrangements was the direct intent of state action in Germany, while in France it was the unintended result of policies adopted for other reasons.

Because the effective use of a particular technology constrains the way men can behave, the evolution and diffusion of technologies in a society will affect the patterns of behavior that typify its culture. The decision to use or develop a technology, of course, is directly affected by existing ideologies, attitudes, and routines. When a technology is adopted, the attitudes and values that men learn as members of their society do not prevent them from learning new ways of behaving which conform to the technological imperatives. This study of organizational change in French electronics firms will demonstrate that the importance these firms have assigned to technological efficiency has determined how closely their organizations were constrained. It appears, then, that both the evolution of technologies and their impact on culture turn on value judgments—often explicitly made in the political arena—about which technological opportunities should be pursued and which constraints will be imposed. This chapter will take up one such problem.

The technological imperatives of science-based, innovation-centered industries, it will be argued here, are incompatible with the organizational patterns that have typified French institutions. We shall consider first the argument that production technology constrains industrial organization, and second the contention that French organizational structures are rooted in French attitudes toward authority and will resist pressures to change. An hypothesis built on the first contention would predict very different organizational structures in the electronics industry than an hypothesis built on the second. The question posed here, and answered in Chapter 4, is whether firms in the electronics industry adapt to technological constraints or persist in maintaining traditional French organizations. The theme of this chapter, then, is the internal organization of the firm; we shall leave for the next chapter a discussion of the position of French firms in the domestic and international electronics industry and their relations with the French state and banks.

Technological Imperatives and Organizational Structure

Empirical studies in England and America suggest that firms depending on continuing technological innovation require particular organizational structures and patterns of individual behavior. An analysis suggests that these structures and behaviors are a response to continuing uncertainty in the firms' internal environment, uncertainty produced by the character of their products and the production process. Because continually innovating organizations must permit easy *horizontal relationships* between separable but intertwined tasks, sharply hierarchical organization slows overall development, raises costs, adversely affects competitiveness, and increases the likelihood of inappropriate solutions to technical problems. The *fluid personal relationships* required to give life to the horizontal connections demand informal and personal mechanisms of management rather than formal, rule-based, and impersonal systems. The task here is first to demonstrate the empirical correlation between production technology and organization, and then to provide a causal explanation for the correlation.

Industrial management theorists have long sought to identify the parameters of "efficient" organization and to spell out the rules for ideal management. Joan Woodward set out to identify empirically the characteristics of successful organizations in a study of the organization of firms in Essex County, England.[4] She found that there was no one ideal form of organization, but rather that the appropriate organization was contingent on the production technology of the firm. Her work was replicated by William Zwerman's study of firms in Minneapolis,[5] and the analysis was supported and extended by Paul Lawrence and Jay Lorsch's study, *Organization and Environment.*[6] The analytic framework of Woodward's work permits us to use production technology as an independent variable and relate it to a series of dependent organizational variables. It allows us, furthermore, to view the different production technologies as part of a historical development.

Production technology is the independent variable in Woodward's analysis. For her, a firm's technology is the "collection of plants, machines, tools, and recipes available at the time for the execution of the production task."[7] A production technology—that collection of plants, machines, tools, and recipes—is thus a function of the production tasks, and it is differences in those production tasks which finally distinguish production technologies.

In this schema the rate of change in products—that is, how often new products are introduced—is the characteristic universal to all production but not tied to any particular product that defines the different categories of production technology. While this schema may be satisfactory in theory, it is often difficult in practice to define or measure the variable "product." A blue automobile is, industrially, no different from a red one. The automobile industry's annual retooling does represent product evolution, but only the possible introduction of the Wankel engine as a replacement for the piston engine, the first such change in sixty years, would approximate the continuing brutal product jumps in electronics that successive generations of components have produced every few years since the second World War.[8]

The Woodward schema distinguishes three different production technologies, each of which contains several sub-types. Only the broad groupings will concern us here; the sub-types are presented to clarify the meaning of each group.[9]

1. Unit and Small-Batch Production
   a. Fabrication of units to customers' requirements
   b. Production of prototypes
   c. Fabrication of large equipment in stages
2. Large-Batch and Mass Production
   a. Production of small batches to customers' orders
   b. Production of large batches
   c. Production of large batches on assembly lines
3. Process Production
   a. Intermittent production of chemicals in multi-purpose plant
   b. Continuous-flow production of liquids, gases, and crystaline substances

This schema represents both a scale of product standardization and of technical complexity in the production system. At one end the chemical industry produces almost entirely standardized products with enormously complicated and often automatic plants, while at the other end craft industries produce individually unique goods in very simple shops. The borderlines between categories are often quite hazy and pose problems, but each group points toward a clearly distinct production task. The production technology as defined by these groupings is the independent variable in Woodward's analysis.

The production technology, then, affects three dependent variables: formal organizational structure, location and basis of specialized skills in the organization, and the management system. Let us consider these dependent variables in order.

1. Organizational structure: for Woodward's purposes, this is the arrangement of formal work roles, each role consisting of particular operations in combination with control of the means to execute that responsibility. This notion of organizational structure, the formal relations of one role to another as defined by rule and custom, allows us to define and describe an organization without reference to the individuals in it. Examining the relationships between five structural characteristics and production technology, Woodward found, in summary, that as one moved up the scale from unit process production, organizational structure also changed—from short, squat forms suggesting little hierarchy and great horizontal connection to tall, narrow, and sharply hierarchical forms.[10]

2. The location of specialized skills in organizations: An organization may be said to have a line or a line-staff structure. In line organizations,

authority flows from the chief executive to various immediate subordinates, and from them to the workers.[11] Each man must possess the specialized skill necessary for his tasks because he cannot turn elsewhere in the organization for help. Line-staff organizations have specialized staffs, whose particular skills supplement the line management where necessary. Because the line operatives can draw on specialized staffs in line-staff organizations, they themselves do not need specialized technical competence.

Line-staff organizations tended to be characteristic of the large-batch and mass-production firms, while line structure existed in four-fifths of the unit-production firms.[12] Three-fifths of the process-production firms had line organizations, and in the rest, executive and advisory responsibilities were so blurred that the formal structure did not matter. *No* large-batch or mass-production systems had line organizations. Thus, it would appear that in unit- and process-production firms the line supervisors must be technically competent, while in mass production they do not have to be. Put differently, in unit- and process-production firms, skill is widely diffused through the organization, while in batch and mass production these skills are collected and concentrated in particular staff positions.

3. Management systems: Broadly speaking, management systems consist of organizational procedures that guide relations between individuals and establish and maintain work roles. Woodward adopted Burns's concepts of "mechanic" and "organic" management systems to distinguish between the managements of the firms she studied.[13] "Mechanistic" systems, a term nearly interchangeable with Weber's bureaucracy, are characterized by a rigid breakdown into functional specialisms; by precise definitions of duties, responsibilities, and power; and by a well-developed command hierarchy to transmit information up and decisions and instructions down. In contrast, "organic systems" are more adaptable; jobs lose much of their formal definition; and communications up and down the hierarchy are more in the "nature of consultation than of passing information up and of receiving orders."[14] The methods of communication between managers differ sharply in these two types of systems. In mechanistic systems, communication is almost entirely written, often involving elaborate interdepartmental memoranda. Organic systems tend toward verbal communication, either face-to-face or over the telephone.[15]

Woodward, and later Zwerman, found that a firm's management style is directly related to its technology.

> Organic management systems predominate among unit and process production systems, whereas mechanistic management systems are associated with large batch and mass production systems.[16]

Clear-cut definition of duties and responsibilities was characteristic
of firms in the middle ranges while flexible organization with a
high degree of delegation both of authority and responsibility for
decision making and with permissive and participating management
was characteristic of firms at the extremes.[17]

To summarize for a moment, an independent variable, production
technology, seems to predict the structure, the management system, and
the distribution of skills in production organization. The predictions are
sharpest at each end of the scale. At the end which concerns us most,
unit production, firms tend to be short and squat in profile, with personalized "organic" management and line operatives who possess skill
sufficient to all aspects of their tasks.

In a subsequent reanalysis of the data, Woodward introduced "control
systems" as an *intermediary variable* between technology and organization. Not only did this addition clarify some of the ambiguities in the
data, but it also suggested a causal basis for the correlations that had
been observed. Schematically the new reasoning was as follows:

Technology——Control Systems——Organizations

This intermediary variable, empirically supported in its own right,
provides a causal linkage between technology and organization, the
character of the control system required by each production category.

Control systems were categorized in two dimensions: whether they were
personal or impersonal and whether they were fragmented or unitary.
Personal control involves one individual's evaluation of another, while an
impersonal control system measures performances against some fixed
standard. A unitary system exists when all departments in an organization
can be judged by the same standard—days absent or profits—but a
fragmented system has different measures of successes for each department. Conflict between departments is more likely in a fragmented system
as each department seeks its goal. Combining these categories, we have
the following table (Joan Woodward, *Industrial Organization Behavior
and Control*, p. 53).

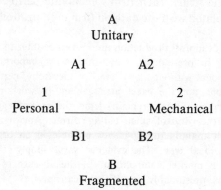

A
Unitary

A1   A2

1   2
Personal _____ Mechanical

B1   B2

B
Fragmented

Data from the original study were adequate to assign each firm to a control category, and definite relations were found between technological type and control system. The data are presented below (Joan Woodward, *Industrial Organization Behavior and Control,* p. 54).

Technological Type of Firm	Control Systems (percent)			
	A1	B1	B2	A2
Unit and small batch production	75	25	—	—
Large batch and mass production	15	35	40	10
Process production	—	—	5	95
Total firms	28	21	18	33

Again, the process and unit firms are clustered at particular control systems, while the large-batch and mass-production firms appear to spread across the board. In fact, the fundamental characteristics of each of the forms of production stand out. All the unit firms had unitary control systems and three-fourths of them had personal control procedures. Ninety-five percent of the process-production firms had unitary and mechanical control systems. Three-fourths of the large-batch and mass-production firms, on the other hand, had fragmented control procedures, although they were evenly divided between personal and mechanical procedures. For the purpose of the argument here, the regularity among unit-production firms will be important.* Recall that all of these had personalized control systems and three-fourths had unitary systems.

The argument that the type of production technology forces firms to adopt or evolve particular organizations to be competitive in market conditions is advanced by Woodward's evidence, which is that organizational structures and management styles associated with each type of production technology were *required* for market success. Prior to the research within the firms, each firm's economic performance had been rated. When correlated with the data on firm organization, the conclusion

---

*The regularities in unit production do not run counter to the overwhelming evidence of variety in pre-industrial cultures. Most importantly, while work control will be personal without many levels of hierarchy, neither the character of authority relations nor the exact arrangement of work roles is specified. The room for enormous variety remains from the assemblage of hundreds of shoemakers under the whip of small cottage firms. Anyway, Woodward does not argue that unit manufacturing is not possible in an organizational form different from the ideal type. The evidence says, simply, that the firm will be less successful in market competition. In the absence of a market, other organizational forms. presumably less efficient, can survive.

was that within each range of technology, successful firms had a particular organizational form—and that in fact, there was one best way of managing each production technology. Again, the Woodward results were confirmed in the Minneapolis replication.

> The re-examination of the organizational figures revealed one other interesting fact; the five successful unit production firms had organizational characteristics in common, so had the five large batch and mass production firms. It was found that the figures relating to the organizational characteristics of successful firms in each production category tended to round the medians for that category as a whole, while the figures of the firms classified as "below average" in success were found at the extreme of the range.[18]

This was found to be true for the figures relating to the span of control of the chief executive, the number of levels in the line of command, labor costs, and the various other labor ratios.

> The fact that organizational characteristics, technology, and success were linked together in this way suggested that not only was the system of production an important variable in the determination of organizational structure, but *also that one particular form of organization was most appropriate for each system of production. In unit production, for example, not only did short and relatively broadly based pyramids predominate, but they also appeared to ensure success.* Process production, on the other hand, would seem to require taller and more narrowly based pyramids.
> It is also interesting to find that in terms of Burns' analysis, *successful firms inside the large production range tended to have mechanistic management systems.* On the other hand, *successful firms outside this range tended to have organic systems.*[19] [My italics.]

"It became apparent that there was a particular form of organization most appropriate to each technological situation."[20] The use of particular technologies, it seems, makes specific organizational demands.

The Woodward argument is supported as well by similar research which proceeds from a slightly different perspective. Traditional management theorists beginning with Taylor have argued that single sets of rules applied to all organizations, that single best ways of organizing existed. Woodward broke, in part, from that orthodoxy by suggesting that the best way of organizing was *contingent* on the *production technology,* but she preserved the faith with her argument that within the realm of each technology a single best organizational form did reign. Her approach is particularly appropriate here because she focuses on the single variable of the production technology inside the firm. In fact, differences in production technology are linked to the rate of product change, or, put differently, to the stability of the internal environment.

Paul Lawrence and Jay Lorsch of the Harvard Business School took the techno-economic environment of the firm as an independent variable, looking therefore at the stability of both the internal and the external environment of the firm.[21] The source of the internal instability, it should be emphasized, can be conceived as a function of the production technology in Woodward's terms. Their sample of firms was from three industries—the specialty plastics industry, which has a market and a technology which are both unstable; a sector of the food industry with an unstable market but a stable technology; and a sector of the container industry in which both market and technology are stable. They contended that the instability forced firms to specialize sharply the three functions of marketing, production, and product development. They argue that this differentiation, as they termed the specialization, was required to adjust to the instability. Sharp differentiation, as measured by attitudes, time perspectives, and definition of the business problems requires some means of integrating the newly separated functions. Lawrence and Lorsch argue that integration in an unstable environment, demanding the adjustment of one division's task to another's, required direct communication between divisions.

Put differently, in a stable environment the limited uncertainties—for example, the adjustment of a production schedule to sales—can be handled at the top of the organization. In a thoroughly unstable environment with many unknowns, decisions must be made at the lower echelons of the hierarchy. In any case, decision-making, the resolution of uncertainty as distinguished from the simple application of rules, always requires face-to-face conflict; but in a stable environment, the unknowns, the decision-making, and thus the face-to-face conflict can be limited to the hierarchical center of the firm. In summary, a stable environment encourages centralized organizations, in which decision-making is impersonal and formally applied from the top, whereas unstable environments demand decentralized and personalized decision-making throughout the firm. Lawrence and Lorsch found that the firms which did not have an appropriate mix of differentiation and integration—in plain English, those that weren't properly organized for their tasks—were less successful in competition.

This evidence is useful in two ways. First, it supports Woodward's contention that proper industrial organization is contingent on the firm's production task. In both studies cited, instability pushes toward personalized and horizontally integrated organization. Lawrence and Lorsch simply add external instability into the analysis. Second, while the theoretical argument to be developed here will continue to focus on the organizational requirements of particular production technologies, the practical reality cannot be ignored: the economic and technical environment of the electronics industry has been violently unstable. The economic situation of the firms studied has reinforced the technologies' tendencies toward personalized and non-hierarchical organization. One would expect that electronics firms must adopt model organization or suffer.

Evolving Technologies and Changing Constraints:
The Emerging Electronics Industries

Innovation-centered research and development oriented (R and D) industries represent, for the most part, a sub-group within the category of unit and small-batch production. To situate this group, of which the portions of the electronics industry studied here form a part, and to clarify the problems particular to it, let us adopt for a moment a historical perspective.

The three technological types discussed in section one—unit production, mass and large-batch production, and process production—were presented as points on a scale of product standardization and technical complexity in the production process, but since the three types developed in chronological sequence each may be seen as a step in a historical development. Since the industrial revolution, product standardization, technical complexity, and capital investment have all increased together. Product standardization allowed greater control over manufacturing because operations could be predicted, coordinated by planning, and automated, and all this resulted in complex production systems requiring higher levels of fixed capital investment. In turn, the physical and financial inflexibility produced long-term industrial perspectives. For example, where unit production, requiring purchase commitments before development begins,[22] moves in short cycles from product to product, process-production plants are only profitable in the very long run. Considered historically, then, the evolution of technology has posed constantly changing demands on industrial organization, specifically on the ways hierarchy and authority need to be organized.

The historical development of technology is clearly expressed if one relabels the categories and refers to the evolution from craft industry to assembly line to automatic production, categories that suggest the social change that was linked with the technologies. Thus, for example, England broke from the world of craft industry when production was divided into a series of specialized and standardized tasks that could be performed repeatedly, using particular technologies, and then combined into a final form. Historically, the technologies for thread-making, for example, were put out into peasant homes, and the products of those specialized tasks were combined elsewhere. Later, when the technical and social possibilities changed, factories appeared where the sub-tasks and the combination could be performed in one place. Mass production and the assembly line are an outgrowth of this progressive sub-division and organization of tasks, while increased standardization and the possibility of auto-matically combining separate operations produced the continuous-flow plants. Of course, as development occurs, earlier forms do not disappear. Each has its application and limitations, and is appropriate to specific objectives, and the older types, although their importance is diminished by the emergence of new technologies, continue to have social and political significance. In France, for example, the political influence of the small businessmen, the *petits commerçants*, and the uneconomic family-owned factory have shaped the pattern of modernization. The new technologies cannot, perhaps, be avoided, but their impact will be mediated by the existing institutions and political structures.[23]

Where in this schema of production technology do we place the new group of high-technology firms—the aerospace firms and the electronics firms—that have made a life of innovation itself, who compete by the continuing technological evolution of their products? Their production task is the development of a rapidly changing range of products whose technical base is continually evolving. Many of these firms, in fact, must be categorized directly as unit and small batch, since they produce their products in very small number, often to existing orders.

However, at this point, an astute reader might remark that, in fact, industries resting on a research and innovation base, as measured by percent of turnover or absolute sums expended on R and D, run the whole gamut—from the batch or even unit production in the case of aircraft or specialty electronics, through the mass production of semi-conductors, to the process production of the plastics industry. He would add that the space program and the rarity of computers in the early years of the industry emphasized and publicized the firms that produced a limited number of exotic products, and would note that the heavy capital cost of process or mass production and the limited markets for the most advanced products might concentrate many small firms at the unit end of the scale. Nonetheless, he could still argue that the value of production generated by the other production types might be greater. He would then contend that the argument as presented is only applicable to a set of firms within the knowledge-based industries.

This argument could be accepted without upsetting the logic of the research simply by choosing our firms from among those producing in unit or small-batch volume. Yet such a restriction is unnecessary. In fact, even semi-conductor firms which mass produce integrated circuits and plastic firms which process produce materials display many of the same communication and control needs of unit-production firms, and their organizational structures reflect these needs. We could, therefore, pose the problem in Lawrence and Lorsch's terms, and emphasize that taken together, the internal and external instability these firms face require organizations incompatible with French tradition. Again, the logic of the research would not be disturbed, although the exclusive focus on an organization's internal operation would be blurred.

Critically, in an important sense all these firms are essentially unit-production firms, though of a very new kind. An intermediary, but fundamental, product of all these firms is the production process itself. The production process must embody the advanced technological characteristics of the product—that is, if the product itself changes, those changes must be reflected in the way it is made. As the final products have undergone waves of radical change, the intermediary product of a production system has undergone fundamental alteration. In the semi-conductor industry, for example, the production process has moved in twenty years from discrete assembly under a microscope to a mass-production planar process. The change in the components' relation to final electronic products has been so profound that products must now be designed around the components, and this has begun to force certain component producers, particularly Texas Instruments, into the equipment field, while equipment producers, such as IBM, have integrated backwards into components. It cannot be overemphasized that in twenty years in the electronics industry, the products have several times undergone technical jumps more fundamental than anything experienced even once in the motor car industry since its very beginnings. New products in electronics are not comparable to the simple retooling of the automobile industry.

The argument, then, is that the high-technology firms are a new form of craft industry, a craft industry based on a new relation to science and focused toward the crafting of the production process itself as an intermediary product. In the electronics industry, particularly, there are four indications that the fundamental, though intermediary, product of these firms is the production system itself.

First, product development is quite literally the creation of a production system. The preliminary version of the product, the prototype, is one step in a process. Firms that once defined the prototype as the end of the product development process have suffered accordingly, and in France these firms have changed their organization to reflect their new understanding of the problem. The product passes from product prototype to pilot production line, a prototype of the production line itself, to the definition of the new production system. Even if the exact characteristics of the product are turned over to a competing firm, it may be months or even years before the other firm can enter the market—because it must develop its own product line. If the product remains stable, then the definition of the production system is a once in a lifetime event, even though it may evolve. *When the difference between products over time are fundamental, there is no question of simply modifying the existing production system; it must be reconceived. That makes production line creation an ongoing feature of that firm's life.*

Second, because product life is short, particularly in the electronics industry, where the life of a product is usually two to four years, and the changes profound enough to be called new generations, the creation of the production system is the central ongoing activity of the firm. The brief life of products is a vital problem in electronics, and its importance cannot be overemphasized.

Third, in many cases changes in product are inseparable from changes in the entire production process. The product jump from individual transistors to integrated circuits, for example, altered the entire focus of production.

Finally, once a production system is created in the most sophisticated firms, it can be cut off and handed over, like a product, to classical production managers. The American semi-conductor firms literally export their production process to the Far East, Hong Kong, and Singapore, where labor costs are low, while they continue their development of the next production system at home.

Thus, whatever the final number of products the continuous creation of a production system makes, the core of the firm develops the central characteristics of a new style of craft industry. The continuous change of product in "unit" firms demands an organization which can control and direct an unstable work environment of shifting tasks. Similarly, the continuous shift in production process generates the same instability. Clearly, the volume of the anticipated production and the characteristics of the product will determine the character of the production system that is "created." However, if the turnover in discrete production systems is continuous, the core of the firm will develop characteristics of a "craft" firm.

Three factors would seem to determine the pace in production system turnover: the rate of basic innovation in final products, the size of the fixed capital investment in the production system, and the ability to defend the firm's market positions with its own older products. In the electronics industry, where the rate of innovation has been high, capital investment low, and older products highly vulnerable to new developments on both a cost and a quality comparison, the turnover in production systems is a central characteristic of the industry.

Let us not forget that this examination of the management of industry is not an end in itself, but a tool for exploring the evolution of industrial society. Each production type is a historical step with particular management styles, organizational structures, and skill levels. The use of each production technology creates constraints and requirements, and these constraints constitute a set of parameters that must be resolved.

The social science problem is how society will adjust to these new parameters.

Uncertainty, Power, and Authority: The Link Between Technology and Structure

The evidence of the previous section correlated the category of production technology to the organizational structure and management system. Apparently, technology presents particularly problems which, in the case of mass production, tend to impose certain control systems. These control systems find their concrete expression in organizational structure and management system.

Taking innovation-centered R and D oriented industry as a sub-group of unit production, this section will extend the causal argument by demonstrating how the specific problems posed by production in these industries and the character of the solutions available limit the possible organizational systems available. Our end purpose, we must recall, is to evaluate technology's influence on the patterns of hierarchy and authority in the industrial sector of advanced societies, but that influence is felt by the organizational problems a technology poses and the solutions it favors.

Two kinds of uncertainty create risk for an organization: uncertainty in its external environment, and uncertainty in its internal production process. A clothes buyer in a retail store faces the external environmental uncertainty called fashion; the internal operations of the store and the specific responsibilities of each person, however, remain relatively unchanged despite changing fashions. Buyers will still buy from a relatively defined number of firms, and sales people will still sell the same category of product to those who enter the store. Of course, sufficient external instability will influence the internal operations; a firm may change the category of products or the physical location of its store, but this is not a recurrent feature of its existence. In contrast, an engineer may face an absolutely stable external market (the product, in fact, may already be sold), but the uncertainty in the production process will remain. Our concern in this section will be production uncertainty, not external environment uncertainty.

The Technical Problem. The continuing risk due to the enormous uncertainty in the production process itself is a fundamental characteristic of industries organized around the innovation of products and technologies. Two separate production problems generate pervasive uncertainty in production. First, a prototype must be created which will demonstrate that a product is technologically feasible. For firms producing only a few units of a particular product for sale the focus of their effort is here. However, for firms producing large batches or mass producing quantities of a product, the prototype is only one part, a part fraught with uncertainties itself, but still only a part of the critical intermediary product—the production system. These firms must develop a production system that will continually produce working and saleable models, not simply prototypes. In industries such as electronics, the development of the prototype and production system opens the floodgates on a sea of uncertainty. Some brief remarks on the organization of uncertainty are needed before a more thorough analysis can be presented.

Within any orgnization there are two simultaneous processes: the subdivision of work into a series of sub-tasks (differentiation), and the coordination of each separate task (integration).[24] Each represents a source of uncertainty in the production process. The less predictable and less controllable each task is, the greater the overall uncertainty in the production will be, and thus the greater the risk faced by the firm. Lack of information and knowledge concerning the means to complete particular tasks on the one hand, and to combine them, on the other, is the central problem.

In the first case (differentiation), if the set of procedures and operations necessary to complete a particular sub-task is unknown, there will be uncertainty as to when, whether, and at what cost the sub-task can be finished. The greater the difficulty, for whatever reason, of establishing those procedures and operations, the greater will be the uncertainty attached to the particular sub-task.

The second source of overall uncertainty (coordination) lies in the interrelation and the interdependence of tasks. How to combine the separate individual tasks may not be known, and as a result, it will be difficult to control or predict the production process. The nature of the relations between tasks determines the appropriate means of coordination. Thompson suggests three possibilities.[25] First, some products are not directly linked, but are combined by pooling the results. For example, when ten men, working independently, each plant a tree to make a grove, they have a *pooled* interdependence. Second, when one task must be completed before the other can begin, the tasks are said to have a *sequential* relationship. Mass production and the assembly line are based on careful planning of sequential operations. Planning is the appropriate coordinating mechanism for this kind of interrelation. Third and finally, tasks may be *mutually dependent* on each other. If one element of a system cannot be changed without simultaneous adjustment of other elements—that is, if the solution of task A depends on the solution chosen for task B and vice versa—then the tasks are mutually dependent. Mutual coordination requires mutual adjustments as the means of coordination, and that in turn requires a continuous knowledge by each work group of the status of work in each other group. Uncertainty can be reduced, the probability that the targets of deadline and cost will be met can be increased, only by transferring information about one work group to another.

To return to our problem, the development of a *prototype* rests on the solution of a series of discrete technological problems of varying difficulty. In the simplest case, a solution existing elsewhere might be directly borrowed. In other cases, existing principles may be applied to the problem at hand. The solution is not known, but the means of arriving at it are. Finally, some problems may require the creation of new principles. Each problem, whatever its solution, represents a source of uncertainty. Project Hindsight, the Department of Defense's analysis of its development projects, reported that on the average only 10 percent of the technologies used in each weapon's system existed when its grandfather, two generations earlier, was in use.[26] Thus, the development of these weapons required an advance in the "state of the art," the discovery of new knowledge, rather than the application of old knowledge. The vast portion of these particular problems can be and is in fact solved by a technologist's university textbook knowledge of science,[27] but in some cases the problems even require advances in science itself.

Few of these tasks, though, are independent of the others. In airplane design, for instance, passenger capacity, range, and engine performance are all dependent on one another. Even after basic problems are broken up and assigned to different groups, the interdependence remains. If passenger capacity is to be increased, then weight will have to be increased. If weight is increased, then either the engines must be made more powerful or range must be reduced. If engine thrust is to be increased, the engines must be bigger or more powerful for the same size. Bigger means increased wing strengths, while achieving more power for the same size may require a costly advance in the state of the art. No decision can be taken in isolation; means must be found to coordinate the choices.

The prototype, we have argued here, should be considered one of the sub-tasks in creating a *production process*. Prototype development is fraught with uncertainty, but the coordination required to establish a production process multiplies the existing problems. Very simply, it is one thing for highly qualified engineers or scientists to make a product in the laboratory under extremely controlled conditions when price is not an object. It is quite another problem to make twenty products for sale using production personnel, and to establish a production line even when skilled labor can be used. Although the development of a production system logically follows the development of a prototype, the two are in fact mutually interdependent tasks. If a prototype is defined without a clear understanding of the problems and limits of production, it will, very simply, have to be redesigned. Moreover, if production engineers wait until the prototype is finished, the firm loses time putting the product on the market. If the production samples do not function, it can be a failure either in the production process or in a design of the product. The developers of a product understand it the best, but it is the production engineer, dependent on the product knowledge of the developers, who must make adjustment if the production "models" have trouble. Unless the two groups are in close rapport with each other, one of two symptoms is likely to appear. The "problem," a non-working product, will be handed back and forth with production engineers claiming a design error is at fault and development engineers claiming that production just won't do what they say. Alternatively, the production division may simply start all over and redevelop the product to fit production logic. Both are slow, costly, and generally disastrous solutions.

In some cases, particularly military contracts, the broad technical outlines of a product have already been defined when it is under development, but when the new product must be sold on the marketplace, the technical product design must emerge in light of commercial considerations. This, of course, further multiplies the pressure for internal coordination. The importance of market uncertainty is infinitely greater when every adjustment by a product-development team may represent a further investment of time and money in applied research and development. At every step uncertainty increases, and the uncertainty multiplies the need for information and thus for communication.

Uncertainty, the inability to predict and control the production process, is related to the amount of information an organization must transfer in order to perform and coordinate its tasks. The more information required for prediction, the greater the uncertainty. Information is needed to solve the problems that individual tasks present; more information is needed to coordinate combinations of tasks. The less information available—or rather, the less appropriate information—the more uncertain it is that an organization can predict and control its production process. The problem, it must be clearly understood, is not simply a technical one of ordering the relations between tasks and establishing adequate channels of information. It is, at its core, a political matter of coordinating a group's activities.

The Question of Power. Power in an organization, according to Crozier, lies within areas of uncertainty because uncertainty allows individual discretion and control over organization resources. Individual choice, created by task uncertainty, can be used to influence the actions of others. When rules and customs establish operating procedures, the bureaucrat (no matter how important his concerns) has no power because he must simply apply a rule created by someone else. Ironically, then, when expertise eliminates uncertainty, it destroys its own power.

Uncertainty thoroughly pervades the production process in innovation-centered industry, creating many centers of power and placing power in the hands of the engineers, the only people with the specialized skills to deal with the particular development problems. Moreover, because each research project generates specialized knowledge, the engineer is further protected from other engineers who might have similar general training.

Yet no one individual, according to this analysis, possesses a great store of power. One engineer by himself will seldom, it would seem, have sufficient strength to produce an organizational crisis, to restructure the organization, or to effect a change in its direction. Because the pervasiveness of uncertainty diffuses power and gives many men control over a small area of operations, the organization in a sense is composed of small pools of power.* *Two problems are posed for the organization:*

*We must distinguish between power within an organization, the ability to influence the internal functioning of an organization, and social power—the ability of someone within the organization to influence those outside. The engineer, whose power rests on the uncertainty in the production process, is very different from the financiers whose power rests on their ability to predict and control an uncertain external financial environment. The financier faces risk because his external environment is uncertain, while Lockheed Aircraft, once its contracts are signed, may face greater risk from internal uncertainties than from external ones. (A changing political environment also contributed to Lockheed's difficulty in the C5A case. New strategic goals—particularly, diminished desire to transport troops abroad—reduced the demands for the plane, and altered Lockheed's profit calculation. However, the uncontrollable rise in cost, resulting from unexpected R and D cost, was at the bottom of the problem.) This is important because it means that all organizational power is not the same; one significant question concerning power is power over what? The power of the financier is often over the possibilities open to sectors and groups in the society. *Thus technology may shift both the meaning and the position of organizational power.*

Power within an organization becomes socially important when it involves contact with and control over the organization's external environment. Organizational power at the engineering levels of the innovation-centered firm becomes social power in two ways. First, the engineers control a scarce economic resource—the knowledge needed to control uncertainty—and as entrepreneurs they can use that resource to found their own firms, and they often do. Secondly, task uncertainty makes both the ultimate characteristics of a product and the delivery date unknowable with any precision. Continual interaction between buyer and seller is required for the continual redefinition of what product is wanted within the limits of what that product can be. This gives the engineer a certain amount of power in the buyers' organization. When the buyer is the government, the production engineer gains a hand in policy.

first, how to transfer the information required to execute and coordinate tasks; and second, how to control these diffuse centers of power, insuring that they move toward a common end.

The Technical Solutions: Information for Uncertainty. Uncertainty in the production process results from not knowing how to perform or combine tasks, a basic lack of information; thus, unless the need for information can be sidestepped, knowledge must be created or information must be transferred from another spot.[28] Pervasive uncertainty, then, means that high-technology firms must transfer enormous amounts of information. The possible organizational solutions push toward informal and personal transfer of this information along horizontal channels, as even the most cursory consideration of the alternatives suggests.

Communication needs can be reduced in several ways, but the "devices" are of limited usefulness for the problems confronting these firms. First, *rules* can specify appropriate behavior, thus ending the need for communication, unless there is a controversy over the rule or the exception. When the operations of a task are unknown or the criteria of mutual dependence and adjustment uncertain, no rule can be exactly pertinent. Even where rules exist, someone must deal with infrequent situations. They can be referred to a higher organizational level for decision, and thus a *hierarchy of authority* may reduce the need for communication by defining exactly who will make which decisions in the case of controversy. Yet if the problem is a lack of engineering or technical knowledge, referring it to a higher authority transfers responsibility, but it usually only succeeds in moving the decision away from the person with the best technical knowledge of the particular problem. Equally important in a situation where uncertainty is the norm, not the exception, the hierarchy will be overwhelmed if each case is moved upward, rather than solved at a lower level. This will be true even if the hierarchical superior is technically more competent than his subordinate. If, on the other hand, the problem is the coordination of mutually dependent tasks, then passing through a hierarchical superior simply adds a step in the transfer process, slowing it down and increasing the probability if inaccuracy. Second, *planning* can eliminate communication by prior consideration of the relationships between tasks, but this requires that the operation of each task and the relations between tasks already be known. When the task is uncertain and mutual adjustment required, this is not possible. Finally, *task differentiation and decentralization*—breaking up one large problem into manageable parts so that decisions can be made closer to the source of information—is certainly a necessary first step in firms that may be highly centralized. Once implemented, however, this decentralization produces its own needs for communication. The task remains uncertain, information must be found for a solution, and the task must be related to other tasks. Further decentralization may in fact multiply the problem of coordination and control.

The alternative is to increase the capacity of an organization to process information, and the characteristics of both unit production and the high-technology sub-group reflect this need; either an informal flow between individuals or an establishment of new organizational mechanisms may increase the information capacity. Let us consider in turn the two problems presented earlier, uncertainty in discrete tasks and mutual adjustment.

The first information problem, the search for technical solutions to the discrete problems of product development, is most effectively solved by informal personal contacts. Technological journals are seldom a source of ideas, since they rarely deal with basic principles, but rather discuss the characteristics of particular pieces of hardware.[29] Nor seemingly are technologists familiar with the scientific literature that could be a source of ideas. Yet the knowledge must be found and developed; and this development is both difficult and expensive.

A number of recent studies show that an increased use of organizational colleagues for information is strongly related to scientific and technological performance.[30] Thomas Allen of MIT has found that both the variety and the number of contacts independently contributed to performance. The problem of mutual adjustment may also be solved by informal personal contact, and in small firms, or for small projects in large firms, this is more important than any formal arrangements. Institutional mechanisms may be created to guide this process. Jay Galbraith of MIT suggests that this can be done in two ways: by continual replanning and by improving lateral relationships.[31] Vertical information systems which transmit information about the state of each task up to a central unit allow continual replanning. Especially under highly uncertain conditions, a plan can warn when delays or difficulties in one sub-task endanger the entire project, and thus replanning becomes a forecasting function, not the rigid guides to action that planning an assembly line implies. This may reduce the continual requirements for communication between units, both because the state of each other's task is continually made known and because the limits around each task are defined. However, to insure that information passed up the line is accurate and sufficient for a sensible readjustment of mutually dependent tasks, those units affected must be involved in the planning process. Replanning may thus reduce the gap between hierarchical levels and act as a lateral arrangement between different tasks.

Galbraith notes several other forms of lateral arrangements which provide communication channels that break the hierarchical, impersonal, sharply functional character of traditional bureaucracy.[32] Direct contact between managers can work when the operations to be controlled are sufficiently standard and predictable that each manager can promise adjustment without consulting anyone closer to the work. The production manager may be able to promise the sales manager more sweaters if he knows he can add another shift. Then the only question is cost. Liaison roles—primarily for transmitting information, not for making decisions—can be successful if the necessary adjustments are automatic when all the information is available. Task forces are institutional mechanisms set up when adjustments of several departments are regularly required. Teams, temporary groups created to solve particular problems, most thoroughly disrupt both authority lines and areas of responsibility. Assignment to them is said to be made primarily on the basis of quite particular intellectual knowledge, not experience, and in American firms senior executives may serve on a team headed by junior engineers. As the task uncertainty increases, the proportion of total decisions made at these lower levels increases also. A danger exists that individual decisions will reflect particular, not general, perspectives and needs. Integrating personnel such as project managers or material managers may serve the function of coordinating, directing, or controlling the discrete choices. In all these devices, the transfer of information involves people, not paper. These committees and roles could serve as mail conduits, but it is the direct personal contact which permits the exchange of views required to determine what in fact is important and to pass on the subtle, but critical, information that a written report often excludes.

Authority and the Control of Diffused Power. Coordination, particularly of mutually dependent tasks, requires more than the transfer of information. It also requires the authoritative choice of direction from amongst technically possible courses, which is a political function. Each group must recognize that performing its task in isolation is futile and perhaps even directly damaging to the firm. Because responsibility and initiative by each of those concerned can help minimize the danger that the multiple tasks will fly in different directions, American firms are often concerned to arrange rewards and sanctions to encourage such individual initiative. At the same time, however, authoritative upper-level decisions may be required, and hierarchy retains its uses. Clearly when several alternative solutions are available, each with different implications for the entire project, then an authoritative decision must be made. Every solution will require a different set of mutual adjustments; hierarchy cannot avoid that problem, but the choice between alternatives made by a hierarchical superior, a choice perhaps reflecting overall goals, might well be different from a negotiated settlement between different groups, which perhaps follows the line of least resistance. Importantly, an authoritative choice by a hierarchical superior requires the involvement of his subordinates, as in the case of replanning, if the options are to be realistically posed. Sharply defined hierarchical gaps may prevent realistic choices between the options facing the overall project.[33]

Thus, while one aspect of organizational contact is insuring the appropriate information flows, getting the right information at the right place, control remains a question of decision making and internal leadership. As a result, in high-technology firms the pervasiveness of uncertainty makes the control of diffuse power centers a critical problem. It would seem reasonable that the instruments of organizational control must be built around solutions to type of uncertainty which diffused power in the first place. Simplistically put, the only solution to technological uncertainty is skill at technological problem solving. Therefore, authority legitimated by skill, the solution to technical uncertainty, may be required to control power that has been diffused by uncertainty. Without skill to understand the problem and evaluate the solutions, the person invested with authority will be dependent on those he is attempting to control. Secondly, since the execution of any choice of development strategy or product strategy requires that further discrete uncertainties be resolved, subordinates retain considerable power to resist unpopular choices. In a sense, therefore, choices must be negotiated, and the respect for the skill of the superior may be critical in these negotiations.

Seen slightly differently, the individual with skill to resolve the uncertainties confronted in the production process has a basis for claiming authority, a claim that may conflict with other bases of authority. Organizational authority has many sources: historical position, seniority, personal prestige, as well as skill. Increasing the importance of one will diminish the importance of the others, and this will hardly occur without resistance. Because skill in science-based industry is not always a product of experience, a conflict between authority bases is nearly inevitable. When experience produces skill, as in traditional craft industries, seniority and skill would be linked together and would be perhaps closely related to hierarchy as well. In the case of science-based industry, skill is produced by engineering or scientific training in the university and may introduce a new conflict into the struggle for authority.

Uncertainty and lack of knowledge may make it possible for men to claim authority by right of skill, but it doesn't mean they can make good this claim. That will depend on the means that others, who base their claims on different rights, can muster to their defense. If the claim is established, and seniority diminishes as a basis of authority, then we would expect authority relationships to become less predictable and more personal. Thus task forces or teams, an institutional means of insuring lateral relationships, will in American firms often be headed by the men judged to have the greatest appropriate skill and not by those in the highest position in a hierarchy.

Several studies offer empirical support for this part of our theoretical expose, particularly for the notion that successful development requires a solution for the mutual adjustment problem. Galbraith, in his study of Boeing Aircraft Company's commercial division, argues that the particular structure and the structural change in the division were a direct and conscious result of the problem of task differentiation and coordination.[34] Jay Lorsch, in *Product Innovation and Organizational Structure*,[35] and Lawrence and Lorsch, in *Environment and Organization*,[36] found that in plastics, success of the firm depended on properly differentiating functions and then coordinating the mutually dependent tasks of development, production, and sales. In a related study of a German plastics firm, Lawrence argues that the rigid hierarchy resulting from German authority patterns was in part responsible for the firm's only modest success.[37] Similarly, a study of innovation in Danish firms has found that the openness of the communication system in the firm was related to its innovativeness.[38] Interestingly, the Bell System, certainly one of the most successful research and development networks in the world, considers the horizontal communications function of utmost importance, even in the physical arrangements of its laboratories.[39] It is a principle that groups working on related problems must never be separated both organizationally and physically. If they are organizationally separated, they must be in close physical proximity, and if they are physically separated, then they must have a formal horizontal organizational connection.

A dominant concern of the management literature has been the *best* way of managing industry—that is, the most efficient use of resources. But the question here is not simply how an industry can be efficiently managed, but rather *what constraints or limits are imposed on social organization by technology or industry.* Because these parameters underlie our discussion throughout, this section has moved slowly and cautiously. In summary, the argument has suggested a causal link between technology on the one hand and organizational structure and management style on the other. Analyzing the sub-group of unit-production technology, we have seen how the structure and management system evolved as solutions to problems raised in the production technology. Short, squat organizations reflect the lateral relationships that are created to allow information transfer. Organic management, fluid and informal, is a response to the shifting basis of authority and the diffuse character of power in the organization. Several organizational parameters for innovation-centered R and D based firms, particularly electronic firms, emerge from the discussion: (1) *fluid and personal communication links,* (2) *flexible definitions of authority,* (3) *the absence of sharply drawn lines between levels of authority,* (4) *authority based on skill,* and (5) *sufficient lower-level responsibility for the coordination of discrete tasks, each with a power base.* Put in different terms, success in these new industries places a premium on face-to-face contact, non-authoritarian relationships, the absence of defined and continuing arenas of authority, and considerable individual initiative and responsibility.

Authority Relations and Organizational Structure in France

French institutions from the state to the firm have traditionally been organized along very different lines from those described above. Observers of many facets of French life have consistently reported institutions to be centralized, segmented on both hierarchical and functional lines by rigid rules, and constipated by an active refusal to participate in the organization and by avoidance of face-to-face relationships. Michel Crozier, in his study of two French administrations, argues that these behaviors and structures are the particular expressions of French culture and French institutions, not simply universal features of bureaucracy.[40] Crozier offers both a specific model of French organizational behavior that has come to be accepted by most American and many French researchers,[42] and also an explicit argument to account for the character of French bureaucracy. Crozier's work will serve as a focus for this discussion and a basis for formulating our first hypothesis about the response of French firms to the production imperatives of electronics technologies.

The French Bureaucratic System. The French bureaucratic system, according to Crozier, is characterized by four important features:

1. The entire system is very centralized with enormous power assigned to the center. The characteristics which follow serve to protect against this enormous central power.[42]

2. Jobs and responsibility are sharply limited and defined. This results in (a) isolation between strata in the hierarchy and (b) isolation between functional categories.[43] This serves to protect against dependence on central authority and on others in the organization. "This freedom from interference—this independence—is therefore another form of the absolutist conception of authority. *To compromise, to make deals, to adjust*

to other people's claims is frowned upon; it is considered better to restrict oneself and to remain free with the narrower limits one has fixed or even those one has had to accept."[44] (My italics.)

3. A refusal to participate actively in achieving the purpose of the organization that might be best characterized as a refusal to take initiatives.[45]

4. This entire system is held together by precise and detailed rules that are adhered to very closely.[46] Change in the system as a whole consequently requires a change in the rules themselves, which can only be accomplished by the full exercise of central authority. The use of such central authority, often on the basis of personal charismatic appeal, is only acceptable during periods of crisis; consequently, the organizations pass through alternating periods of stultifying routine and centralizing crisis.

Crozier's argument is that the features of French bureaucracy emerge from the individual Frenchman's efforts to resolve a dilemma in his attitudes toward authority. "[The French] . . . cannot bear the omnipotent authority which they feel is indispensable if any kind of cooperative activity is to succeed.[47] Face-to-face dependency relationships (or conflicts)[48] are . . . perceived as difficult to bear in the French cultural setting. Yet the prevailing view of authority is still that of universalism and absolutism."[49] The features of French bureaucracy resolve this dilemma for the individual in the organization by carefully restricting the realm of action, the discretion and thus the real power of the central authority, which remains all-powerful in principle. Individuals' discretion in performing their work tasks provides them power within the organization which then can be used to achieve personal ends. Because these individual goals are shaped by the culture, bureaucracies should be expected to develop features which are specific to the cultures of which they are a part.

Crozier seeks to establish the generality of his model by identifying the characteristic features of the authority relationships he observed in the case studies in other aspects of French life; the school system, labor-industrial relationships, the colonial system, and bourgeois business structures. He draws, moreover, on a variety of sociological studies of French community and political life and its historical evolution. A subsequent study of Schonfeld provides an independent test of the model in a different domain and supports, without major disagreement, the important tenets of the original study.[50] Schonfeld's study, in addition, demonstrates some of the mechanisms by which characteristic authority relationships are learned. He argues that patterns of authority are taught by the schools at an early age, but once formed they shape the way individuals resolve crises. Children learn particular authority patterns in school because certain behaviors are rewarded, and they then apply these models of conflict and conflict resolution in later years.

Since Crozier's work and that of Schonfeld was based on the analysis of government administration, we should not simply assume that the same organizational features will appear in business organizations. The argument is that French institutions develop certain characteristic features as a response to the authority attitudes of individuals. The organization resolves an authority dilemma that members bring with them when they come to the organization. Any organization, therefore, composed of people with these distinctive attitudes, be it a business organization or a government administration, should display similar features. A bureaucracy, in Crozier's analysis, is an organization unable to learn from its mistakes, and a business can develop bureaucratic dysfunctions as easily as an administration.

A recent study of business management in four developed countries based on case studies of French and British firms, as well as secondary materials from America and the Soviet Union, support this argument and provide substantial evidence that French businesses display the organizational features described by Crozier, in sharp contrast with practices in other countries.[51] The French firms were highly centralized in "sharp contrast" to their British counterparts, but that centralism did not imply effective control. Despite the centralism, the bulk of the firms "seem to have been quite out of control. The management did not receive enough information to make rational choices."[52] Sharp and virtually impenetrable divisions were found between the hierarchical divisions within the firms, and equally sharp lines existed between functional areas. This isolation was further exaggerated by the unusually long time a French manager spent in a single post. In one company in which management careers were studied in detail, Granick concluded that "a situation prevailed in which not only was a movement between factory and headquarters positions virtually nil, but in which there was also very little movement between functions at the same broad managerial level."[53]

Both American practice and British experience were quite different. In several of the French companies, managers spent an average of eight or more years in the same post. The middle managers, who in fact controlled the operations of the company, moreover, were characterized as refusing to accept responsibility for the goals of their firms. "Middle managers cannot be counted upon to work either for the goals held by top management of for sub-optimizing objectives which would at least promote the well being of the individual units in the company. Instead their goals seem quite divorced from company objectives of any sort."[54] Finally, evaluation and promotion depended on external and impersonal criteria rather than on direct personal evaluation, as is characteristic of American and British firms. It appears, then, that French business is plagued by many of the same organizational difficulties as the government administrations studied by Crozier.

Even if one accepts Crozier's model as a general explanation of French organizational behavior, one must still ask whether these features appear in the bureaucracies of other countries. Crozier attempted in two ways to isolate the features peculiar to the French system from those elements universal to all bureaucracies. He contrasted his data on inter-group and inter-personal relationships with similar studies of American bureaucracies to establish that the isolation and centralism of the French model did not appear in the American materials. Then, drawing on other sociological studies, he drew the outlines of the Russian and American bureaucratic systems to suggest how power relationships produce culturally distinct bureaucratic forms. Charles Sabel, in an unpublished paper inspired by Crozier's work, has developed a model of German authority relationships based on materials from labor history.[55] The general lines of the argument, particularly the importance of participation as a value, sharply differentiate it from the French example.

That these bureaucratic features and the cultural values that give rise to them are incompatible with the technological imperatives for organization described earlier should be quite clear, but let us draw the lines of conflict as sharply as possible. The fundamental production problem, widespread uncertainty, means substantial discretion in work tasks, and thus should provide individuals with enormous power in the organization to achieve their individual ends. In the case of French firms we might hypothesize that a diffusion of power would result in a mushrooming of small fortresses of personal autonomy. The mutual adjustment of tasks by direct personal negotiation, which is required by the technology, is therefore a danger to be guarded against by the culture. Face-to-face authority relationships and loosely defined areas of personal responsibility tied together by individual initiative, both solutions to the problems of information transfer and organizational control, would be difficult to implement in a French atmosphere where rules, active non-participation, and sharply drawn responsibility lines are a part of the game and are valued in their own right.

Perhaps a concrete case can make this conflict between technology and culture more vivid. Earlier, it was noted that personal exchange of technical information was found to be directly related to success in solving the particular technological problems. Despite the benefits of such contact, oral communication is extremely infrequent, even in American firms. Allen argues that the cost of such contact, acknowledging inferiority, is extremely high.[56] The comment of one engineer he interviewed is revealing: "Either you are afraid you are going to look like a schnook when it's all over or you are afraid that this guy may not have enough time. I think everybody goes through this ever since they were kids." Another engineer remarked: "When you come into a place as a junior engineer, you ask everybody anything and they accept the fact that you are real dumb. After you have stayed awhile you ask fewer people fewer things . . . you are a bit querulous about displaying ignorance."

Interpersonal communication in interpersonal judgment situations clearly has inherent costs. In American firms, though, social relationships and friendships provide conduits for job-oriented communication.[57] In France, the problem would appear unsurmountable. First, given real costs of communication, the cultural tendency to avoid stressful interpersonal judgment situations would be an additional barrier to the necessary, but painful, face-to-face communication. Second, the French, as Crozier's evidence shows, avoid social relationships with work colleagues away from the job. This eliminates one solution that is available to American firms, which encourage off-the-job contact among employees.

Put in Woodward's terms, the technology asks for personal, flexible control of work but French culture tends to impose mechanical, impersonal control systems. Very simply, can a firm in which continuous change —technological and organizational innovation—is the daily routine, be grown on soil where change has traditionally been difficult without crisis? Unless the technological demands on the organization can alter the paradigm itself, Crozier's argument would lead us to expect that French high-technology firms would die of hardening of the arteries almost as soon as they were created.

The Conditions for Change in French Bureaucracy. Because the kind of organization required by the production technology of innovation-centered industry is clearly the reverse of the traditional French organization, the issue is whether French traditions and attitudes of authority will block the organizational changes required for industrial efficiency or whether these traditions and attitudes will themselves be changed. Crozier's model fails to specify what actions or outcomes are precluded by the style of French authority relations, and thus does not provide a direct answer to this question. The model's implication is that France is immune to change, but what may actually have been demonstrated is that although change occurs, some things remain constant throughout the process. Several arguments seem possible at this point.

Crozier's notion is that individual attitudes toward authority shape the structure and behavior of organizations. The very character of the argument implies that the "authority dilemma" is something which Frenchmen carry with them and must resolve wherever they go. Frenchmen in organizations, then, will use their personal power to force the construction of a structure that will solve the dilemma for them, a dilemma they bring with them when they come. Neither the schoolchildren in Naville nor the peasants in the Vaucluse, to take two cases cited by Crozier, are able to sustain face-to-face authority conflicts long enough to establish organizations or peer groups. Yet, assuming that authority attitudes are not in the genes, they are formed by the environment in which people grow up and live. The question that follows, of course is what are the mechanism by which they are learned, and what possibility of change exists? Crozier does not consider the conditions under which existing attitudes or an existing model of organization can change nor does he directly articulate theoretical assumptions about the way a cultural model of authority attitudes and organizational behavior is created and maintained.

Crozier takes another route of explanation at the same time, looking for the historical origins of the "dilemma" in the creation of the nation-state, the king's struggle to establish his power, and the bourgeoisie's effort to establish its social position. The implication is that actual conflicts in the social and political development of France taught the nationals certain "general" principles about authority which are preserved and perpetuated directly in the individual attitudes toward authority and indirectly in the organizations Frenchmen create. Yet, the linkage between this historical development and the individual authority attitudes that mold the orgnizational environment today is not spelled out. Crozier's approach, though, suggests the alternative explanation that the distinctive features of French bureaucracy resolve an organization's problems of dealing with the external environment. The internal patterns will change, then, when the external problems change. This argument serves as the basis for the second hypothesis, which is developed in the next chapter.

Finally, an important issue is how change occurs, if it does, and how it is successfully opposed, if it does not. The empirical results of this study, presented in Chapter 4, should help us spell out some of the conditions of change and stability in authority patterns and the process by which technological evolution provokes social change.

Hypothesis: The Conflict Between Technology and Culture

The conflict developed in this chapter must now be posed as a testable hypothesis. The two explanations presented here, one technological and one cultural, rest, it should be noted, on analyses of the internal workings of an institution in isolation from its environment. In this instance, clearly, they predict different organizations amongst French electronics firms. The hypothesis will draw the line as sharply as possible by assuming that the existing patterns will resist pressure to change and block organizational adjustment required by high-technology industry.

Organizational structure and management styles that favor success in the electronics industry appear incompatible with organizational structures and styles that resolve the French authority dilemma. *Given this conflict, and despite the greater efficiency and competitiveness of firms that are appropriately organized, the hypothesis is that the organization of the French electronics firms will reflect this authority dilemma by displaying the characteristics outlined by Crozier. The firms will not, as a result, organize appropriately to resolve their technological tasks, and therefore will not resolve the problems or display the characteristics outlined in this chapter.* The question immediately arises, how can the hypothesis be denied or affirmed?

The hypothesis can be denied in two ways. First, if it can be shown that the French electronics firms organize to resolve the problems of their technology, displaying the characteristics of American and English high-technology and unit firms, and not the characteristics outlined by Crozier, the hypothesis will be denied. In this case we will presume that the existing cultural rules do not prevent change. Second, if the French firms manage to resolve their technological problem within the constraints of the French organizational model, then we must presume the theoretical link between technology and organization reflects Anglo-American culture more than technological imperatives; this also will deny the hypothesis. The evidence on which the theoretical argument was built, after all, was drawn from studies in America and England, and it is possible that the firms display cultural characteristics as much as technological ones. The hypothesis will be *confirmed* only if it can be shown that the firms retain their French model organizations and display obvious difficulties solving the technological problems they face. Finally, the hypothesis and the problem must be *re-examined* if the French model organization is retained, not for the latent function of resolving the authority dilemma, but because it serves one or another functional purpose for the organization. The question of how organizational change can be measured will be considered when the evidence is introduced in Chapter 4.

The alternation of stultifying routine and explosive crisis with a charismatic leader seizing centralized authority to break up social logjams is often described as a fundamental pattern of French politics as well as French organizations.[58] The patterns of authority typical of politics, it is observed, can be found in other organized activity—a congruence sometimes explained by common attitudes toward authority throughout a society. (A discussion of this theoretical issue will be presented in Chapter 6). Crozier himself extends his arguments about the character and basis of French organization to a broader interpretation of French politics and French society.[59] It should be noted that if his arguments about French organizations are questioned, any extension of the argument to explain patterns in French society must also be examined.

3

A Competitive Industry in a
Protective Tradition

Because French firms have been insulated from the
marketplace by tariff protection, state subsidy, and cartel arrangements,
the issue of whether they adapt their organizations to the imperatives
of technology is a political one, not simply a technical matter of
industrial efficiency. The case of the electronics industry attracts attention
because the imperatives of its technology represent pressure for change in
traditionally organized French firms. The industry is all the more interesting because the devices of state protection and promotion of industry
that have long formed part of French economic and political life, and
which have proved successful in other industries, have been unable to
exclude or control the intense competitive pressure of the international
electronics industry. At least in electronics, the French, whether they like
it or not, are indeed part of an international industry, facing foreign
competitors at home and fighting for markets outside of France, and
therefore unable to escape the need for efficiency in the continuous
product development that rapid innovation requires.

The state, nonetheless, has been able to place a protective umbrella
over some firms in certain sectors of the market. This intervention has
created short-run alternatives to full-scale product competition for those
firms so favored. Though there are limits to the protection that can be
provided, the action of the state offers a political option to the competitive marketplace and its requirements for efficiency. Two worlds, then,
co-exist, one sheltered and one unprotected. For firms not in the protected
circle of favorites, the rapid technological evolution in electronics makes
continuing product development at an internationally competitive pace a
fact of life, and even in the protected sector the state can reduce

49

but not eliminate that pressure. The coexistence of a sheltered segment of the industry with a competitive segment means that we can observe the influence of state protectionism on the organization of the firm and, more broadly, the influence of politics on society's response to technological development. While the previous chapter considered the ways in which an evolving technology could provoke changes in social institutions, this chapter will focus on the fashion on which the action of the state and politics in general can blunt or contain these technologies' pressures for change. Put differently, the concern here is the business firm's relations with other institutions of the economy, most particularly the state, rather than with its purely internal dynamics.

The pattern of relations between business, the banks, and the state sets the structure within which particular crises are confronted or programs evolved, although clearly the solutions to one particular problem may involve changes in those patterns. This chapter will consider, first, the structure of business-state relations in France, which emerged from a common effort to suppress or at least control market competition. Only by viewing the relations between business and the state can we consider the state bureaucrat's perception of the problem, the available policy instruments, and the actual strategies adopted. In fact, electronics policy was one element of a larger strategy of state intervention in several critical industries, a strategy that is particularly clear in the oil and steel industries. The second section of the chapter will set forth that strategy. Therefore, before analyzing electronics policy, the dimensions of state activity in oil and steel will be considered briefly. In these industries, it should be emphasized, the state policies proved effective. After that, the evolution of the electronics industry will be examined to suggest why this general policy, when applied to electronics, was unable to insulate French firms in that industry from international competition, and thus how a competitive and a protected sector emerged. Judgments about this strategy for critical industries ought to be suspended until the final chapter allows the somewhat dismal electronics experience to be put into a broader perspective.

Finally, it will be argued that the influence of state policy on the firms in the electronics industry has been to encourage traditional centralized and functional organizations that are inappropriate to the imperatives of technology. In the sector where the state plays a role, guaranteed markets, development aid, and direct subsidy all combine to blunt the competitive pressure for organizational change; at the same time, the forms of the state's relationships to the firms, the techniques of granting and controlling the funds and of selecting state suppliers, encourage firms to mimic the centralized and funcitonal form of the state, or at least not to disrupt their existing and vital ties to the government. In France, that means preserving hierarchical organizations.

This chapter thus presents three arguments; first, one about the structure of business-state relations in France; then one about the nature of policy for critical industries; and finally, one about the impact of business-state relations in a critical industry, electronics, on the internal organization of the firm.

The Structure of Business-State Relationships in a Protective Tradition

The anti-market tradition in France has its origins in the very process of industrialization, which was initiated by a strong and centralized state and tended to leave in place and even reinforce many of the institutions and social groups of the traditional economy. The French have always had a "fundamental mistrust of market mechanisms,"[1] which have been viewed as threats to the ideal of a balanced and coherent society and as sources of social anarchy and economic waste. The market system implies that every commodity has a price, an exchange value set by buyers and sellers in the marketplace, and that each element in production—land, men, and money—can be treated as a commodity with a price set by exchange. The value and use of each commodity, then, is set by the activities of buyers and sellers and unrestricted either by social custom or by the intervention of the state. In a non-market society, economic relationships are submerged in social relationships; social custom and the political power that is synonymous with social position direct and dictate the uses of land, men, and money and the terms of exchange between them and between available commodities. One can, of course, have marketplaces for the exchange of goods without a full-blown market system, but the goods exchanged will be limited and their values constrained. An unrestricted market system, though, reverses matters: "the control of the economic system by the market is of overwhelming consequence to the whole organization of society; it means no less than the running of society as an adjunct to the market. Instead of economy being imbedded in social relations, social relations are imbedded in the economic system."[2] Such a system is not a natural occurrence, and intense political activity is required to set up its institutions and to break land, labor, and capital free from the social restrictions on their uses and values. In France the marketplace was never really allowed to impose its will on the community; a full-blown market system was slow in evolving, and the structure of social relationships preserved in the political arena set the channels through which industrialization would flow. Closed borders, active entrepreneurial intervention by the state, and negotiation rather than competition between businesses within France have all served to insulate the economy from the market. The French heritage of social protection against economic disturbance, of explicit limits on the operation of the market system, can be understood by examining the evolution of the agricultural sector and the economic role of the state bureaucracy.

In England, where the market system first emerged, agricultural relationships became commercialized very early—that is, obligations between landlord and peasant of goods and services. Moreover, important parts of the English peasantry were uprooted from the land, generating saleable land parcels and a pool of excess labor. This dual process created markets for land, labor, and capital.[3] In France, subsistence agriculture survived until the nineteenth century, and barter was the predominant form of exchange with only limited regional markets for grain.[4] The peasant remained rooted to the land. The French Revolution, in fact, reinforced the peasantry. At the time of the revolution, despite the feudal social hierarchy, the control of agricultural operations was in the hands of the peasants, not the nobility. The destruction of the feudal political structure during the revolution, therefore, did not require a reorganization of agriculture because it merely removed an intermediary, the nobility, which had been consuming the surplus but contributing little in return.[5] In fact, having seized control of the land in the revolution, the peasants were able to demand land guarantees as the price of their participation in the governments that followed.

An important part of France thus remained tied to a subsistence form of agriculture and, consequently, the old economic structure was left basically undisturbed despite the rise of some modern elements. Not only did this restrict the growth of disposable rural income, and thus the quantitative demand in the economy, but it blocked the establishment of a national market as well. Equally important, a powerful political clientele remained committed to a traditional economy. One lesson of the revolution was that the urban disorders could be contained if the peasants did not mobilize. Thus, state initiatives in the industrial sector, intended to bolster state power, could not be permitted to disturb the social calm in the rural areas, which was essential for the stability of any French regime. The revolution created a modern state, but it entrenched a traditional economy.

Before the rise of the doctrines of economic liberalism, the regulation of commerce and manufacturing by the state was a matter of course. The mercantilist creed, which Adam Smith was to repudiate in the *Wealth of Nations,* called for the use of the state apparatus to promote national economic power and later a unified national economy. In France, in sharp contrast to England, the state maintained such a role and guided the economy through the period of industrialization. John Neff suggests that the English crown had the same aims as the French king of harnessing and directing the national economy, but was unable to establish its claim.[6] In England, he argues, enforcement of the industrial regulations depended in large measure on independent local officials whose personal financial interests increasingly came to be attached to the private development of industry. Thus, the interests of those responsible for administering the state's will were at odds with the crown's goals. In France, however the king had begun to establish a centralized administration whose members were dependent on him both for status as members of the nobility and for financial well-being. The centralized state machinery, which never permitted its agents to form a local political base, gave the king a means of enforcing his claim to regulate economic life. Ironically, the institutional device through which the state exerted its economic will before the revolution was the old guild structure, again emphasizing that the traditional aspects of the economic structure persisted even as the political apparatus was modernized.

At any rate, once the state preempted the field of industrial investment, business success depended as much on royal favors as on entrepreneurial skill or efficiency. The state, some would argue, ended by creating the bourgeoisie as a political and economic class through its grants of economic power to nobles who brought neither capital nor technical skills to their positions.[7] The nobility disdained industry, and as a result no group existed which would challenge the state's assertion of economic power in these early years of industrialization. Since many businesses were political creations rather than entrepreneurial acts, it is not surprising that the bourgeoisie looked for political action by the state to resolve their economic problems, and only secondarily sought their solutions in greater efficiency and competitiveness. Protection, not competition, was the theme.

While the English bourgeoisie saw the government as an external force from which little good might come, the French had come to view the state as a necessary agent for the protection of established positions and an instrument for the creation of new wealth. Not only older families, but the newly rich as well, had built their wealth with the protection of the state.[8] Thus at the time of the revolution, "although new techniques, new forms of business organization and finance were implanted . . . they had not yet proved strong enough to affect a structural tradition. . . . The forces which tended to conserve the old structures and forms of economy remained deeply entrenched."[9] Industrial development from the beginning was closely bound up with the old regime and the state bureaucracy, and was never to become an irresistible force for change.

France, of course, developed after England and more slowly, and one might find in the difficulties of overcoming such relative backwardness a second explanation for the state's role in the economy. Alexander

Gerschenkron argues that in late-developing countries the necessities of a sudden burst to overcome the obstacles to development mean that the "more backward a country, the more likely its industrialization was to proceed under some organized direction; depending on the degree of backwardness the seat of such direction could be found in investment banks, in investment banks acting under the aegis of the state, or in bureaucratic control."[10] The need for greater organization results in part from the technical problems of creating the greater scale of plant and firm required by steel as opposed to textile technology, in part from the absence of a broad pool of entrepreneurs to spark the process spontaneously, and in part from the rapid change required to provide simultaneously all the technical perquisites of growth and to obtain its fruits before one's enemies advanced. Such organization, of course, entails suppression of the market and conscious planning of the direction of industrialization.

In the French case, though, this seems only a partial explanation of the state's dominant place in the story of industrialization. In the early part of the nineteenth century it was textiles, not steel, that led industrialization, and French industry held to "putting-out" production methods much longer than in England.[11] The enduring small scale of French enterprise, perpetually fighting off the banks, also suggests a piecemeal family investment with slow-paced growth rather than an organized burst. In the second half of the nineteenth century, when admittedly industrialization was proceeding more intensely in France, the question centers around the different roles played by the state, the banks, and individual entrepreneurs in organizing and initiating industry. The relationship between bank and state was certainly intimate, the state depending on the *hautes banques* for important pieces of finance[12] and the banks finding finance of the modern state to be the first massive investment market, but their relations in the course of industrialization are not clear. We need an analysis of the initiation and development of the industries fundamental to French growth, an analysis that would delineate who sponsored the investment possibility, who initiated investment, who organized the capital, and whether the state or the banks sought to guarantee profitable conditions for the firm. Only in this fashion could one estimate the various roles played by state, banks, and business entrepreneurs in nineteenth-century French growth. Gerschenkron attributes great importance to the emergence of industrial banking in France under Napoleon III.[13] The Crédit Mobilier offered a model that spread across Europe, but he makes no clear argument about the importance of industrial banking to French industrialization. Landes argues that the industrial or investment banks played a greater part in the story of German industrialization than they did in France, though the innovation was clearly French.[14] Investment bankers in France, he contends, simply could not find profitable investments in their own country, or, more exactly, those enterprises that seemed promising refused bank interference. Bouvier goes further, in fact, and argues that the banks in France always played a passive role, and developed by following rather than leading growth.[15] The investment banks undoubtedly affected the reorganization of particular industries after the Second World War, and in prior years most certainly aided the process of cartelization. While they are a powerful and autonomous force, they are by no means a directing conductor in the French economy.

Two distinct traditions of business-state relations emerged from the early and enduring involvement of the state in French industrial growth, each tradition expressed and supported by a different set of institutional relationships, a separate structure. The tradition of arbitrator encompasses the protective tariff, the cartel, and the trade association, whereas the state entrepreneurial tradition is linked to the system of Grand Corps, as Friedberg argues. In its *paternalistic role* as the arbitrator of social conflict the state acted to maintain social harmony by defending established rights and positions. Industrial growth was deliberately slowed down to preserve the agricultural sector, while high tariffs sealed France off from outside competition. Negotiations and agreement, then, limited competition within her borders. The market was something to be controlled by business arrangement and political action, not something to which one adapted, and certainly the notion of self-balancing economy has been alien to French thought up to the present time. John Luethy put it well when he wrote: "They [the French administration and business community] are all imbued with the same spirit and the same mercantilist tradition, sheltered by the same legislation and legal tradition which regards every *situation acquise* as worthy of protection and every *fond de commerce* as a claim to hereditary income, and they are all fenced around with the same protectionism."[16] In sum, the state was not considered an alien force to be limited, but an instrument for protecting against the unknown and guarding what one had already gained.[17]

Central to all such policies was the protective tariff. From before the revolution, French tariff barriers were among the most restrictive in Europe, and in the mid-fifties on the eve of the Treaty of Rome they were the highest in the European community. Only at two brief moments were French tariffs driven down, and each time the decrease was imposed by an autocratic ruler against the wishes of the nation's industrialists. The treaty of 1786, which reduced restrictions on British goods, was implemented for political reasons, but protests against it are to be found in the *Cahiers* of grievances that preceded the revolution some three years later.[18] Some seventy years later Napoleon III concluded the Commercial Treaty of 1860 with England, with the intention of stimulating French producers to adjust to the most advanced world standards, even at the risk of losing their own home markets. Although these two reductions of government restrictions on trade were "liberal" in form, the policy was not at all aimed at removing the government from the economy. Since the government granted dislocation loans to facilitate readjustment, it was left in the position of directing industrial development. The policy "was based on a recognition that national power was bound up inextricably with industrialization and it was intended to impel manufacturers to improve their technical efficiency in the national cause. In other directions, indeed, policy was interventionist rather than liberal."[19]

Otherwise, throughout the nineteenth and early twentieth centuries, protectionism ran rampant in France. Since entrepreneurs sought to hold on to what they already had rather than run risks in expanding their holdings, tariff protection of the home market was more important than any opportunities abroad that might be created by free trade. The growing British industrial advantage only served to further fuel the protectionist fires. After Napoleon Bonaparte, protectionist policy firmly gripped France, and the nearly reflex character of this instinct for economic isolation and security is suggested by the high, even prohibitive, tariffs on resources, such as coal and iron, which were in short supply in France.[20] In fact, the manufacturers were correct in their belief that penetration of the national market by cheap English commodities would force difficult business readjustments and might mean failure; and thus, although some economists and publicists might trumpet the argument for free trade, there was no constituency ready to make tariff reduction into a vibrant political issue. "Every sectional and local interest, with but few exceptions, contributed its quota to the protectionist pressure."[21] As a result, French manufacturers tended to slumber behind the tariff wall and to specialize in high-cost luxury goods that did not require either a mass market or low-cost production and technical innovation.

Napoleon III's experiment in state-imposed free trade ended with the establishment of the Third Republic and stands as a brief gap between two long periods of protectionism. The protectionist movement that emerged in the Third Republic was even more broadly based than that which had preceded the Empire. As the peasants were slowly drawn into the market economy, they, too, became vulnerable to price shifts in the world economy. In particular, the large-scale cereal growers were hit by a sudden jump in world supply made possible by lower transport costs, and they became ready allies for the industrialists who had never really accepted the Commercial Treaty of 1860. Thiers, head of the government at the start of the Third Republic and a committed protectionist, broke the commercial treaties and used the need for increased revenue as a pretext to raise tariffs in 1872, but the real pressure for prohibitive tariffs did not flower until the 1880s. During the long depression from 1882 to 1899, French industry retreated behind the seeming security of tariff walls, and the movement culminated with the Meline Tariff of 1892. This law was reinforced in 1910, and France was not again to depart from her protectionist doctrines until she entered the Common Market in the 1950s.[22]

The tariff and other restrictions served to exclude foreigners who were not part of the national bargain and allowed French producers to manage the marketplace. Within France, business life has long been arranged and negotiated by the state or between the businessmen themselves. Dividing the market assured the survival of the inefficient firm and guaranteed a stable environment with steady profits for the low-cost producer. Thus, industrial growth could proceed without disturbing the acquired position of the inefficient. The best-known mechanism of the arranged market, the formal cartel, did not become important until after the First World War, but by the eve of the Second World War there were thousands of cartels, each controlling 80 to 85 percent of the production in their particular industrial sector.[23] In some industries the arrangements were simply gentlemen's agreements, while in others, of which cement was one, they were so strictly regulated that quotas had a market value.[24] The collective management of the marketplace even extended into joint borrowing arrangements that gave the industry as a whole control over the growth of productive capacity of each of its members. Joint ventures by established producers preserved the existing structure of industry while at the same time permitting some new technologies, facilities, and products to be created. During the Third Republic, the cartels were generally run through the particular industry's business association and often housed in the same building,[25] and some business interests even demanded that arrangements be made compulsory if a majority of the industry supported them. During the Vichy years, they became the instrument of state industrial planning. Immediately after the war some efforts were made to weaken the cartels, but they continued to operate. In the middle 1960s Bruce Scott and John McArthur wrote: "It would appear that the state not only tolerated, but in some cases encouraged seller concentration and that a number of cartels were under state supervision at the time of our research."[26]

When stable arrangements could not be established among the producers themselves, the state has often intervened to regulate competition and manage the division of markets. Despite a criss-crossing of financial control, the electronics industry, for example, never appears to have been stably cartelized. French businessmen have acknowledged that efforts were made to control competition, but claim that the implantation of American firms and the instability of product lines as a result of rapid innovation has blocked these efforts. Government purchasing, by military and civilian agencies alike, has nonetheless systematically divided the market on politico-economic criteria rather than through procurement open to competition.

The cartels served to organize production and manage the marketplace, while their counterpart, the trade associations, served to keep the state at arm's length. In industries composed of small and medium-sized and often family-owned firms, as most of French industry was until quite recently, the trade association acts as a filter for the contacts of an individual company with the state, and as a result relationships between firm and state can only be distant and impersonal.[27] In fact, they are often quite hostile. These trade associations are organized along both product and geographic lines as a confederation of equals. With social as well as economic interests frequently linking the members, they are often said to be corporatist in character, aiming as they do at the self-regulation of industrial sectors. The state is expected to provide protection against outside competition and general and impersonal support which will not benefit one firm at the expense of another, while arrangements in the marketplace are to be left to the industry to work out, usually within the structure of the trade association.

Such a protected environment, of course, tends simply to reproduce itself and to suppress elements of spontaneous change and expansion.[28] In part because restrictions and regulations limited the industrial change and innovation that was possible, the state became the important source of pressure for industrial development, and came to play an *entrepreneurial role* in the economy. Colbert, whose name has been linked to an activist role for the state, was motivated by a concern with the power and security of the government, not with economic growth as it was later to be conceived. He created, nonetheless, a tradition of state subsidy and encouragement for larger manufacturers. In Colbert's period, the manufacturers of the state, which included arsenals and luxury goods such as Gobelins tapestries, "were strictly artificial creations set up to serve the needs of the state, to reduce dependence on foreign imports, or for other reasons of non-economic kind."[29] More recently, the creation of an independent oil company or the less successful history of the French computer company shows that the state is still ready to play a central and dynamic role. But today, as before, state intervention is not motivated by economic reasoning.

These entrepreneurial activities of the state, though, have generated arrangements entirely different from the trade-association and cartel patterns. In sectors such as metals, electronics, and particularly oil (where government action virtually created an independent industry) strong, direct, and unified state action is facilitated by the interpenetration of state and business leaders. "Contacts and relations between the two are easy, frequent, direct, and informal with a constant flow of information both ways, giving especially the state an opportunity to be well informed and build up the kind of industrial and economic expertise it needs for its interventions."[30] Government officials and business leaders are united by common education in the Grandes Écoles, particularly Polytechnique, and membership in the Grands Corps of state administrators which monopolize areas of state decision making and guide the careers of their members.

Admission to Polytechnique, or more recently to the École Nationale d'Administration (ENA) is virtually a requirement for career in the top echelons of government administration and business. A competitive exam determines which students will fill the handful of places at Polytechnique and at ENA, but this elite is further filtered as it leaves the school. Only the top students win a place in the Grands Corps. These corps are independent organizations, or perhaps better considered as unions, of high civil servants that in fact control different pieces of the state administrative machinery. A large corps like the Ponts et Chaussées contains only 1200 members, while a small corps such as the Inspection des Finances is restricted to 300 members. In the most prestigious corps all members are recruited from the top graduating members of the ENA or Polytechnique class. Certain corps recruit only from ENA, others only from Polytechnique. The more technical corps are usually from Polytechnique, the administrative corps from ENA. Polytechnique's control of the highest positions in the state administration is now challenged, though, by the alumni of the École Nationale d'Administration, a school established after the Second World War to modernize the training of the very top echelon of state administrators. However, the principle of selecting a tiny elite on the basis of a competitive exam remains the same, as does the competition between the corps within the administration. The alumni of ENA simply are a new entrant in the competition for power. The monopoly of these corps in segments of government decision-making machinery allows them to assure their members tailor-made and prestigious careers, and after serving the government the members of the corps can go on to claim the top management posts in private business.

In the world of private affairs the rivalry between corps and ecoles continues as each corps attempts to dominate different companies in order to provide new careers for its members. Writing about the Corps des Ponts et Chaussées, Jean Claude Thoenig explained this strategy:

> Spectacular initiatives are launched in the direction of the business world. Certainly the corps has occupied positions in the private sector for many years, but these placements are now being multiplied. The strategy which is pursued is intended to create new and solid footholds that will allow the corps to control certain branches; electrical construction, road and bridge building, transportation and the like. Georges Peberau's departure for the CGE in 1969 is a symptom of this strategy. Having completed a reform of the Ministry of Equipment, the head of the corps left the government to take up a post in one of the most powerful businesses and he took with him a whole series of his comrades from the corps.[31]

In companies with close links to the state, members of a particular corps may dominate the top general management positions. More generally, Polytechnicians are a significant factor in most important companies. Twenty-three of the fifty largest companies in France had a graduate of Polytechnique as chairman or president or both, and another fifteen had at least one Polytechnician as a vice-president.[32] The result is a tight network of professional and personal ties that connects the managers of the firms with their government counterparts who are likely one day to be their successors.

Both patterns of business-state relations continue in modern France, although one or the other may predominate in a particular sector. Many techniques, in fact, remain the same, even if the exact mixture and emphasis of state policy has shifted over the years. Protection from foreign competition and the internal management of the market continued until after the war. French entry into the Common Market, however, broke up the game of protection and market sharing as it had been played under the Third Republic. "By 1969 . . . most French enterprise was competing directly in its own traditional markets not only with the subsidiaries of foreign firms but with goods produced in other countries. At the same time French industry was selling industrial goods abroad in ever increasing quantities."[33]

Increased French competition with her industrial partners did not mean, however, that the role of the state as protector and entrepreneur in the economy was abandoned or that bloodthirsty competition had come to France. The external pressures, and consequently many of the tactics, did change; some of the weak have been "retired" or a future retirement presaged, but others possess sufficient political strength to prevent their elimination. Furthermore, the rearrangement of industrial holdings by the banks and government in many industries suggests that a position in the old protected world was entitlement to a stake and consideration in the revised game. At worst, the weak are usually paid a price for abandoning the field. The state has taken an active hand in reorganizing certain strategic sectors, not to encourage internal struggle but with the intent of protecting France by making her leading firms internationally competitive. In other sectors the impact of the Treaty of Rome has been delayed or cushioned by compensatory state action, and one might speak of administrative rather than tariff protection. Competition, at any rate, retains a special meaning in France and certainly is not exposed to the penalties for weaknesses which abound elsewhere.

Emphasing the continuity of the government's role in the French economy should not, however, disguise the fundamentally new elements in the equation. The removal of trade barriers has forced the French economy to integrate into the European and world markets and has brought organizational and strategic changes in the firms. The logic of competition and measures of industrial performance have been introduced as guiding principles in the industrial reorganization that has occurred. Such measures of performance focus government attention on the behavior of the individual firm, the fundamental producing and selling unit in the economy, and French enterprises are less able to hide their inefficiency in the shadows of industry statistics. The global figures and industry performance which average the results of the firms and could serve for industry-wide negotiations with the government are no longer a defense for the individual firm against outside competition.

The state is no longer satisfied to guard a static balance in the economy, but is carefully and selectively prodding business to adopt competitive policies of growth. The strategy, in essence, is the one adopted by Napoleon III one hundred years ago. Foreign competition and the threat of such competition is used to give the state leverage in reshaping the economy, while tax incentives and outright intervention, particularly under the Fifth and Sixth Plans (covering the decade 1965-1975), encouraged mergers and rationalizations of certain sectors. Whether as a result of these policies, or increasing competition, or changing entrepreneurial motivation, industrial concentration did begin to rise. The number of firms in 41 industrial sectors declined from 400,000 in 1955 to 355,000 in 1963 and the market share controlled by the ten largest firms was slowly increasing, reflecting a recognition that the small, ineffective firms were hardly suited for the rough terrain of a competitive Europe.[34] While the increase in concentration was modest, it is a sharp change from the steady levels in previous decades, and the trend has remained the same since 1963. At the same time, strategies of the largest firms have become more competitive, and the structures of the firms have been correspondingly rationalized.

The most explicit use of state power to create competitive firms has been the careful nurturing of "national champions."[35] These businesses are aided by the state in their reorganization and expansion so that they may serve as defenders of the French market and flag bearers abroad. Friedberg described this strategy as follows: ". . . develop and if necessary create a few important companies able to hold their own on world markets. For this, all means are good, and especially reducing competition by product specialization and administrative regulations, thereby guaranteeing each company a predominant and sizable share of the French market as well as protection from competition abroad."[36] The contrast of gargantuan American firms with the abnormally small French firms, reinforced by the French popularization of the Galbraithian vision that the technological and industrial future lay with the giant firms, urged a quick promotion of a few large firms, particularly the fusion of small firms into bigger ones; but in the rush— as is increasingly acknowledged—the potentially important role of medium-sized and small firms was overlooked.

The French have now come to recognize that large size does not mean competitiveness, but of course competition was never a goal in itself. It was considered a device to obtain politically defined goals. State policy walks a delicate tightrope when it promotes firms that will be competitive on the world market without introducing "socially destructive" competition at home, since it is difficult for a firm to play entirely different roles at home and abroad. This dilemma is reflected in the very way the national champions were fostered. A national champion could be created in two ways, either by merging together existing small firms into one large firm, or by encouraging the rapid internal growth of a small or medium-sized firm well suited for combat. Merging small firms avoided internal competition and permitted producers to be paid for their existing market positions rather than driven out of business by a hungry competitor. Gentlemanly mergers, though, have often resulted in serious internal problems that have weakened the firm in the international market.

The policy of national champions also has sources in the administrative needs of the government. In arguing for a *dirigiste* policy of creating competitive French firms, Lionel Stoleru, an American-trained economist who has long worked with Giscard, argues, in fact, that the state should aid only one, not several, firms in each sector: *"Assistance, but for whom?* For one company, and not for two. . . . It is appropriate therefore that the state have opposite itself one single point of decision that can take the responsibility for each of the industrial objectives that might be pursued."[37] (My translation, author's italics.) Such a policy certainly reflects the concern that French industry not waste its energies with internal combat, but it also suggests a government need for a single strong industrial counterpart with whom it can negotiate its industrial policies. The tendency, moreover, has been to infiltrate Grand Corps members into upper management, thus providing the state bureaucrat with a personal counterpart.

Clearly, then, the shift in emphasis of state policy away from protection and toward promotion has entailed changes in the structure of relations between individual businesses and government. An entrepreneurial industrial policy intending to encourage the competitiveness of particular firms and hoping to influence the development of particular sectors requires direct communication between businessmen and civil servants. The trade association as an intermediary simply stands in the way of such a relationship and has been increasingly bypassed through devices such as the coordinating committees of the National Economic Plan. The shift of emphasis in government policy, therefore, has encouraged the expansion of the second, or Grandes Écoles, model of business-state relations and has expanded the power of ex-civil servants in the top management of important industrial groups.[38] Some industries now present a melange of the two patterns. In electronics, for example, the large firms deal directly with the state while the trade association represents the interests of the others. In this industry the implantation of American firms who then join the trade associations makes these associations thoroughly inappropriate for national economic planning.

Both patterns of business-state relationships allow for planned control of the marketplace, it should be emphasized. The difference between them is in who shall carry out that planning. In the trade-association model, businessmen arrange matters amongst themselves, while in the Grandes Écoles model the state plays a dominant role.

The change in emphasis of state policy toward active intervention also brought changes within the apparatus of the state during the presidencies of de Gaulle and Georges Pompidou. Power and responsibility were moved away from ministries with sectoral responsibility, such as the Ministry of Industry and Scientific Research, toward administrations with more general responsibilities, such as the Planning Commission attached to the Prime Minister or the Ministry of Finance.

The Ministry of Industry, importantly, preserved the trade-association pattern of industry-state relations in its own structure. Divided into seven sectoral administrations, each with a specific tutelary responsibility for the well-being of particular industries as a whole, the Ministry's objective is to wheedle and cajole the firms to assure a "harmonious development." Such harmony means assurance that there were no sudden layoffs or other sudden dislocations. To gain a voice in the affairs of industry, the Ministry becomes a lobby for industry within the government "to show that it is capable of obtaining the aid of the state."[39] Before entry to the Common Market, it was largely responsible for tariff policy,[40] and it remains concerned with even-handed and impersonal mechanisms of state support or programs which permit small gifts to be widely distributed. Its influence has diminished as policies of intervention in favor of particular objectives or specific firms have increased the importance of financial assistance and incentives in the governmental gamebag.

The elaboration of a general industrial policy using financial incentives has increased the importance of the Prime Minister with his technical staffs, which include the Planning Commission, and the Minister of Finance, who has control of the budget and an iron grip on all expenditures through the network of finance inspectors. In the electronics industry, there was little question that policy was being formulated in the cabinet of the Prime Minister and the Minister of Finance and imposed on the operating agencies. In ministries with general, not sectional, responsibilities, decisions cease to be simply technical and involve difficult political choices and exchanges between different sectors and often between particular firms. The result, according to Friedberg, is an increased politicizing of industrial planning. At any rate, when the Prime Minister and the Minister of Finance are in agreement, they can swing the weight of the centralized state apparatus behind their joint policy; but when they have differing perspectives and responsibilities, conflict is inevitable. The continuing conflicts between the Prime Minister's industrial planning service, the Commissariat Général du Plan, and the Minister of Finance could be characterized in several ways. McArthur and Scott remarked on a "recurring opposition between agencies mainly committed to growth (e.g., the Planning Commission) and agencies mainly committed to fiscal stability (e.g., the Minister of Finance)."[41] It is the Prime Minister and his staffs who are responsible for drawing up the long-term plans of the government, but the Ministry of Finance has the greatest influence in their execution, and thus there is inevitable conflict between long-term objectives and daily constraints. The daily constraints are not simply financial but also political, and planning officials point out that short-term political considerations are often central in the decisions of the

Prime Minister. Since the Minister of Finance calls on firms to adopt policies that are politically but not economically profitable—policies such as maintaining production in an inefficient plant to sustain regional employment—it is hardly surprising that he is responsive when demands are made on him by the firms. Such cooperation tends to protect both the firm and the state from the consequences of the market-place; both profits and political stability are preserved. The intimate ties between the leaders of business and state make possible this kind of give and take.

In sum, each ministry in its own way expresses a distrust of the market mechanism, either in overtly supporting the firms or in attempting to manipulate industrial organization and firm structure so that market outcomes will be more politically acceptable. With the Ministry of Finance providing short-term support for political reasons and the Ministry of Industry attempting to pass around prizes to maximize its influence, even a policy intending to prod firms into becoming more competitive can easily degenerate into a simple arrangement of subsidy and a shelter from the marketplace. Everyone wants change, but no one wants the pains; we can therefore expect that any adjustments to demands of the market that are directed by the state will be slow and partial.

With Giscard's presidency the power and purposes of different ministries have been altered and some tactics of state intervention are shifting. The emphasis since his election in 1974 seems to be on the *coordination* of state power toward specific and selected ends rather than on a continuing effort to maintain coherence in the economy. The Planning Commission's influence is diminished, and many of its officials have left seeking more promising careers. A high level "planning" group that includes the President, the Minister of Finance, the Minister of Industry, and the head of the Planning Commission now meets monthly to consider specific problems of industrial and economic policy. Under Giscard, in fact, the Planning Commission may find its role as the technical arm of this inter-ministerial group. Less effort will be made to direct the evolution of particular industries, which in some ways reflects an ideological emphasis on private power and in part expresses an acquiescence in the growing power of the major companies. Similarly, there are some signs that in high-technology areas less emphasis will be placed on the purely French character of projects and more on the economics and market feasibility.

State Intervention in Critical Industries

The state's assumption of an activist role in electronics, then, had well-established precedent, and an array of institutional devices for intervention was available. In fact, government policy closely followed the broad strategy pursued in both the oil and the steel industries: a state alliance with financial holding companies—often backed by one or several banque d'affaires or the direct control of access to financial markets—to initiate new firms or to amalgamate old ones for particular policy ends. Common to the three cases was the state's definition that each industry was critical to the national well-being because it provided a vital input to industrial production and national defense. Because the industry was defined as vital, the state sought to insure a structure of ownership and production that would allow French national control over the industrial operations.

The striking difference between the three industries is that the policy was successful for oil and steel but not for electronics. Success here is defined as the establishment and maintainance of an industry structure satisfactory to the state; or put differently, that the state could make the industry conform to some acceptable version of its original image without being stymied by political opposition or economic difficulty.* It will be argued in a later chapter that the difference in policy *outcomes* in the three cases results from differences in the *requirements* of success in the three industries and the possibilities of state leverage, suggesting the strengths and difficulties of state industrial intervention in France. When evaluated as a whole, it must be emphasized, the record of state industrial intervention is much brighter than if electronics is considered alone.

In this chapter, the task is only to suggest the similarities in policy approaches and to trace the evolution of the electronics industry in order to demonstrate the state's inability to achieve its purposes. The main effort in the next sections will be to examine the impact of state policy on the three French industries—oil, steel, and electronics. Following these industry discussions, a section will focus on the impact of state policy on firm organization.

Oil. Since the early twentieth century, a vocal and powerful segment of the French bureaucracy has perceived oil to be a political problem for the state, not simply a matter of profit for private firms. The dual purposes of policy have been to assure French-controlled oil supplies with a minimum of strain on the balance of payments position. Two state-created oil companies have served as the instrument of this policy.

*This in no sense implies that some magical economic optimum was achieved or even sought, since the French bureaucrat will often reject on social or political grounds the American economists' definition of the concept of economic optimum. The definition here is similar to that used by Harvey Sapolsky in his study of the U.S. Navy's development of the Polaris submarine.

In the years before the First World War, the French oil industry consisted of a handful of small distributing companies, none of which were refining facilities, let alone its own oil reserves, and all of which were dependent on Standard Oil of New Jersey.[42] These companies known as the Cartel des Dix, were organized in a traditional fashion, using market sharing agreements and tariff protection to avoid competition. Then, in the 1920s the international majors launched an invasion of the French market, buying up the distributing companies they had been supplying and making them into direct subsidiaries. Foreign capture of a potentially profitable sector of the economy was not well received, the Banque de Paris et des Pays-Bas in particular having interests in this area, but security issues and perhaps the vaguer notion of the integrity of French supply were at stake as well. During the First World War the French war effort had been threatened by an oil shortage, created in part because American ships were withdrawn from the dangerous North Atlantic route. Thus, as in the case of electronics later, the refusal of American companies or the U.S. government to supply a vital resource provided the incident that gave substance to fear of French dependence on foreign sources of supply.

Two political initiatives, one domestic and one international, allowed the French to recapture part of their own market. First, the state established a quota and licensing system to regulate oil imports, limiting the importation of refined products in order to prompt the construction of refineries in France.[43] Critically, this system allowed the government to insure a place in the market for the production of any French company it might choose to create or support. The problem remained, of course, where a French company would obtain oil to import, refine, and sell. Through diplomatic initiatives the French government won and preserved Middle Eastern oil concessions. After the First World War, German rights in the Turkish Petroleum Company were transfered to the French government, and the right to develop these oil lands was assigned to a newly created firm, the Compagnie Française des Pétroles (CFP) which thus became a member of the Iraq Petroleum Company and each of the other cartel arrangements amongst the international majors.[44]

The CFP, suggested by Poincaré, was set up to combine the interests of all existing French petroleum companies, as well as of the major investment banks. Its first president was Ernest Mercier, a Polytechnician who had gained experience in oil matters during his service in the Ministry of Armaments. His career in oil, though, was made by his friendship with the director of the Banque de Paris et des Pays-Bas, who was actively promoting a French presence in oil. Mercier was, at the same time, on good terms with the other major banque d'affaire involved, the Union Parisienne, and thus he was able to mediate amongst the principal French interests. Interestingly, he then staffed the CFP with ex-Polytechnicians.[45] The organizational form of the firm proved quite difficult to settle, however, because business interests were pushing for a purely private company. In fact, private groups resisted the formation of any single firm, whether public or private, for fear the state could control one firm more easily than many small ones—a fear that proved well founded. A sudden and substantial oil discovery combined with fear of a leftist electoral victory brought quick agreement in 1924, leaving the company primarily in private hands with limited state involvement. In 1929 foreign minority stockholders, allied with French independent companies that also held stock in CFP, tried to prevent the company from supplying finished products. To repulse this bid the state purchased 25 percent of the stock and took its one-fourth of the seats on the board of directors. The firm, at any rate, was created at the initiative of the state in alliance with currently operating companies and the major banks; it was intended to "farm" an oil concession handed to it by the state for sale in a market guaranteed it by the state.

In the 1960s the state-controlled share of the oil sector was the Enterprise de Recherches et d'Activité Pétrolières (ERAP), in which a majority of shares were publicly held. This firm was established to exploit the Saharan oil fields that had been opened by massive French government expenditures for exploration. State companies had initiated the exploration and development of Saharan oil, and to provide an outlet for this new supply the state "bought its way into the refining and marketing business"[46] by purchasing 60 percent of the French refining and marketing system of one of the majors, Caltex. Then in 1963, when import quotas were renewed, it provided an increased market share for ERAP and forced other companies operating in France to take up part of the Algerian oil that ERAP was producing.

This enterprise was motivated by concerns for the balance of payments problems created by increasing French dependence on oil for energy, a conscious decision that formed a part of the Fifth Plan. Coal production declined absolutely, and therefore oil as a percentage of French energy needs grew substantially. This dependence on energy purchased outside of France was intended to be a temporary matter until large-scale nuclear power could be brought on line in the 1980s. Since this transition was consciously planned by state bureaucrats, provision was made to accommodate the increased expenditures for imports. As long as Algeria was part of France, which it was when the plan was initially drawn, Saharan oil could be treated as domestic production, but even after Algerian independence there were important advantages in importing Saharan oil through French companies.[47] First, if a French company —particularly a state-owned company—produced and imported the oil, only royalties paid to the host government represented increased imports that would have to be compensated by greater exports. Secondly, direct government-to-government dealings, as between a public French company and the Algerian oil ministry, permit direct barter agreements of manufactured goods for oil, so that payment to the economy as a whole is settled before any balance of payments problem can begin. For the French, with a history of protection and insulation from international markets, it seemed a most unattractive gamble to assume that the increased imports could be paid for by some spontaneous and independent increase in exports when it was possible to settle matters on a direct government-to-government basis. Thus bilateral government-to-government dealings in the oil arena, a feature of French policy long before the current oil crisis, have their roots in the mechanism of state intervention at home. However, at least until the radical price increases of 1973, Algerian oil was more expensive than other Middle Eastern oil, with the higher cost simply being passed on to the French public in higher retail prices. Similarly, the rationalization of the coal industry was financed by artificially high electricity charges. Higher prices, as long as the problem was one of internal distribution and not balances, were not obstacles to a policy of energy independence for France.

Steel. In the steel sector after World War II, the state faced a fully developed industry composed of myriad medium-sized and small companies linked together through a crosshatching of financial holdings which presented a united front through its trade association. Perhaps because the industry had been so effectively cartelized—for many years the steel industry had collectively managed its own production and investment levels on both a national and an international steel basis[48]—the state was able to deal with it effectively through the mediation of a trade association, when in most other instances the trade association simply filtered out government influence. The reorganization of the steel industry, at any rate, was accomplished in two phases, each phase tied to a conjunction of circumstances that allowed the state to force basic changes in industry structure.

The first phase ran from the end of the Second World War through the early years of the European Coal and Steel Community (ECSC). Steel was the pivot of postwar efforts to plan reconstruction, and in those early years the planners sought to insure that investment in capital facilities would be on as efficient a scale as possible, and that capacity would be expanded to allow for the planned growth of the economy. Immediately following the war the firms were entirely unable to finance new investment themselves; and the state had control of the newly nationalized deposit banks and was able to allocate funds from the Marshall Plan to projects it might choose. The threat of competition implicit in the creation of the Coal and Steel Community was, clearly, the other government instrument during these years. Not unexpectedly, it made the firms more-amenable to promptings for greater efficiency. The creation of the Coal and Steel Community represented an institutional commitment by France to the principle of continued economic expansion. In fact, one might argue that the ECSC simply replaced the formal International Steel Cartel that existed before the war. The important difference was that the ECSC allowed direct government influence on steel-industry plans, and that as an institution the ECSC was committed to expansion while the cartels were tied to stabilization by restriction.[49] At any rate, as will be argued later, the ECSC did not bring about a reorganization of the steel industry across national boundaries, but rather drove the firms more closely toward their own governments.[50] Only in Belgium and the Netherlands did adjustment to the Common Market bring internationalization.

In France, state action to prompt economic growth was a new idea, though, and the planners sought to enlist industry cooperation for its plans, rather than to compel acceptance. This was not simply a technical choice of how planning might best be accomplished, though the planners do not appear to have been ideologically enamored of administrative planning, but a broader political strategy of securing a constituency for their activity, by demonstrating to the capitalists that planning was a profitable matter.[51] Consequently, the patterns of ownership in steel, which were often antithetical to economic efficiency, were left fundamentally untouched during these years, although all of the major steel groups were reorganized between 1945 and 1956. These reorganizations involved some 75 percent of total French steel capacity. About half the reorganization occurred as part of the period of reconstruction, but the other half seems to have been a response to the creation of the Coal and Steel Community.[52] The initiative in these matters of ownership, though, seems to have been left to the industry. Throughout the fifties and early sixties the government continued to influence corporate investment strategies, and even the structures of steel firms, but only in the middle sixties did its influence come to predominate.[53]

A formal contractual agreement between the steel industry and the state signed in 1966 involved basic changes in the structure of production and ownership. After extended negotiations and much against its will, the industry, in the form of its trade association, agreed to the plan because it was in desperate need of substantial government financial assistance. After a virtual doubling of steel sales between 1955 and 1959 in France, demand stabilized both in France and abroad, leaving substantial excess capacity throughout the world.[54] At the same time, strict steel price controls established to fight inflation—controls imposed in direct violation of the rules of the ECSC—squeezed the profit margins and cash reserves of the companies. Modernization and expansion thus required outside financing, which was available only as debt rather than increased equity in that period in France, and the debt position of the firms was already so great that further borrowing would have been difficult and even servicing the current debt was hard. As McArthur and Scott put it: "In short, the industry was financially overextended, and neither domestic nor export markets seemed likely to improve very quickly. . . . Some firms were better off, some worse. Indeed some of the older firms were virtually bankrupt and were being kept alive only by support from the state."[55]

Finally, changes in steel-making technology began to make seaside locations more competitive than inland locations closer to national coal and ore sources, thus outmoding nearly the entirety of French steel capacity. Steel firms, it must be remembered, were accustomed to reaching agreement on investment plans amongst themselves and then collectively approaching the banks through the agency of the trade association, which borrowed funds for the entire industry. Such collective borrowing protected the loans of the bank by spreading the risk of all banks across the entire industry, while the internal agreements that led to the collective loan request tended to insure the financial position of the banks. In negotiating the 1966 steel convention, the state therefore simply played the traditional role of the lending banks, making massive investment funds available at especially favorable rates in return for a virtually contractual agreement from the industry to fulfill a plan of reorganization. The state, unlike the lending banks, though, was interested in the productive structure of the industry, not simply in the security of its investments. Thus, instead of simply acquiescing to a plan agreed to by the firms, the state pushed its own plan. Formal "contracts" between the state and industry were an innovation of the Fifth Plan. The counterpart in electronics is the Plan Calcul, to be discussed later.

Despite the powerful position of the state at this juncture, intense negotiation was required to force private firms with important political resources to give way. The negotiations were successful, it appears, because the trade association was able to maintain its position as spokesman for the entire industry. In fact, though, there is no clear political picture of the bureaucratic and political maneuvering that produced the agreement or of the continuing negotiation associated with its implementation. The implementation of the plan has wrought such basic changes, it should be noted, that it cannot be said whether the trade association will be able to retain the role it has played until now. The increasing concentration of ownership and professionalization of management may allow for increased penetration of the firms by the Grands Corps and more direct state negotiation with particular firms.

Formally, a virtual duopoly has been established in the steel industry (leaving out special steels): domination in the north by Usinor/Lorraine Escaut, and in the south by de Wendel-Sidelor, with the state financing development of a seaside production facility for each group.[56] The signing of the 1966 steel convention was hardly the end of negotiation and conflict, as firms and groups large and small maneuvered to retain independence during the industry reorganization, or at least to assure an advantage position in the series of mergers and fusions.

Although the number of firms has been reduced, the industry remains archaic in many ways. The maneuvering of financial holdings that formally constituted two steel groups has not clearly been accompanied by a unification of operating control or a fundamental rationalization of production. Horizontal financial interconnections between steel companies—that is, ties amongst firms producing identical or similar goods rather than vertical connections in which one firm produces inputs for another—are common in France and particularly prevalent in the steel industry.[58] Such arrangements have served to manage competition by implicating everyone in everyone else's affairs. New production, moreover, is often organized as a joint venture, which avoids competitive investments by providing something for all. The large French firm organized as a "Groupe" is more closely equivalent to an American holding company than a corporation. That is, central management focuses on financial maneuvering and is distanced from productive operations, and since conflicting interests are often included in French "groups," operating changes cannot be simply administered by management but must be negotiated amongst the interests that form the holding. Therefore, awkward and divided management structures have often been the outcome of financial fusions. This has, however, allowed a certain degree of family control to be retained in steel, and has preserved smaller firms and inefficient plants as well. Particularly in the de Wendel family empire, it is reported that certain plants have been preserved for their historical and sentimental value despite their complete obsolescence.[59] Jack Hayward has summarized the arrangements in steel quite well:

The trend to concentration, however, did not guarantee the achievement of larger production units. In keeping with French precedents, combinations in France's steel industry were achieved by horizontal rather than vertical integration, accentuating the industry's "closed" and introverted character. Concentration took a financial rather than industrial form, leading to the creation of larger holding companies, but not necessarily to bigger production units. This process was facilitated by the fact that all the major and even some of the smaller steel companies were linked with investment banks. A prime motivation in the strategic choices of the French steel industry was the preservation of some measure of family control. This was imperiled by any form of merger, but much more by mergers of physical facilities than by financial mergers alone. Accordingly hierarchies of holding companies and joint subsidiaries were created among the producing firms. These, together with a multiplicity of bilateral agreements sharing out markets and sources of supply, were staging points in the process of eliminating competition. . . . Like the government, the major steel firms wanted to dominate and control market forces rather than submit to them.[60]

Consequently, improvements in productivity have been much slower than those that would in fact have been possible if the traditional ownership and production pattern could simply have been stripped away. Clearly the firms had political resources substantial enough to prevent their simple elimination. Particular families and interests had political power and the state bureaucracy was concerned that French control, at least over a partially modernized industry, be maintained. In fact, some evidence exists that the gap between productivity in French steel and the productivity of its continental neighbors which existed before this reorganization has in fact grown. That is, French productivity, which was initially low, has improved, but the productivity in other continental steel industries has improved more rapidly.[61] Productivity improvements, though, have been adequate to preserve the French steel industry without unduly high steel costs that would have threatened the competitive position of the rest of French industry. Thus, since the improvements achieved since the war would have been unlikely without state intervention, and since the reorganizations have avoided any serious crisis for the French economy and have maintained French control of its own steel supply, the state intervention in this sector must be judged a success.

Electronics. During the middle 1960s the survival of an advanced electronics industry became a national priority. Whatever the exact events which prompted this concern, the logic justifying government support is clear; an independent electronics industry consisting of firms controlled by French capital and not dependent on American technology is required for a French military and economic independence. The mythology has it that the American government's refusal in 1966 to permit Control Data to sell a scientific computer required for weapons development the year after the French firm of Machines Bull was lost to General Electric sparked the French government's active interest in the industry.[62] In fact, the concern was more general, although those events undoubtedly shaped the form of the government's intervention.

One government committee, in addition to invoking the national defense, also called up the image of a France mired in hopeless underdevelopment as a justification of increased government support: "The importance of electronics is not measured solely by the production of sales figures of the branch, which only represent 1.5 percent of the Gross National Product, nor by the number of employees, which only represent 0.6 percent of the active population. . . . In fact our country cannot give up an electronics industry, and a complete electronics industry, without entering onto the road to underdevelopment.[63] (My translation.)

For a country willing to pay the costs, national self-sufficiency for military reasons is a political choice, not a technical question; but the economic value of a technically and financially independent production capacity, distinct from the capability to utilize or absorb new production and communication processes, is unclear. Whether the state's economic return on investment in the increasing the *use* of computers, process-control production, and numerically controlled machine tools would have been higher than its return on investment in the support of a financially and technically independent French computer company was a question left undiscussed. The notion of national self-sufficiency and technological glory was, by the time the choice was made, an unquestioned value. The government intervened to achieve a political goal of technological independence, not an economic goal, however defined.

A distinction, though, must be made at this juncture between programs and activities to support the electronics industry as a whole, and the Plan Calcul, which established a French computer company as the joint subsidiary of major firms. The Plan Calcul was directed by the Délégation à l'Informatique and emphasized data-processing policy. In the Planning Commission, however, there was another group, COPEP (the permanent electronics commission, the only permanently constituted industry group at the Planning Commission, which concerned itself with the industry as a whole). Although separate institutions charged with different responsibilities existed, not too much must be made of the distinction, since the two policies intimately affected each other and the same actors within the state and in the industry were involved in each case. The head of COPEP in fact became second in command at the Délégation à l'Informatique. The plan for the data-processing industry, which envisioned computers playing a central role, was the most elaborately formulated, spelling out even precise product strategies and levels of state support, while the policy for the industry as a whole evolved on a more piecemeal basis. The computer plan, though, gave a technological rather than commercial cast to the whole policy. Let us, then, first consider the original choices of the Plan Calcul.

Whatever the wisdom of the decision to create a French computer firm, it certainly appears that once again the government bureaucrats chose to do what they knew best—wield the power of the state and manipulate the web of school and social ties between the top-echelon businessmen and government officials—to create operating companies, direct capital flows, and establish guaranteed markets.[64] Broadly speaking, there were two decisions to be taken. First, what would the goals of the state be, and after technological independence became the objective, what would the goals mean in operational terms? Second, who in the state and the private sector would organize the activities of the industry and thus be the instrument of policy and the recipient of state assistance; and after a commitment was made to a state-supported computer company, who would organize it and control it? Those who set the options and took the choice, it should be noted, had working experience inside the government ministries managing state research of production facilities, managing companies almost exclusively dependent on state purchasing for success, or in the politics of merger and joint venture. Virtually no one had experience managing a market-oriented company, let alone a company in the competitive and difficult field of computers and components. Two commercially based strategies were proposed, but neither found strong allies in the government, and in the end all the policy options were defined as means of achieving technological independence for France. The options themselves reflected the responsibilities of the agencies involved, while the common experiences of all the state officials tended to exclude a competitive and dynamic business strategy as an option.[65]

The policy choices were finally formulated by the head of the Planning Commission. One set of proposals came from the permanent planning group for electronics (COPEP), set up at the Planning Commission even before the Machines Bull affair. A second early lead came jointly from the civilian and military research agencies. Throughout, the planning group was more concerned with the impact of the computer industry in the economy as a whole, while the research agencies were more concerned with scientific and military applications. Each emphasis became a formal policy option. Neither group really focused on what was required to foster a competitive and profitable computer company. The question of business strategy was addressed only after the different purposes each agency urged on the government were defined. The computer subsidiary of Schneider and an independent consulting firm urged a strategy of aggressively exploiting competence in particular sectors, but they seem never to have found widespread support in the business community or in the government. Certain holding companies and banks urged an entirely different solution—some kind of agreement with Bull-G.E.—to assure a profitable but not autonomous French presence. However, since French independence was decided as one of the objectives of the plan, this approach was rejected.

Each of the final options was linked to a different notion of independence. If strategic independence meant the ability to develop the atomic weapons required by the Gaullist Force de Frappe, then large-scale computers primarily for scientific use, such as those of Control Data, were required. If independence meant the ability to use and produce computers when needed, then support could be given to companies to exploit the market niches in which they had the greatest competence. If independence meant the ability to develop an industrial capacity in the range of computers of greatest importance to industry and business, then medium-sized computers similar to those already produced by IBM were required. Although this last option was thought of as an economic strategy, it is dubious that subsidizing the use of French-produced business computers in French firms, products they could have in any case and which were not strategically important, would be of more economic value than competitive companies turning a profit in a less difficult sector of the market. This last strategy, though, was chosen, and it meant that the new company would find itself in direct competition with the bread-and-butter line of IBM. The government, it was thought, would make this strategy viable by a combination of subsidy and a guaranteed market amongst state agencies. Equally important as the profit strategy, the large-scale effort involved permitted a merging of the computer subsidiaries of nearly all the large groups, thereby assuring everyone a piece of the action.

In April 1967 the agreement between the electronics industry and the state was signed. The computer plan would force existing companies and the banks that supported them to pool resources in a single joint subsidiary. This produced enormous organizational problems that would handicap the new firm, Compagnie Internationale de l'Informatique (CII), but it did solve the political problem of *who* would control the company. An elaborately specified program of aid and assured markets was to nurture this infant through its early years, but although hopes of profits were expressed early on, these dreams faded quickly and the real message that the computer plan conveyed to the firms was that they should turn their face toward the state, not the marketplace. This would affect the entire industry.

After the Plan Calcul was formulated, there was general agreement and a unity of purpose about the direction of policy for the industry as a whole, so much so that one may speak of a "French" policy for the electronics industry. During the Fifth Plan, the efforts of the Planning Commission to encourage fusions and to promote a national champion meshed with the efforts of the Ministry of Industry to win substantial subsidies for the sector. The Ministry of Finance, which is said to have incurred important political debts to the French group (of Thomson-Houston), strongly supported subsidies for this firm during the Fifth Plan in the second half of the 1960s. While the various ministries used similar policies for divergent purposes, there was, of course, substantial dissent. For example, the client ministries, the PTT (postal, telephone, and telegraph service) and the military, did not support efforts at fusion that would saddle them with a single supplier and thereby limit their price-quality negotiating power. Similarly, the DGRST in the early 1970s unsuccessfully opposed efforts to use R and D funds to direct subsidies to particular groups. However, because the Plan Calcul, the Minister of Finance's Cabinet, and the Prime Minister's Cabinet are said to have taken an active role in policy formulation, dissent was effectively squashed and a coordination of policy achieved.

By the time the French state intervened, American firms had already taken up powerful positions in computers and semi-conductors. From the beginning, the structure of the international industry which favored the Americans in certain products was a set of obstacles to French electronics policy, not a set of constraints on an industrial strategy. The initial problem, therefore, was to protect French firms from the consequences of the market, not to help them adapt to it. French policy was intended to compensate for what were seen as three weaknesses in the competitive position of French firms: the firms themselves were too small; the French market was too limited; and American firms were subsidized by military and space programs. (For an analysis of the French perception of their competitive position, see Chapter 5.) Intervention, then, took three important forms: the fusion of small firms and the creation of a national champion firm; the support of French exports in semi-competitive markets; and the creation of internally protected markets for the national champion and other privileged firms, and the outright subsidy of these firms.

The Thomson-Houston group emerged from a decade of positioning and fusions as the French electronics champion. (CII is a subsidiary of this firm.) Its president, Paul Richard, certainly expressed the conventional wisdom when he argued that "without the efforts of Thomson during the last four years, French electronics would no longer exist . . . there would no longer be today a French electronics industry capable of playing an international role."[66] As national champion, Thomson has the right to claim the aid of the state to maintain the position of the firm and thus of the French government. As Richard expressed it, "I ought, moreover, to underline that this effort, indispensable for maintaining French electronics in the first rank position it occupies on the world market, could not be pursued without satisfactory financing of research, studies, and development, equivalent to that which all the major foreign companies received in their respective countries."[67] Thomson's demands have been met, and it has been the single greatest beneficiary of the state programs, though not the only one.

Active government support for exports to the Eastern bloc and Third World countries, where competition has been more political than commercial and technical, has been the second part of the electronics policy. The justification of what sometimes sounds like a de-emphasis of efforts directed at truly competitive markets has been the argument that French presence should be extended throughout the world. Occasionally such a policy is even overtly defended, as when the weekly paper of the French electronics industry commented on export figures showing that over two-thirds of French exports went to the Third World: "Contrary to the situation in other industries, French electronics judge that it is better to make an effort all over the globe than in the Common Market. The industry believes in effect that assuring a strong position in these markets against international competitors, including America, is a priority. This will permit the realization of future hopes for markets closer to home."[68] (My translation.)

The result, in practical terms, is the extension of a protective umbrella over at least a portion of the market, reducing the pressure on French firms to match the international development pace or to develop their own competitively based export policy. Some industry observers contend that these state-supported exports are essential to a continued French electronics capability in many areas. Not only do they provide important income to firms such as Thomson, which exports 25 percent of its production,[69] but they may also provide sufficient production to reduce average costs, and thus the price of these products to the government, to acceptable levels. Furthermore, these exports tend to cover the import of advanced products from the United States. A strategy emphasizing export to the industrial world would have forced firms in the state to develop *an economically based commercial and business strategy* in order to effectively enter the market. Eastern bloc and Third World exports, at the same time that they reduce competitive pressure, permit the continuation of a bias toward technological self-sufficiency.

Such export markets, of course, simply supplement the market that the state can provide through administrative purchases, made primarily by the military and the government-controlled telecommunications system. Government markets, of course, are not created to support the electronics industry, but they can be manipulated to serve industrial objectives. Both the PTT and the military have offices of industrial policy which serve to coordinate their purchasing with the more general industrial strategy of the government.

The third technique has been direct subsidy of particular firms. Aid has passed through a variety of programs, some, like the Plan Calcul, aimed directly at the electronics industry, and some such as the DGRST's (the Délégation à la Recherche Scientifique et Technique) *action concertée*, aimed at industry in general. The two primary goals have been to subsidize the development of particular technologies and to create a French national champion as an instrument of that technology polity. As discussed above, the Plan Calcul and its sister program, the Plan des Composants, for example, were outgrowths of the Bull affair. The core of the program was the creation of CII (Compagnie Internationale de l'Informatique) as a joint venture among three electronics groups—CSF (then independent of Thomson), CGE, and Schneider. This firm was then provided certain guaranteed markets in the administration and aid for development and research to create the products. Computer technology, though, is so directly dependent on component technology that support for the semi-conductor industry was also required and provided through the Plan des Composants. Since CII and the component firm, SESCOSEM, are now both subsidiaries of Thomson (after the plan was initiated, in fact, SESCOSEM was absorbed into Thomson), the bulk of the assistance has gone to one firm.

There are, in addition, programs of aid for research and development that are, in effect, subsidies of particular companies. In absolute terms, the subsidies represented by the Plan Calcul are larger than the other forms of aid, but R and D subsidy is untied money that can be used to support particular firms or to bail them out. Prior to the 1960s, the subsidy was pure and simple, and a shift to more formal contracting methods, although it may have broadened the number of firms receiving funds, changed very little.

Unlike the oil and steel sectors, however, policies of state promotion and protection in electronics have not been particularly successful in helping French firms retain control over the national market.* The structure of the French electronics industry was created by these efforts

---

*This discussion is not concerned with the consumer-goods sector of the industry, which is a different problem and story. In an important way, though, many problems were a product of the difficulty of relating consumer policy to industrial policy.

at state protection in a viciously competitive international industry. The intense pace of new product development meant that only outright prohibition on imports and the implantation of foreign companies could have moderated the competitive forces. The French, with a small and vulnerable segment of the market and committed to an international economy with at least formal open access, had no way of slowing the competitive pace to a more convenient tempo. The state has been able to shelter some firms, but the rest have had to face the strong headwinds of competition. Since continuous and rapid technological innovation was a central element in this competition, no firm could escape the need for ongoing product development. The culture-technology conflict outlined in the second chapter cannot, therefore, be quietly sidestepped.

The competitive pressures and technological advances in each of the vast variety of electronics goods, from complicated computers and radars to such basic and simple elements of industrial control as detectors of proximity, cannot be reviewed separately, but perhaps they can be summarized by describing the evolution of the active components which are the industry's building blocks and which establish the limits of the capabilities of electronic goods. In the fifty years of commercial production, active components have undergone three fundamental revolutions, representing quite distinct generations: electron tubes, discrete semiconductors, and integrated circuits. Both the jump from one generation to the next and the rapid development within each basic component conception have altered the size, the reliability, and the price of the components, which in turn have affected all electronic products.

The electronic tube, the industrial realization of years of fundamental research and development work, is the grandfather of active components. It works by altering an electric current as it passes through the space enclosed by the tube that contains either a vacuum or an inert gas. Until the 1960s all electronic products were built from electron tubes, and although the capabilities of these tubes increased enormously from the early efforts at radio until the development of sophisticated radars, they all have important and inherent limitations: (1) because heat is used to operate the components, they must be cooled and other parts protected against the heat; (2) the tubes burn out—that is, they have a theoretically finite lifetime causing reliability problems in any system such as a computer or a telephone exchange that uses thousands of tubes; (3) the design of the tube inherently limits reduction in price and size; and (4) they are fragile and easily damaged by shock.

The transistor, first produced at Bell Telephone Laboratories around 1950, performs the same functions as a tube, but it operates within the bulk of a semi-conductor material—that is, a solid material which conducts less well than a highly conductive material but better than an insulator. Transistors, which have in actual industrial practice been made first from germanium and then from silicon, have four primary advantages; (1) the transistor does not require heating; (2) its size is much smaller than the vacuum tube; (3) it has no time-dependent failures—that is, no inherent reason why it cannot operate forever; and (4) it is less vulnerable to shock. Because the Bell Telephone System is an enormously complicated electronic circuit or a collection of such circuits, and thus always faces problems of reliability and repair, it provides an enormous captive market for any component advances that might emerge from its laboratories. Thus even without military interest in component advances, Bell would almost certainly have brought the invention of the transistor to the commercial stage. Equally important, Bell was under an antitrust ruling forbidding it to become a general component vendor, though it could produce for its own needs. It stood to benefit, therefore, by royalties and cross-licensing agreements from the general diffusion of the new technology, and Bell, as a result, encouraged the rapid diffusion of the transistor.

The integrated circuit was a logical development that would have been developed without military assistance, but the active interest of the armed forces held out the lure of vast military markets and at least the assurance that successful development efforts could be quickly amortized. This attracted the interest of existing giants and small but ambitious companies. The integrated circuit, a combination of two or more elements— specifically, two or more transistors, diodes, and passive components which are inseparably associated within a silicon crystal—began to appear on the markets in the 1960s. Integration further increased reliability, decreased size, and as the technology matured the cost of any given element within the circuit began to drop radically.

These two technological jumps were not, strictly speaking, the result of the economics of competition *within* the industry, since the transistor was supplied and diffused by Bell Laboratories and the development of the integrated circuit was a response to a unique and tantalizing military market. Within each component generation, though, several factors favored the rapid and continued development and commercial exploitation of the original breakthrough.

Although learning-curve economies occur in all branches of industrial production, they are critical to an understanding of the component business because they have a peculiar impact on business strategy in the active component industry. The cost of producing semi-conductors appears to decline by 20 to 30 percent every time the total number of units produced doubles.[70] That is, with every doubling of the total number produced, the manufacturer learns enough to permit that substantial reduction in his costs. Since the initial market for the product is very small, every production run is limited to tens or hundreds of an item. Production volumes build very rapidly during the short lifetime of a particular product to millions of units a month, and the price declines resulting from learning economies are spectacular. As a result, a firm that enters the market early and captures a sizable portion of that small market can defend it with growing ease against would-be intruders. If a firm captures a larger share than any other producer, its costs will decline more rapidly, allowing it to take a predominant position in a particular product. *In a sense, the only defense in this business is a total offense, in which early market entry is critical.* Some firms even sell products at a loss in the early stages to capture a sufficiently strong market position and the benefits of the learning curve. Cases are reported of firms that sign contracts to sell a large volume of a product at a price below its current production costs, fully confident that the continuing decline in production costs will allow it to make a profit on the entire contract. Product advances will therefore be exploited because an early edge by a competitor may never be overcome. Furthermore, once forced out of one product, a firm will direct its efforts toward creating new products because it can recapture its position by rapidly commercializing the next advance. Because entry into the market by small newcomers was easy in America during the 1960s, this pace could not be controlled by agreements between the leaders.

The transistor and the integrated circuit changed the technical limits on electronics product design, but it was the continued price decline which made it possible to use these new components in industrial and consumer products where price is an important part of competition. Initially costs were high, making the first market military and space equipment, a market where reliability, resistance to shock, and small size are of prime importance and cost control is a decidedly secondary consideration. As prices declined, industrial and consumer applications became possible. The pace of this price decline was as important as the technical possibilities in determining the rate at which manufacturers substituted new components for old and thus the rate at which new products were developed. Between 1963 and 1968, the average price in the United States for integrated circuits dropped by more than 90 percent,[71] but this was only a prelude to the full-scale price war of 1971 that was launched as over-capacity appeared from military and space cutbacks.

This simultaneous and continuous increase in the technical capabilities of components combined with the decline in their prices has had a powerful impact on firms making electronic products. Entirely new products have become possible, and existing products have been redesigned. Hand calculators could not have been made from tubes, and the performance gap between one generation of computers and another makes it difficult to market old models.

Several competitive factors maintained the innovative pace among equipment manufacturers. An innovative firm can reap a monopoly profit until its product is duplicated and marketed, which certainly attracts interest in exploiting technical possibilities. Moreover, since product innovation always demands lead time for development, even a firm not eager to push the pace of innovation must undertake defensive R and D to protect itself, and once development is underway, there is certainly a temptation to reap the benefits. Equally important, the ease of entry even to equipment markets has certainly encouraged existing producers to keep out new entries by marketing new products.

Any effort, furthermore, to control the overall pace of innovation by implicit or explicit agreement would be complicated by the international character of the industry. Not only do electronic goods have a high weight-to-value ratio, making shipment a small portion of costs, but the temporary monopoly that exists between the time a foreign producer invades the market and the first national producer begins production reduces the effectiveness of tariff barriers as a means of isolating a single national market. Even more important, the low capital costs of electronic production facilitate the implantation of factories in any market. Only utter prohibition of imports or foreign implantation can isolate a national market.

Product competition on continuing innovation is therefore a fundamental feature of the electronics industry that French firms could neither control nor avoid. Faced with competition, though, they have fared well, and evidence of French difficulty is certainly abundant. Foreign companies implanted in France dominate the industry, and the American grip on the French market for components and computers has particularly disturbed the government by sparking fears that French destiny—or more exactly, Gaullist military policy—was slipping into American hands. In the computer business, American firms—principally IBM, Honeywell-Bull, and Control Data—control 75 percent of the French market.[72] In semi-conductors, American firms and Phillips of Holland entirely dominate the market for the more advanced product lines. Certainly in these two fields no broadline French producer would exist had it not been for the continued entrepreneurial and financial aid of the state. Even with substantial assistance, CII, the state-promoted computer company, can only sell its smaller machines in the competitive market, the rest of its sales going to administratively controlled or influenced purchasers. SESCOSEM, the component company of France, was recently absorbed as a special division of Thomson Houston-CSF, also the parent company of CII, because its losses had reached unacceptable proportions.

In all, French-controlled firms produce only 45 to 48 percent of the value of non-consumer electronic products actually manufactured in

France. Protective policies are only successful in heavy electronic equipment, where the state is the principal final purchaser and can provide a guaranteed market. In the more competitive sectors, French firms represent only 35 percent of total production.[73] In addition, part of the market is filled by imports and part of that 35 percent figure still represents direct state purchases. Thus, French firms are virtually unable to defend the home market, except when the state is the immediate client.

The French are heavy trade debtors to the United States and the other advanced countries, financing this deficit with substantial export to the Third World and Eastern Europe. Often these exports are made possible by the direct political intervention of the state. Some observers contend that these exports do more than simply even the trade balances, but are essential to the survival of French-controlled industry. Not only do they provide needed income, but in certain cases they represent the marginal production necessary to reduce unit costs to a competitive position. Thus, although the French cover their electronics imports with exports, the geographic and product mix of that trade does not reflect strength but weakness.[74]

A number of stronger French entries in the industry, such as Machines Bull and CSF, have, moreover, met with sudden death from financial crisis. Bull was taken over by G.E., which later sold Bull to another American, Honeywell. CSF was merged with Thomson-Houston and Hotchkiss-Brandt, following a financial crisis in which its development expenditures had soared and its market position weakened. Thomson-Houston was primarily an electrical consumer-goods company, usually producing more advanced electronic products under license from G.E. Since the absorption of CSF, the original firm has become a holding company, and Thomson-Houston-CSF its professional electronics subsidiary. This holding company represents some 60 percent in sales figures of the purely French electronics capability.[75] Many observers contend that it is a very sick company, despite its sophisticated technological capacity, and that it would die without continued government tending in the form of administrative protection (exhortations to "but French," export assistance, and direct subsidy). It is important to note, then, that the French firms have not simply been squeezed by American pressures, but have died from internal weakness as well.

French business leaders and policy-makers attribute the weakness to the enormous American military and space expenditures that created the electronics boom, while American firms, although acknowledging that they reaped certain benefits from these government programs, hastily point to the signs of weakness in the product development and commercial efforts of the French firms. Finally, there are those who blame French government policy, but their critiques are divided between assertions that the government provided too little support and claims that the nationalistic and technological character of the policy destroyed whatever chances French firms might have had in the first place. (See Chapter 5 for an analysis of the dilemmas and difficulties of French policy in electronics.) Whatever the causes, the weakness of the French firms and the state efforts to compensate for them are evident in the shape of the French electronics industry.

The postwar evolution of the electronics industry has been characterized by the implantation of foreign subsidiaries and the sharp rise of imports, by the regroupment of the French firms as they have attempted to form a defense, and by the active intervention of the state to maintain a French presence in this strategic industry. The result has been a bipolar industry that at once expresses the competitive pressures of the internal electronics firms and the protective heritage of France. Very schematically, the larger firms that now dominate the industry were created by two distinct processes that represent quite different business instincts and purposes. On the one hand, there were the subsidiaries of foreign companies that settled in France with the intention of capturing a portion of the French market as part of the parent company's strategy. Among the American firms, there are those like IBM, which had been established in France for many years before the postwar electronics revolution, and others like Texas Instruments and Honeywell, which have entered only in recent years.

The second group are French firms that grew to their current size by merger and acquisitions rather than by internal growth. Though no reliable data exists, industry sources unanimously report a steady increase in mergers and fusions among the French firms. In the 1950s the industry was composed of a few medium-sized and many small firms. The number of firms has remained the same, but the domestic market has continually expanded.[76] The smallest firms have exited, and their place has been taken by American firms producing in France and by small, specialized equipment manufacturers. In fact, these two processes—American penetration and French regroupment—have been intimately connected because the French state, faced with the American domination of what it perceived to be a critical industry, acted to encourage fusion and merger among French firms.

Interestingly, industry sources and trade-association officials contend that the industry was never formally cartelized, but the criss-crossing of financial control was a sure sign of the negotiated environment of the early 1950s. Thus the regroupment required not simply fusion to increase size, but a reorganization of industrial holdings to permit even a first effort at rational management. Direct participation by one group in the stock of another was not unusual, and CGE—the largest electrical equipment group with small interest in electronics—controlled 10 percent of CSF, the government electronics favorite in the fifties and sixties.[77] Similarly, investment houses such as the Banque de Paris et des Pays Bas have had a hand in several of the important firms of the time, including Machines Bull and CSF, and thus they provided a second link between the firms. Nonetheless, despite the interlocking of interests, and the efforts acknowledged by former executives to cartelize, the arrangements were never stable or binding. Apparently the presence of American firms and the pace of innovation blocked actual cartelization. It is difficult to imagine IBM with its brutally competitive history, or Texas Instruments, riding the wave of its spectacular growth, agreeing to a restricted section of the market. Yet even when competing with the Americans, the French instincts toward cartelization showed through. Certain industry officials argue that the best solution of the Machines Bull affair would have been a market-sharing agreement with IBM, although recognizing it would have been difficult to implement.

In fact, the presence of the American firms limited the value of any purely French agreements, and left to themselves, some argue, the French firms would have eventually cartelized. Even among French producers, though, the evolving technology upset efforts at comfortable arrangements. Firms would enter agreements about existing products confident that their development groups held an ace that would improve their position for marketing future products. Competition did exist between Thomson and CSF in certain important sectors, such as radar and consumer television. In sectors where the government was the dominant buyer, though, it could and did impose market sharing by manipulating selective purchasing.

In summary, then, French electronics firms find themselves (as *electronics* firms) in an intensely competitive international industry, but they are part of a *French* business community that has historically been protected and anti-competitive. In fact, the highly competitive electronics industry growing on a protected soil has resulted in two coexisting but distinct business worlds; or, more exactly, a protected preserve for favored firms has been maintained in a wild jungle of competition. In the competitive world a firm must adopt an industrial and economic strategy, identifying promising markets and entering quickly with competitively priced products, while in the protected world a suitable political strategy to draw on the state's resources is more important than market performance. (The serious policy dilemmas posed by this partial protection will be considered in Chapter 5.)

No specific evidence developed in this research would demonstrate conclusively why particular firms fell into the two "segments" of the market. Once in the competitive or the state "segment," it would be difficult for a firm to switch strategies. There are powerful political barriers against access to direct state support. For example, the firms camped under the state umbrella, and often the banks to which they are tied, have remarkable access to the bureaucracy and would fight admission of new members to the club; in certain cases such as telephone equipment, these firms are a formally defined group. Firms with the support of the state, and the close ties of social and educational background which such support usually implies, would probably never imagine giving up that support. It would appear, most generally speaking, that firms emerged, often with initial bank support, either to serve the state or to enter the competitive markets, or at some specific point used specific state needs to gain admittance to the circle of favorites. The collapse of CSF forced the state, in a reverse of that pattern, to apply pressure to Thomson-Houston, then standing with several toes in the state sector, to absorb CSF and play the role CSF alone played before. These then, with the exception of the Thomson-CSF merger, are historical choices, not made during the period of this research effort.

The Organizational Consequences of
State Policy in Electronics

Two strategies, then, are found among French electronics firms: either they compete on a price and quality basis with electronics firms of other national origins, or alternatively, they seek the direct and indirect protection of the state and follow a political as well as an economic strategy.[78] A central problem of the first strategy is efficiency and product development, and the organization might be expected to reflect this need. However, if the firm depends on the state-guaranteed markets, development aid and direct subsidy reduce the competitive pressure for organizational change, and the ongoing political problem of obtaining that assistance from the state encourages the firms not to disrupt existing and vital ties to the government. In France this has meant maintaining traditional centralized and functional organizations that are not appropriate to the imperatives of the technology.

The argument, therefore, is that the company strategy poses or emphasizes different sets of problems for the firm and that the organizational structure will reflect the efforts to resolve them. The internal technological pressure for change is mediated by the strategy a firm adopts. We will hypothesize, therefore, that if change does occur in the organization of electronics firms, it will come more completely and more quickly to firms competing in the marketplace than to firms that have adopted a strategy of state protection and support. Let us therefore consider first how French policies may have dampened any technological pressure for reorganization. Next, let us analyze the manner in which the techniques of purchasing and granting funds have pushed firms to mimic the structure of the state.

Dampening Organizational Change. The organizational structure typical of firms in an industry can change either when new firms enter the market and bring with them new organizational ideas or when old firms abandon their traditional ways. These two processes, of course, may be linked because the entry of new firms may pressure the older ones into changing. Nonetheless, in France, where the growth of small firms is at best difficult, state support appears to have reduced the pressure on firms under its tutelage to adopt structures more suited to their technological and market problems. As one government official involved in industrial planning for the electronics industry remarked in an interview, "Aid intended to make firms competitive has in fact often simply put them to sleep." Once the cycle of aid is begun, moreover, a firm in trouble will seek help from the state rather than trying to correct the problems in their own operations.

The difficulty of starting up new firms in France means that our focus here must be on change in older firms. Creating a new firm and nurturing its rapid growth requires considerable managerial skill anywhere, but in France the structure of the financial markets, the pattern of government contracting, and the attitudes of many officials add to the already hazardous life of the new firm. The meteoric growth of a firm like Texas Instruments, which grew in less than twenty years from a medium-sized firm with sales of 20 million dollars to the stature of a worldwide giant, would be impossible in France. Moreover, the routes to success open to a new firm, particularly routes leading into the circle of the government favorites, tend to socialize the newcomer in the traditional ways of the business community. The result, for our purposes, is that a new firm's thrust as a force for organizational change is at best weakened. There are several questions that must be answered.

In France, access to capital either to create a firm or to finance its expansion is extremely limited. The general lack of risk capital and the reported tendency of the French to hold their gold or invest in real estate as an inflation hedge are expressed in the weakness of the stock market. An entrepreneur, consequently, has difficulty raising capital or realizing a capital gain through the sale of stock. Not only does this slow the growth of the firm, but it ties even venture-capital groups to the established institutions of finance, because venture-capital companies must realize their profits through the sale of the stock in small companies either to an existing company or to a bank or holding group.

Medium and long-term debt is as difficult to obtain as capital, further complicating the problem of financing growth. In addition, small businessmen fear that involvement with a bank risks their control over their own business, and their fears are not at all unjustified. In a banking structure where a commercial bank making short-term loans can also act as an investment bank and undertake substantial participation in the firm, short-term indebtedness can be used, and often is, to obtain bank control of the business. This threat pushes the entrepreneur back on his own financial resources to finance growth.

Entering the circle of government contracting and support is at least as difficult as obtaining capital financing, which amounts to a serious problem in any industry where the quality-conscious government market can serve as an aid to a small firm. Government purchases and research support in France are a political as well as a technical matter (as explained below), and the choice of firms from whom the military will purchase, for example, is in part a negotiation with the Ministry of Industry which has the *tutelle*—that is, the formal government responsibility for the well-being of the electronics industry—and which is charged with developing a plan for its growth.* Not only does the policy of a national champion, whatever its legitimacy or justification, express a conscious decision to favor the large over the small, but some government officials simply view the small, growing firm as a dangerous intruder. In an interview, one government official with control over electronics industry funds remarked that "the profit conscious small firm simply doesn't know the rules of the game, and I would oppose providing them with funds." That political game is even more thoroughly weighted against the small firm in government programs of research and development support, where the committees that grant the funds include members from the dominant companies. Not unexpectedly, perhaps, 85 percent of the money for one such

*It may be argued justly that American purchases are also political matters, but there are at least three important differences that affect the small firm: (1) the political game in America is decentralized, leaving more access for a small firm; (2) contracting is often based on a technical competition that is more open; and (3) the Small Business Administration encourages subcontracting on major projects.

program over a period of eight years has gone to four firms. New French firms, therefore, are not likely to be either a source of new organizational ideas or a competitive threat to the existing firms, and we must focus therefore on organizational change in old and established firms.

To consider the influence of state aid on organizational evolution in the established firm we must have some notion, however vague and implicit, of the process of organizational change. Organizations, we might assume, change only in response to pressure, Alfred Chandler's study of the emergence of the divisionalized corporate structure in the American business enterprise in the first half of this century suggests a model by which an organizational problem initiates change.[79] First, an organizational deficiency which creates serious inefficiencies must exist. Second, someone in the organization must become aware both that the firm has problems and that they are produced by the organizational structure. Third, a plan must be developed. Finally, senior executives must accept it, and generally this is as the result of a crisis. Critically, then, although functional and centralized organizations were inappropriate to the technological problems, state subsidy meant that the costs of the organizational deficiency were low enough that they were not always perceived, or if perceived, not entirely corrected.

Inefficiencies in the electronics firms might be felt in several ways: a change in some measure of market performance or market share, the anguished cries of a captive client such as the state, or the frustration of overworked chief executives with too little time to handle all the problems that are pushed up to them in a centralized system. *State aid removed the market measures of performance. as pressures for organizational change.* With guaranteed markets, inefficient development is acceptable because no competitor can capitalize on delays, and cost overruns can be passed on to the purchaser. Subsidy, similarly, removes the threat of failure and prevents the kinds of crisis that might be necessary to spark change. Again, the firm might never perceive the inefficiency of its current structures, might not search for a solution if it did perceive the problem, and might not face a crisis that would require implementation of the plan.

Selective purchasing from national producers has become an important form of administrative protection in many countries. Our concern here is not with the economic or political justifications of such policy but with its impact on the organization of the firm. The impact of this form of protection will be a function of the price-quality deterioration that the state is willing to accept in order to purchase from a home firm, and the number of national firms that then compete for the state's purchases in that protected market. As the preference accorded a national producer increases to the limit where a product is not made within the country at any price or quality and the number of national producers declines, competitive pressures on the firm will be reduced. Taking a further step, the minimum package of quality, delivery delay, and price acceptable to the government before it decides to purchase from a foreign firm represents the minimum efficiency in development and production required from the national firm.

If the company can meet these lowered standards without changing its organization, then it will never feel a pressure for change. However, if there is more than one national producer, one would expect competition for the national market to push the package produced by the most efficient national producer away from the minimally acceptable toward the internationally competitive. This intra-national competition, then, may still encourage the firm to adopt a more efficient organization. In this analysis, *the organization of the firm represents a factor of production, or perhaps better a process of production, that affects the production function, and thus the set of price-quality packages a firm can produce.* If the competitive price-quality package in the protected market represents a level of efficiency incompatible with the traditional organization, then the theoretical implication is that the firm will sense the inefficiency through government protests or loss of orders.

In fact, both the acceptable minimum package and the desired degree of competition vary from ministry to ministry. The ministries that are the clients of the electronics industry, particularly the military, desire high quality, low price, and domestic competition to insure both, while ministries more generally responsible for the well-being of French firms have argued that international competition is sufficient pressure and that French firms should arrange matters among themselves or simply merge.

It is not important to specify the exact degree of protection or the size of the state market. What matters is that for many firms this special market of government purchases and supported exports represents an alternative to full-scale competition and the increased efficiency it would require. This strategy can be clearly seen in the product choices of some firms. In one case, a development project was underway to create a xerox copying process. Given the implantation of Xerox, the interest of IBM in the field, and the high development costs, this hardly seemed like a profitable use of the firm's resources. However, the firm's president remarked that if and when they ever managed to make the product, he had a guaranteed market in the administration.

Similarly, *direct subsidy* of government favorites tends to reduce the pressure to adopt competitive strategies and efficient organization, and often directly absorbs the losses when these firms are unable to develop and to market products profitably. The inefficiencies may not be hidden, but there is little incentive for change. As discussed above, the state has underwritten the development of firms such as CII through the computer plan, but the R and D efforts of many firms have also been subsidized and even the losses of these companies are underwritten. An industrial policy undertaken through subsidies for research, development, or anything else can easily become indirect subsidy of losses. French experience, moreover, suggests that subsidies of losses are often quite direct. Several firms have been directly floated by the state through subsidies disguised as aid to development or assistance for research. This line of the budget, as one official remarked, is seldom scrutinized. An unsigned memo in the DGRST's public files, dated February 13, 1968, outlined one such case: "Nothing of that was realized. The components plan is only a rescue operation intended to save . . . Firm X . . . exactly at the moment where the deficit of that company—by the fault of its management—has become catastrophic."

Replicating the Structure of the State: Techniques of Support for the Firm. State subsidy, whether direct in the form of grants of money or indirect in the form of preferential purchasing, removes the classical instrument of a liberal economy for insuring the efficiency of the firm—the threat of market exit or, more exactly, of failure or decline. In return, however, the state's loyalty and the firm's dependence give the state a considerable voice in the affairs of the firm,[80] a voice that is inevitably amplified in France where the officers of the major companies are former *hautes functionaires* in the ministries and alumni of the same handful of schools. Although the firms are sheltered from the market, the cost of the subsidies and the failure of French firms to produce certain products successfully have provoked pressures from the state for changes in the firms. However, the efficiency of the internal organization was not of primary importance, and the state's potential for influence in the affairs of the firms was used to force the merger of smaller firms and to divide and rationalize the marketplace. Whether the gains from forcing an internal restructuring would have been greater than benefits of increased size is in retrospect unimportant, because the civil servants had no idea of what changes would be required and no understanding of why they were necessary.

It is of importance here, however, that the content of the state's demands in the industry did not encourage the internal reorganization the technology required. At least as important, *the centralized and functional structure of the state's procurement funding procedures provided strong incentives for the firms not only to retain but perhaps even to create functional and centralized organizations.* Government purchases and subsidies in the electronics industry are allocated among firms according to a formula negotiated not simply within each ministry, but within several ministries as part of a general industrial plan.

Faced with this centralization of the state and a politicizing of the firm's technical choices, the general management of the firm probably must retain considerable control over the product and market strategies of the firm. Insofar as the choices must be made as part of a cohesive political strategy and not on technical and market criteria, the corporate general management is almost certainly in the best position to make these choices. Since technical choices made at the lower levels of the state machinery reflect the political negotiations at higher levels, the general management probably must remain involved in the negotiation, even on a technical basis. Because there is not a single point of choice after which the project becomes a technical problem, but several points at which the negotiations are reopened, the general management is further encouraged to retain a hand in the ongoing project. Second, the ministries which are the clients of the industry, primarily the PTT and the military, are sharply divided into functional services for research, development, and purchasing. The military, it should be noted, has been changing. Each of these services deals with its counterparts in the private firms and is free to pass a contract with a functional division of the firm. Certainly the firm can impose a product organization and insist that all divisions of the state deal with the product manager, but unquestionably the firm is confronted with a very solid organizational model and pattern of funding that at best reinforces existing functional divisions within the firm. Put differently, a shift to closer integration of functions or product organization means not only a disruption of internal relations within the firm, but more vitally, *a disruption of external relations with the government that may be quite satisfactory.*[81]

This influence supporting functional and centralized organization can best be understood by examining the procurement and funding processes in the four major programs that touch the electronics industry: weapons acquisition by the Minister of Defense; product procurement by the PTT; aid to research and development offered by the DGRST; and the major civilian electronics intervention of the Minister of the Industry—the Plan Calcul.

1. The military's acquisition of weapons.[82] Three aspects of the weapons acquisition process in France are of importance to this argument: first, suppliers are chosen in part to fit an industrial plan; second, the weapons acquisition process is broken down into administratively separate steps; and finally, there is a historical organizational division between the functional steps in the weapons development process.

Since weapons development and acquisition for each of the fighting services—air, sea, and land—are centralized in the Direction Ministérielle Pour l'Armament (DMA), it is possible in France to speak of the *military's* industrial policy. More exactly, since the formal responsibility —the *tutelle*—for the well-being of the electronics industry rests in the Ministry of Industry and Scientific Development, the military acts as a lobby to insure that its particular needs are represented in the overall government policy. The military would like to maintain competition among French suppliers to increase its bargaining power over price, quality, and delay negotiations, but it accepts—at least formally and publicly—the argument that the long-run interests of the industry require increased concentration. A firm, then, must not only enter the ranks of military suppliers, which is difficult since there are generally no open requests for proposals, but it must defend its right to a position in the marketplace at an inter-ministerial level. In the United States, by contrast, the acquisition system is much more decentralized and dispersed, with each service maintaining its own development service and set of suppliers. Certainly the smaller French market and the more limited number of national suppliers constrains the choice of the state, and the concentration of its efforts is probably necessary; however, the centralization and politicized nature of the acquisition process cannot help but touch the firms.

The French major weapons acquisition process proceeds in discrete steps with a separate contract let for each of these steps. Furthermore, until recently the development and production functions were organizationally divided within the military itself. Several important consequences for the organization of the firm apparently follow. The responsibility of each service within the firm might tend to be sharply and functionally articulated in accordance with the responsibilities defined by the military contractor. The responsibility of each functional service might tend to be to its military counterpart passing the contract, and much less toward the other services within the firm than would be the case if the firm had a unified responsibility for a product. Thus the functional organization represents not simply a solution to the problems within the firm, but maintenance of the firm's ties to the government as well. Since only an estimated one-third of the projects that enter the early stages of research are developed as prototypes, and not all of those are produced, the R and D group can enter each project without any presumption that it would some day have to work out the industrialization and production problems. This attitude is reinforced since the services within the firm report to organizationally distinct groups within the military. Thus, not only were divisions awarded contracts for separate functional tasks, but they were given the contracts by different organizational units. Since 1960 the military has slowly developed a project director organization to assure the coordination of its complex weapons systems. The evolution reportedly began with the Force de Frappe, but it was only in the early 1970s that a project manager became a requirement. In one of the four purchasing and development services, the position of projector director is reportedly a fiction covering continued organizational distinctions between development and production.

Furthermore, the French do not name a prime contractor on the industry side—that is, one firm which assumes the general management responsibility for the coordination of the entire project—preferring instead to assure systems unity and coordination in the military administration. The supervisory responsibility of the military is thus multiplied, and, moreover, many firms that might have been subcontractors to a single large firm are tied directly to the functionally divided system of the military. At the same time, the pressure on any industrialist to organize to assure coordination of a system is reduced, since the final responsibility will not be his.

2. The PTT, or Ministry of Telecommunications. At the PTT, the functional division of the ministry is even more serious than it ever was in the military, with an apparently serious effect on the entire system. Responsibility for system definition—that is, the definition of characteristics of the telephone equipment—and the initiation of research and development for new equipment lies with the CNET (Centre National d'Etudes des Télécommunications). The CNET, however, does not purchase or use the equipment; those functions are in the Ministry of the PTT, and the Minister of the PTT is the only formal link between the two. The not-unexpected result that is a reported overconcern with technical aspects of the system without an adequate regard for economic consequences. The president of one electronics firm said, "They are always quick to demand a 10 percent improvement over the characteristics of the equivalent American component even if the marginal cost of the improvement is 70 percent, for example." One telecommunications development engineer admitted this problem and said, "We seek a certain perfection. (Nous sommes plus exigeant qu'il faut. C'est vrai que nous ne savons pas comment dire, ça suffit.)"

Equally serious, the engineers of the CNET are primarily in contact with the engineers from the research laboratories of the firm, not with the production unit. For one component product, the CNET engineer reported that he was rarely ever spoke with the development group of the producing firm until the product definition had been completed.

Similarly, it is reported that the production engineers at the PTT are primarily tied to the production units in the firms. Since, as was the case in the military, separate contracts are passed for each step of the process, one again finds the possibility for each functional division of the firm to become just as attached to its counterpart in the government as it is to its collaborators inside the firm. The result, according to one former CNET engineer in an interview, was this: *each negotiation, each passage from one step to another and thus one service to another, required the arbitrage and intervention of the president of the firm.*

The choice of supplier is also very centralized. The set of potential suppliers to the PTT forms two legally defined groups, the SOCATEL and the SOTELEC. Overt quotas are said to divide the PTT market among the firms that compose these two clubs, the quotas being decided on, as one official put it, at "the highest levels," and then debated on a case-by-case basis. Although hoping to preserve some competition by including smaller firms in this group, the two primary official goals of the industrial policy are to encourage exports and to support Thomson-Houston and CGE. The conflict between a technically optimal choice of supplier and the industrial policy was clear in the PTT's resistance to strong pressure that it require its equipment producers to purchase semi-conductor components from SESCOSEM, the then semi-conductor subsidiary of Thomson. The compromise has been an oral encouragement rather than a formal order. For firms in this network, the political problem is at least as important as the technical and economic ones.

3. Aid for industrial research and development from the Delegation à la Recherche Scientifique et Technique (DGRST). (The DGRST, attached to the Ministry of Industry, has had responsibility for coordinating non-military research activities, but has had limited independent funds.) The aid for research and development granted by the DGRST is not an enourmous sum; a total of 950 million francs have been passed to all industry since 1966, of which approximately one-fourth has gone into the electronics industry, but the programs do represent a conscious effort by the government to intervene in the industrial research and development process. Once again, the centralized and political character of funding and the institutionalization of a functional and fragmented conception of product development stand out, all the more clearly because the decision making is more open to public view.

The funding process for the two major DGRST programs, Aid for Development and Concerted Action, was characterized by its inter-ministerial character, the direct representation of the major firms of the bodies granting funds, and its apparently ingrained political character. The result, in the case of the Concerted Action program in electronics, has been that 90 percent of the funds now go to the laboratories of the organizations, public as well as private, that are represented on the committees.

The unsystematic analysis of the composition of the committees suggests not only that the several bureaucracies of the state are represented along with the dominant firms in the sector, but that the representatives are of high rank. This is not unusual because the firms are typically represented either by the director of research, a vice-president, or the president. For example, in one of the early work groups in electronics, the two firms present were represented in one case by the president and in the other case by the vice-president who six years later became president. The interests of the state's favorite in the 1960s, CSF, were more often than not represented by the president, Ponte, or the vice-president, Danzin.[83]

Moreover, the mechanisms not only reflected industrial policy made at a level above the DGRST, but often contained formal techniques to aid the implementation of such an industrial policy. The following instructions on grant procedures for the program of aid to development were jointly issued by the Minister of Industrial and Scientific Development, the Minister of Finance, and the Secretary of State for Economics and Finances in 1970 in a memo: "To allow the Administration and the Committee to consider the contract demands presented by the large companies apart from a general perspective of the policy of research, the General Delegate and the technical officials invite those responsible for development in the major industrial groups to give them each year, confidentially of course, an indication of their program of research. . . ."

The Crédit National, it should be noted, is a para-public financial institution that is one of the few sources of medium-range and long-range financing. Therefore the instructions are an effort to coordinate subsidy with access to financing, and the funding decisions are clearly not simply technical ones, made in the committees or by the Minister of Industry, but ultimately by the government in coordination with the Minister of Finance. One former civil servant remarked that a portion of funds was allocated on direct instruction from the Minister of Finance to fulfill some promise of support made to particular firms. According to some observers, the program was really introduced to permit the state to purchase information about the plans of the major companies.[84] Importantly, neither the process nor its outcome should be considered a form of political corruption, but rather an expression of the centralization of government industrial policy, the holdovers of an era of negotiated rather than competitive business strategies, and the intimate ties between current civil servants and the businessmen who were often their predecessors.

The programs also tend to institutionalize a notion that technical innovation proceeds in sharp jumps that begin with basic research, proceed through development, then blossom into production. Thus, the Concerted Action programs were an attempt to unite the research efforts of the government labs, the university labs, and the industrial labs along axes of common interests and economic importance. The contracts, therefore, were not aimed at specific product development. Later, a second program of aid to development was begun to speed the flow of ideas from research toward actual products. This notion, expressed in this extract from a 1963 DGRST report, remains the government's working notion of the role of R and D in the economy:

> The definition of "development" flows from the place which this form of research occupies in the chain which goes from basic research to the industrialization of a process or the first commercialization of a product. Development supposes above all a satisfactory result obtained in the laboratory and the idea that this result can have a useful and beneficial application on techniques in use or for the manufacture of a product. This is then the intermediary phase of verifying a research result which, at the laboratory level, appears likely to generate an industrial innovation.

This is a summary of the "innovation chain" idea that was popular during the 1950s in America. The Project Hindsight study of the role of research in new defense systems was an early part of a reconsideration of the process of innovation that emphasized the role of market demand. The American funding structures also assign a much greater role to product development, with research serving as a filler for problems insoluble with current knowledge.

This definition of the role of research underlay the original structures of firms such as CSF, and the structure of government that divides the process into organizationally separate steps can only serve to reinforce such an idea, both intellectually and concretely, in the form of funding procedures.

The techniques of government funding are centralized and functionally specialized. Since the individual choices about particular projects in part express a negotiated allocation of government support, it is important that a firm be represent by its higher officials in the ongoing negotiations about these allocations. Strategic planning is therefore political planning that must involve the president and other high officers in the technical details of the firm. At the same time, the funding within the government is structured around the steps of a line model of innovation that begins in the laboratory. Certainly it would be possible for a firm to insist that the different organs of the state negotiate with a single product-division manager, but the government's functional division inevitably created limited, functional, and stepping-stone definitions of responsi-bility that could easily be picked up within a firm. If the firm is already functionally organized, as were the firms studied in this research, the division of the state supports the traditional structure by insulating it from forces for change. Finally, if the vital government contacts are organized on a functional basis, there must be a hesitation to reorganize or disrupt them, whatever the technological pressure.

Hypothesis on The Relations Between Organizational Structure and State Policy. We are arguing, then, that when a firm accepts the guidance and protection of the state and adopts a strategy aimed at state markets, the technological problems of product development become less pressing. On the one hand, there is less pressure for organizational efficiency, and on the other, the interaction with the state encourages a functional and centralized structure. Two predictions are possible: first, all firms oriented toward the state are and will remain more centralized and functional than firms oriented toward the market; or, second, when other characteristics such as size and product are the same, those firms which are oriented toward the state are and will remain more centralized and functionally structured than those that are market-oriented. The first prediction compares *all* state-oriented firms with all market-oriented firms. The second prediction first divides firms into sub-groups of firm size and product, then compares market-oriented and state-oriented firms.

The French electronics firms, then, find themselves wedged between the market and the state, pressed on the one hand by the requirements of industrial efficiency and on the other by the problems of negotiating with the French government. It begins to appear that the characteristic cultural features of an organization are part of its adjustment to the environment, part of its institutional strategy, and not simply an ex-pression of the attitudes toward authority or other psychological pro-pensities of the members.

II

Evolution in Firm and Industry:
The Evidence

4

Organizational Tradition and Change in the French Electronics Industry

This chapter will consider the organizational change that occurred within French electronics firms in order to test the two hypotheses developed in Part I. To accommodate readers with widely different interests, its organization will be somewhat unorthodox: first, a summary of the research conclusions, then a preliminary interpretation of the results, then the analytic framework and data from which these conclusions were drawn, and finally a longer interpretation of the results. The reader can therefore choose for himself how deeply he wishes to plunge into the evidence.

A Summary of Conclusions

The first research hypothesis predicted that the organization of firms in the French electronics industry would reflect the authority dilemma of French culture, and would maintain traditional organizational structures even when these produced serious industrial inefficiencies. The second and contrary hypothesis would predict that despite the cultural traditions, the pressures of the technological task would produce the more fluid and flexible organizations required in this industry. The evidence presented in this chapter, based on a survey of the structure of eighteen electronics firms and case studies of organizational structure and change in four of these firms, will deny both of these simple hypotheses about the relationship between technological imperatives and traditional authority patterns. Three general conclusions emerge:

1. There was a general movement away from centralized, rule-ordered organizations with sharply defined areas of responsibility toward decentralized organizations depending on initiative and flexible job definitions. The firms responded to the pressures of the technological task when the problems were clearly understood and when the pressure for success at the task was high.

2. Neither an aversion to face-to-face conflict nor an unwillingness to accept responsibility can be said to have blocked organizational change. After a period of adjustment to the new organizational rules, the managers often found the new environment more satisfactory. In the few cases where personal conflicts occurred, they appeared to have been almost inevitably *provoked* by the firm's structure. In the firms where change did not take place, there was scant evidence that the inability of lower-level managers to take responsibility or accept the conflicts involved was the cause, although the desire of the boss to retain his power could often be seen.

3. Change did not occur in all firms, nor could it have been said to be fully satisfactory in very many. In the process toward decentralization, the heritage described by Crozier left its traces.

The problem, then, is to explain the pattern of change that really did occur, and to distinguish those firms that tended to change from those that retained traditional organizations. The second hypothesis, developed in Chapter 2, argued that when a firm accepts the guidance and protection of the state and adopts a strategy aimed at state markets, the technological problems of product development become less pressing. The evidence supports the hypothesis that when characteristics such as a firm's size and product are held constant, firms oriented toward the state are more centralized and functionally organized than their market-oriented counterparts. (The date presented here were gathered during a nineteen-month period from January 1972 through July 1973. Unless otherwise noted, the data refer to this period.)

Two forms of evidence were developed from a sample of eighteen firms in the electronics industry, of which four were selected as case studies. One form of evidence was the formal organizational structure and the other patterns of individual interactions. The aspects of formal organization considered were centralization versus decentralization, the formal location within the firm at which product choices are made, the organizational arrangements for passing a product from development into production, and the mechanisms for integrating functions. Decentralization, product choice at the level of product-development groups, institutionalized ties between development and production, and formal integrating roles constituted evidence of adjustment to technological requirements. The interactions of individuals were evaluated to determine whether they accepted decentralized responsibility and initiative and face-to-face conflict, or whether they were able to resolve the technological problems without decentralization and conflict and to define their jobs and the permissible demands of authority on them in such a way as to avoid decentralized responsibility and face-to-face conflict.

The current organization of the firms in the sample was balanced between centralized and decentralized structures. We must note, however that several of the formally centralized firms were smaller concerns in which horizontal communication and the integration of functions was assured by long-standing personal relations between the managers. Two of the centralized operations, in addition, were in the market sector where the technological pressures for change were the lowest. The weight of the evidence suggests change and adjustment in the industry.

The limited evidence for the evolution of the firm's formal structures indicated a growth away from centralized and functional organization toward more decentralized structures. The case studies suggest that this evolution was a response to problems of making product choices and putting products into production after development, as well as a response by chief executives who had been over-worked by the demands on their time generated by overly centralized organization. The production problem of passing a product from lab to production line was, interestingly, perceived more often and corrected more quickly than problems of product choice, which perhaps reflects either French industry's production bias or the continuing protection of certain markets.

Decentralization, the lower-level integration of functions, and the face-to-face work environment that resulted did not apparently generate great tension, although a period of adjustment was reported. In fact, managers reported fewer conflicts and appeared to welcome both the new responsibility that was placed on them and the initiative it demanded. Conversely, organizational barriers that separated interdependent functions tended to *generate* conflict, in part at least because the sharply different measures of success for intertwined tasks made cooperation inherently difficult. This suggests that the behaviors which Crozier argues are the product of French attitudes and produce particular organizational systems may have in fact been *provoked* by the organization.

When faced with organizational barriers the managers and engineers did appear to respond in very traditional ways and sought to preserve their areas of organizational independence, but when the barriers were removed, they learned to behave differently. The centralized functional organization and the decentralized-product structure appeared to have different informal rules that guided members' behavior. At a firm we shall call "Industrial Electronics", one engineer noted that the functional structure had permitted him an independence and isolation he valued, while a colleague noted that with the decentralized and integrated structure one tended to take account of the needs of other team members because this avoided the otherwise inevitable conflicts in team meetings. Although the limited evidence here does not permit a general conclusion, the younger engineers reported and were reported to have had little problem working in the decentralized environment, while the older engineers appear to have required a difficult period of transition. This would suggest either that the cultural upbringing was different in the two generations or that the traditional work environment itself had shaped the behavior of the older engineers. Since the older men finally did adjust to decentralization, we must suppose that the existing work environment tends to socialize individuals in the ways of a firm, and that a change in the work environment can produce important changes among those who have already learned one work style.

The evidence, however, would hardly permit us to conclude that the requirements of the technological problems had swept away the traditional centralized and hierarchical organization and heralded a new age of decentralized and fluid organization in France. The adjustments do not appear to have been easy or complete. Many firms retain centralized structures, and others have only partially adjusted, and then only under very considerable pressures.

The changes themselves, interestingly, appear to have followed the older pattern of centralized authority. When change did come, it was not the result of insistent demands from lower-level management that the organization be adjusted to the problems the faced. It was rather imposed—often as a brutal break with the past—by top management. Dividing the firm into product lines did not, moreover, insure that functional distinctions were wiped away at the product-group level. "Industrial Electronics" (code names have been assigned to firms in the case study), for example, has broken into product divisions and subdivided many of these divisions into product lines, but at the lowest level, the functions of Research, Development, Production, and Sales were often still separated by important organizational barriers. Decentralization at one level recreated the same problems of functional divisions and centralized decisions for the head of a product line. Many firms, in fact, might be said to have recentralized power at a lower level. Each decentralization unquestionably reduced the height of the organizational barriers between any two services, in part because at each progressively lower level the services themselves would be smaller and the physical distances between them less, but it hardly insured a full lower-level integration of these services.

The implementation of one adjustment would simply point up the need for another. Thus, for example, "Industrial Electronics" divisionalized, but the Electronic Equipment Division remained centralized. Later the development and production functions at the Electronic Equipment Division were directly integrated, but the marketing remained isolated. Now the continuing of the marketing is seen as a problem and another organizational adjustment is being prepared.

In all firms, the break with the old ways was made step by cautious step. *The evolution that took place was shaped by the existing traditions of structure and authority even as it was provoked by the new problems of the technology.* Change unquestionably occurred; the next problem is to account for the pattern it took.

Not all firms have evolved, and the depth of change in those that have is quite varied. In the largest firms some decentralization around product lines appeared to be necessary, while some of the smaller firms were able to preserve centralized and functionally structured organizations. When firm size and product were held constant, the changes in the firms subsidized and protected by the state were slower and less complete than in the market-oriented firms. This relation held up in an analysis of matched pairs, (matching market-oriented and state-oriented firms of similar size and product characteristics), involving ten firms.

Looking more closely at the case studies, "Genset Products" has followed a competitive strategy and profoundly decentralized, while "Norgood Electronics" remains entirely dependent on the state and has only partially decentralized. "Genset" has decentralized product choices, development responsibilities, instituted profit accounting, and developed a mission-oriented sense of responsibility. "Norgood" has allowed sharp barriers between development-production responsibilities and commercial responsibilities to remain, and as a result responsibility for production costs, but not for profits, have been reorganized on a product basis. Even inside "Norgood" the same relation between market-orientation and decentralization seems to hold. The Hudson Division at "Norwood" is more directly and heavily involved with the state than the other division. It is also more centralized and has not found a means of bridging organizational divisions between development and production services. Minor product-improvement decisions have been decentralized but major product choices are made at the general management level, not even at the level of the division head. These choices, importantly, are not simply whether or not to enter a product area—a choice often made at general-management levels in this country—but whether to change product characteristics and research direction, matters usually left to a lower level. The Missouri Division has effectively decentralized production and development functions, integrating them under a product manager who is responsible for product choices. At Norgood, state *tutelle* appeared to be directly linked to the failure to decentralize responsibility for product choices and profit.

While Thomson (the only firm whose real name is used) has been torn by the politics of forced mergers and a struggle for presidential succession that has involved the state administration, "Industrial Electronics" has responded to the problem of product diversity with the now classical solution of division. This division-making has permitted effective decentralization of tactical operations and central control of strategy. Thomson, in contrast, has been unable to establish effective control over those of its operating units that were previously either independent companies or quite separate subsidiaries. Thomson might nominally be called divisionalized, but in fact it operates more like a federation or a holding company. Despite a confused decentralization, many tactical choices are centralized at Thomson. The extreme example is the development strategy for CII, the French computer company, which was formally drawn up as part of a negotiation between the state and the companies that formed this joint venture. Thomson is known for sharp hierarchical divisions, while "Industrial Electronics" is reputed to have forged unusually close links between the top and bottom of the firm. In the one product area shared by the two firms, the division of Industrial Electronics appears to have been more successfully integrated in functional services. In fact, Thomson's subsidiary, which receives important subsidies of all kinds from the state, is said to have increasingly centralized with each crisis it faced, while Industrial Electronics' division is fighting for its life in this sector and has progressively evolved more decentralized management.

Two recent studies of decentralization as a response to product diversity in French firms have provided supplementary evidence with which to contrast these results. Gareth Pooley-Dyas's examination of the formal structure of France's one-hundred largest firms also indicated that French cultural traditions have not blocked organizational change that required decentralization.[1] George Trepo's case-study approach to the same problem takes sharp exception to this conclusion, but his results in fact suggest only that the process of decentralization is shaped by French traditions, not that change is impossible.[2]

Pooley's evidence suggests that increased product diversity which requires divisionalization for efficient management had brought greater decentralization to French firms. Not only had there been an increase in the total number of firms which were not specialized by tasks immediately below the level of the general management, but the number of division-alized firms with decentralized authority had increased within each category of product diversity, except where only one product was pro-duced. The number of multi-divisional companies increased from 6 in 1950 to 54 in 1970, while the number of firms with a strictly functional organization declined from 50 to 14.[3] Pooley-Dyas concluded that "vir-tually all change in structure could be described as being in the direc-tion of structures with some general management responsibilities at lower levels in the organization."[4] This tends to confirm our conclusions that French cultural traditions do not block organizational adjustments which require new patterns of authority, and also indicates that similar results would have been found with a different sample of electronics firms.

Pooley-Dyas argues that the movement toward greater product diversity and organizational decentralization began in France much later than in the United States. The end of the "negotiated environment" and the increase in European competition provoked changes in both strategy and subsequent structural adjustments. He suggests that protected markets tended to support traditional centralized structures in French firms. Similarly, McArthur and Scott conclude that the traditional French centralism and over emphasis on production problems was a heritage from years of protected markets and cartels.

George Trepo makes the opposite argument, contending that tradi-tional authority patterns in France actually did block meaningful change in business organizations.[5] The behavior he describes certainly suggests that a simple change of formal structure does not wash away existing hierarchy or patterns of interaction. Nonetheless, from the data Trepo presents it is difficult to reach his conclusion that change did not take place and that the new management structures amounted to little more than changes in ritual. Most importantly, there is no definition of the problem that was to be resolved by the division-making, therefore it is impossible to know whether the organizational change resolved the problem. If it did, then we could conclude that although authority patterns tended to continue, more than one organizational form can be developed from those patterns. If that appeared unlikely then we would have to consider whether behaviors had changed. Very simply, since change does not require a sharp and total break with the past, the continuance of tradition does not mean that change has not occurred. Thus the failure to measure current behavior against some norm, either past or present, makes it impossible to conclude whether change was "real" or "ritual."

Three of the changes occurred quite recently and quite rapidly without full preparation. Since a difficult transition period was found in the electronics firms studied in this project, there is no reason to assume that the immediate problems would continue or that these problems meant that the change was empty. In the fourth case, where decentralization has occurred and does work, Trepo finds evidence in the form of denial of certain responsibilities for the idea that nothing has changed. This case, in fact, directly supports the argument developed here: that change occurs, but is accommodated within the terms of the past.

The Research Results

The Problems of Evidence. Two problems of evidence must be considered before the research results are introduced. What forms of evidence can allow us to judge whether the two hypotheses are confirmed or denied? Can the manner in which the research was conducted permit us to have confidence in the data that constitutes our evidence?

To test the hypotheses, we must be able to evaluate whether the organizational structure and behavior of the firms adapted to the demands of the technology; or, put differently, whether the structure of the organization is constrained and the resolution of the technological problems blocked by the attitudes toward authority and the resulting behavior of the individuals in the firms.

We can consider how the structure and behavior of the firms, each taken as a unit of observation, have responded to the requirements of technology. This can be observed in the formal arrangements of jobs and the formal responsibilities of individuals placed in different positions to make particular decisions. If the organizations observed do not display the characteristics said to resolve the French authority dilemma but instead reflect the demands of the technology, then we might conclude that traditional attitudes and authority patterns do not block the evolution of the organizations required by the technology. This approach permits a larger sample because it does not require intimate access or extended research in the firm. The difficulty is that such evidence depends on individuals' reports of their own and of their colleagues' behavior. Similarly, the role of attitudes toward authority or the patterns of behavior and responsibility in shaping the organization can only be inferred.

Alternatively, the interactions of individuals can be observed to see how they resolve the development problems that confront them. This will allow us to determine whether (a) they accept the decentralized responsibility and initiative and the face-to-face conflict seemingly required by the technology; (b) whether they are able to resolve the technological problems without such decentralization and conflict; and (c) whether they are able to define their jobs and the permissable demands of authority on them in such a way as to avoid decentralized responsibility or face-to-face conflict by appealing to a centralized authority that arbitrates conflicts. Here the unit observed is the individual and the evidence is his behavior. The obvious advantage is that the researcher is not dependent on individuals' reports of their own behavior and can judge directly whether behavior toward authority interferes with their organizational tasks. The difficulty, of course, is that for one researcher the time required within each firm would sharply limit the number of cases he could examine. At the same time, much greater cooperation from the firm is required, increasing the problems of access.

Both approaches were used in this research. Both the mix and the sample of particular firms were the result of the concrete difficulties of research, particularly problems of access, rather than the outcome of a theoretically neat research design. Access to firms depended almost entirely on personal introduction—more exactly, on permission to use the name of a friend or business acquaintance in requesting the interviews. The sample emerged from this chain of personal links, and experience throughout the research suggested that it would have been impossible to have made a random selection of firms and then have gained access with a formal written request. It is difficult to know what biases this sample introduced; but because the industry was so small, a number of firms included in this study would have been picked in any random sample that first divided the population into sub-groups by size, product, and ties to the state. Interviews were conducted in twenty-one different French-controlled firms, but only in eighteen was sufficient evidence developed to include the firms in the analysis presented here. The median number of persons interviewed in a firm was four, although there were usually continuing contacts. In three of the firms, only one person was interviewed, in two cases the president and in the other case the vice-president. Of the firms visited, six produced components, ten produced final products, and five produced both. Of the final product manufacturers, five produced primarily for government markets and nine produced primarily for industry, and one was divided. In retrospect, one possible bias in the sample as a whole may have been to understate the number of firms selling primarily to the state. This bias, if it was one, was reduced by a conscious matching of firms for the case studies. The distribution of the final sample of firms by number of employees is given on the right below, while on the left is the distribution of all French electronics firms (figures taken from Planning Commission data).

Employees	All French Electronics Firms with More than 10 Employees in 1969	Firms in this Sample—1973
1000+	18 or 5.9% (60%)	8 or 44%
200-1000	76 or 24.3% (27.0%)	3 or 16%
100-200	51 or 16.4% (5%)	3 or 16%
10-100	164 or 52.9% (5%)	4 or 22%

Figures in parentheses approximate percentages of employees in electronics industry included in this category.

The sample, therefore, was also biased toward the larger firms, which accounted for the vast bulk of employment and production in the industry.

I was never formally granted open access to an entire firm—that is, permission to come and go as I pleased and to interview whom I liked, though I had such access to parts of firms. I had to move within a firm with introductions from one man to another. With several exceptions, I was never passed up the hierarchy of the organization, and the initial point of entry would be the highest point unless I had another outside introduction. This, incidentally, was in sharp contrast to my more limited experience in American firms, where I was passed up, down, and around on the basis of formal introductions. Eventually in certain firms, I was informally able to develop a general and open access. This depended on the time required to cultivate my contacts and on having several outside introductions that provided independent routes inside the firm. The only clear bias this may have introduced is that I never had a long-term, intimate view of the small equipment manufacturers.

The interviews focused on how and by whom product choices are made and how and by whom the product is passed from research and development into production. My original project design focused on the coordination of tasks within the development process of a particular project, but it quickly appeared that the critical problems in electronics was not here but in the coordination of different functions of marketing, development, and production. In several cases the actual organization of development work was investigated, but often the number of people working on a project was so small that it was a matter of small-group relations rather than one of hierarchy and large-scale organization. This contrasts sharply with aircraft development, where the overall project represents a large-scale system and the development group is a large organization in itself. In several cases the separation of basic research from development posed serious problems, but these tended to reflect themselves in product choices and the difficulty of getting a product conception to work, either as a prototype or in final production.

With these two basic questions, both the *organization* and the *strategy* of the firm could be explored; and this permitted, finally, the analysis of organization as an interaction between a firm's technology and its external environment. Both of the activities, product choice and product development, require coordination of the three functions of the firm, and consideration of how they were carried out would define the structure, responsibilities, and boundaries of each component. At the same time, actual product choices, the criteria for those choices, and the delays tolerated in getting a product on the market or to the client expressed the firm's strategy.

No systematic effort was made to review the literature on each of the firms included in the sample, but their current activity was closely followed in the professional and business press.

The Survey of Organizational Structures. Four features are used to describe the current organizations of the firms and the evolution of a subset of these firms. These features are: (1) the basic axis around which the firm is organized; (2) the mechanism integrating the functions; (3) the formal location of the product choices; and (4) the organizational arrangement for passing a product from development into production. Let us consider these measures in turn.

Axis of the Organization. There were two basic axes around which the firms were organized: functions and products. In a functional organization the major divisions within the firm are determined by the tasks that individuals perform; people performing similar tasks are grouped together. In simplified terms such an organization would appear as follows:

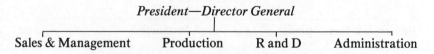

President—Director General

| Sales & Management | Production | R and D | Administration |

As Gareth Pooley-Dyas states it, "Management tasks [in functional organization] are specialized at the level immediately below top management by functional areas such as sales and manufacturing."[6] Formally, the only point at which the functions can be integrated is at the top of the organization. Unless some form of intermediary exists, the structure of the organization will tend to isolate the functions from each other. The organizational wall, furthermore, can easily be buttressed by definitions of responsibility and measures of success that relate to the performance of the isolated task, such as prototype development or sales volume, rather than the mission. The type of financial control that assigns a budget to each service to accomplish its task, which is usually the case in functional organization, means that accepting responsibility for the adjustments of one task to another benefits no one. No person's job performance, if strictly measured, will improve from efforts to integrate tasks; instead, the resources of each service will simply be drawn off. In this environment, distinctions between tasks, jobs, and responsibilities can become important. Thus, strictly functional organization depends entirely on the informal links between services for the lower-level integration required by the technology, and it arranges incentives in such a way that these exchanges are not encouraged.

In contrast, in a *product* structure jobs are grouped by the final outcome of the work, the development, production, and sale of a product to a particular market. Such a structure might appear as follows:

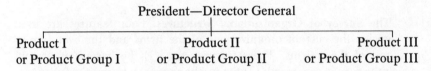

If the subdivision is a product group there might be a further subdivision of product responsibility:

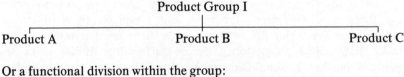

Or a functional division within the group:

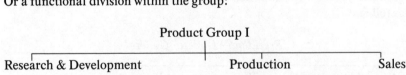

In this latter case the problem of integration of functions is pushed down to a lower point in the organization and might well result in a *recentralization* at that lower level. However, an organization built around products presumes some decentralization of power; it does not *require* such sharp definitions of jobs according to functional task, and it permits a closer attachment of the sub-groups' responsibilities to the firm's goals because the group can be judged on profit or growth criteria.*

Of course, neither structure will determine whether the system is in fact centralized, whether there is isolation between strata and functional divisions, whether individuals refuse to take initiative, or whether the system is rule-bound. Decentralized product groups might well build up walls against the influence of the center and refuse the firm's goals. However, the presumption must be of a greater degree of lower-level responsibility and authority, and a closer integration of functions. In fact there are a number of forms of partial product decentralization that we must consider here: several product groups may be created, but the president may retain control over one or several groups; production may be decentralized along product lines but product groups, including sales and development, may not be created; development and production functions may be decentralized, but not sales activities. A final possibility, the decentralization of production and sales functions but not of development work, did not appear. Clearly, decentralization by product line or the reorientation of the axes of a firm is not necessarily a question of one or another, or an abrupt transition; it may mean a partial adjustment or a slower evolution as well.

The formal location of product choice. The choice of products in a rapidly evolving industry such as electronics represents substantial power over the future growth of the firm. Therefore, the official assignment of that responsibility indicates the presumed distribution of actual control, whatever the axes of the organization. Here the term product

*Division-making in major corporations represents a similar movement from functional to product-based organization, but while the solution is similar, the *problem* is quite different. Division-making is a response to the *complexity* of internal exchanges created by diversity among products. Thus, for example, if a firm produces refrigerators, bathtubs, and toothpaste, each aimed at separate markets, the crossing of internal exchanges between sales and production services may make it difficult to balance sales and production and allocate resources between products. Thus product organization represents a simplification of exchanges that groups together those portions of sales and productions, for example, that are concerned with the same product. No presumption can be made that sales and production are any more closely integrated than before; that will depend on the character of the market and the product.

Decentralization around product lines or particular products in the electronics industry, in contrast, responds to the need for the lower-level integration required by the technology, to use the analysis presented in Chapter 1, or the instability of the environment in the terms of Lawrence and Lorsch. Thus two semi-conductor products may be organzationally separated to permit closer integration between R and D, Sales, and Production.

choice means the choice of the next product with *existing* lines of development for a particular market. It does not imply the right to commit the firm to a new line of growth. That choice will be said to be centralized if it is made by the president or general director and his immediate entourage of general managers; and it will be considered decentralized if the official points of choice, whatever the patterns of influence, are located further down in the organization. In several cases there were several points of influence spread throughout the organization. We therefore distinguish between centralized, decentralized, and spread-choice structures. Both of the second and third presume decentralized and lower-level initiative.

The integration of functions. Since the functions of Research and Development, Production, and Sales must be integrated, some mechanism must be developed to permit the activities to adjust to one another. One way of doing that is to decentralize product responsibility and to permit the product-group leader to act as an integrator. If the group is small enough he can coordinate the activities himself, even if he does not further decentralize his power. The integration between tasks that have a different functional focus may, however, be increased by overlapping the defined or understood responsibilities between these tasks. Thus, within a product group, one might find a sharp break between functionally oriented tasks or an overlapping of jobs aimed at accomplishing certain missions. Thus, one measure will be whether there are overlapping definitions of functions.

However, if the firm remains organized around functions or if a product group maintains sharp distinctions between functions, the problem of coordination may press even more seriously. To provide for this coordination someone may be designated as product manager or integrator. Thus an individual might have the responsibility for coordinating sales and development relationships or for supervising the development of a particular product. Whether a product manager exists will therefore be a second measure.

If the only formal mechanism for coordination is at the organizational center, it will tend to move all conflicts to the center, where they can be settled by the arbitration of conflicting claims. Face-to-face conflicts between these groups can therefore be avoided by recourse to higher-level arbitration of conflicting claims. Each movement toward lower-level integration involves increased demands on individuals to resolve through unarbitrated conflict the differences that separate them.

Passage from development to production (from the lab to the line). As argued earlier (see Chapter 2), taking a product from the laboratory or development group and putting it into production is a delicate and critical moment in the electronics industry. How well those two functions are integrated will deeply influence the firm. Thus, our fourth measure focuses on one aspect of integration: whether the product must move from one service within the firm to another (for example, from a sharply defined laboratory group), or whether the transition takes place within the same service. If product transition takes place within one service then functional tasks are more effectively integrated—that is, their isolation is broken, because sharp distinctions between tasks are less likely. *At the same time, direct negotiation of conflicts is demanded.* In contrast, shift from service to service, even within a decentralized product group, implies a jump over organizational boundaries and a sharp limitation of the responsibilities of each group.

Table 1, which summarizes the four features of the current organization of the eighteen firms, suggests the division between firms organized on functional and centralized lines and those organized around product and decentralized lines. Two of the companies were small, young, single-product firms where there was no sharp distinction of functions. One-half of the remaining firms were organized around functions, the other half around products. Product organization, however, meant several different things. In only two cases were R and D, Production, and Sales clearly and entirely decentralized along product lines. There was one case in which two product lines were decentralized and the third continued to report to the president; this appeared, however, to be a transitional moment in that firm, because the existing product groups were thoroughly and effectively decentralized, and specific problems blocked the immediate creation of a third product group, reporting to the president. There was one case where production was decentralized but sales and development were not—that is, a series of autonomous production units were evolved, each producing a limited series of products that had generally been sold before production from a general laboratory. There were two cases where production and development were decentralized, but sales remained centralized. Finally, there were two cases where a variety of arrangements were created for the different sub-units, and the firms could not be classified in any of the preceding categories. In seven of the firms there was a decentralization of product choice or a clear sharing of product choice responsibility between the center of the firm and the sub-units.

The other two measures of organizational structure also suggest division between those firms that tend to maintain a sharp distinction between functions and those that have decentralized and loosened their organizational structure to meet the demands of the technology. Six of the firms integrated all three of the functions only at the very top of the organization (these six included several that were in name decentralized by products), while nine of the firms had someone responsible specifically for the integration of those functions—an intermediary or liaison, if you will. In four cases the integration went a step further and involved overlapping definitions of responsibility. This tendency toward integration at a lower level of the organization was reflected in seven firms where products passed from development into production within the same service.

A full picture requires several comments about certain firms. Two of the eight firms that remained organized around functions were passive component producers, one with a direct licensing arrangement with an American firm. Because the passive components sector has been touched the least by the pace of innovation in the industry, and a direct licensing agreement further reduces internal development needs, the pressure on these two firms to change their organizations for the reasons argued in Chapter 2 was certainly reduced. In addition, three of the

Table 1

FORMAL ORGANIZATION OF THE FIRM

Structure	Number of Firms
1. Axes of Organization	
a. Functional	8
b. Product	8
(1) Entire	2
(2) Product line partially functional, partially product	1
(3) Decentralized production but not sales or development	1
(4) Decentralized development but not sales	2
(5) Decentralization of production and sales but not development	
2. Integration of functions	
a. None except at the top	6
b. Integrator with formal responsibility	9
c. Overlapping definition of function	4
3. Location of Product Choice	
a. Centralized	4
b. Decentralized	7
4. Passage from Lab to Line	
a. From one service to another	7
b. Within same service	7

Note: Not all firms could be measured on all criteria.

eight functional firms produced what amounted to a single product line. Thus in some sense they might represent a product subdivision of a larger firm divided along product lines. Each had developed reasonably effective means of integration, but their current form of organization is certain to pose problems as the firms grow. The two largest firms, however, were initially organized around product distinctions, but in each of them there was recentralization of power at the level of the operating sub-unit.

The next problem is to identify the cluster of characteristics that appeared in the firms. We might distinguish an extreme functionally oriented and centralized organization from an extreme product-oriented and decentralized organization. Our extreme functionally oriented organization would, of course, be organized around functions, have no integration of functions except at the top, centralize product choice, and pass products from one service to another without an intermediary. (The firm would display characteristics 1a, 2a, 3a, and 4a on Table 1.) There were four such firms, and one other which, while heavily functional and centralized, did provide some means of lower-level integration. In two of these firms, however, the firm was medium-sized and work relationships had been built up over many years. Thus, despite the formal structure, some integration of functions had been worked out. A fully product-oriented and decentralized firm would be defined by characteristics 1b (1), 2b, 3b, and 4b. There were three such firms, with the remainder falling somewhere in between.

Table 2

IDEAL FIRM TYPES

Extreme Functionally Oriented and Centralized Firm
  1. Functional organization axis
  2. Integration of functions only at the top
  3. Formally centralized product choice
  4. Product passage from lab to line from one service to another

Examples: 5

Extreme Product-Oriented and Decentralized Firm
  1. Entire firm organized along product lines
  2. Either an integrator with formal responsibilities and power or overlapping definitions of functions
  3. Decentralized product choices
  4. Passage from lab to line within the same service

Examples: 3

Table 3

ORGANIZATIONAL CHARACTERISTICS OF FRENCH ELECTRONICS FIRMS

A. INTEGRATION OF FUNCTIONS				
Organizational axes	At top	Formal integrator	Overlapping definition	Ambiguous or heterogeneous
Functional	4	4	—	—
Product	2	4	4	2

B. FORMAL LOCATION OF PRODUCT CHOICE		
Centralized or spread	Decentralized	Ambiguous or heterogeneous
Functional	—	2
Product	5	—

C. PASSAGE FROM LAB TO LINE		
Organizational axes	From one service to another	Within same service	Ambiguous
Functional	8	6	2
Product	—	—	—

Several matters become clear when we consider the relationships between the axis of the organization and the other three characteristics. Although product axes for the organization may decentralize the control and the point of integration of certain functions, it does not insure complete decentralization or lower-level integration of functions. Even organizations that are *functionally* organized feel the need for lower-level integration, and fulfill these needs by creating a position of integrator. Similarly, even functionally organized firms decentralize product choice or spread it out between the hierarchical center and lower-level managers. Lastly, a product axis tended to insure a closer link between the factory and the laboratory.

We can draw from this two important conclusions. First, when we add the qualitative observation that the three firms (out of four) which formally retained all power at the center appeared to be those in which long years of cooperation between the important actors insured continuing informal and often social contacts, it appears that even the functionally organized firms felt and responded to the technological pressure to link the functions horizontally and reduce the distance between strata in the organization. Second, when firms undertook partial reorganization along product lines, retaining some functional divisions, it was always the sales group that was left in isolation. Responsibility for production costs but not for profits would then be decentralized.

We might then hypothesize that it was the difficulty of putting a product into production, rather than financial or commercial problems, that brought about a product axis. Interestingly, this usually happened in state-oriented firms.

Our analysis has thus far focused only on the current organization of the firms, but in nine of the cases the organizational history of the firm could be developed from some point in the past (not always the same one), to the present. In two other cases two points in the organizational history could be established, although the firms have since gone out of existence in their previous forms. While the sample is very limited, it does indicate an evolution from functional to produce axes for organization, as shown in this tabulation:

Organizational Axes	Point in Past	Present
Functional	9	4
Product	0	5

In two cases not included in the tabulation, one firm attempted to decentralize power into more clearly defined product divisins before disappearing in a merger, while the other attempted, unsuccessfully, to establish defined lines of decentralized authority which would have involved wresting some independence from legally autonomous subsidiaries. It appears, therefore, that firms with product axes, decentralized and defined responsibility, and lower-level horizontal integration of functions are the product of an evolution, and not simply continuing features of the industry from the past. We cannot, of course, directly conclude anything about the role that technological demands may have played in this evolution.

The firms in the sample have until now been treated as undifferentiated units. The question remains, however, whether characteristics of the firms will distinguish between those that have adapted, as it were, to the pressures of technology and those that have retained functional and hierarchical organizations. Of the characteristics considered, including age and ownership, only two appeared to be important —the size of the firm and its relationship to the state.

Large size—that is, more than 1000 employees—appeared to make some form of decentralization necessary among the electronics firms in this sample. All the firms with more than 1000 employees, or half the sample, eventually instituted some system of decentralized authority on a product-line basis. Their success, as will be seen in the case studies, was widely different, but all at least began the effort. Of the firms smaller than 1000, only one was thoroughly decentralized on a product basis, but two others had institutionalized means for directly integrating the functions. Of the remaining five firms, two had the technologically most stable products. Very simple, it appeared that the fluidity and face-to-face contact required by the technology remained possible in a functionally organized *medium-sized* company but was impossible in the larger firms. In at least three of the five cases of functionally organized firms (in the other two I would not hazard a guess) it did appear that greater decentralization and closer integration of the functions would have been very useful, but the problems did not pose themselves as crises.

A firm's relation to the state did help explain the pattern of organizational change that appeared in the industry. A crude interpretation that firms oriented toward the state would as a group remain more centralized and functional than the others is not supported by the evidence, but when characteristics such as size and product are held constant they do appear to be more decentralized.

Testing this proposition requires a matched set of firms distinguished only by their orientation toward the state and some scale of decentralization and integration of functions. Four sets of matched pairs could be chosen from the sample. By early good fortune and later intention, the four case studies were matchable; the first two were of relatively the same size and produced different forms of the same product, while the second two were both very large firms that produced a variety of products. Six other firms could be matched. There was one reasonably direct match and one firm in the state sector that was comparable with three different firms in the competitive sectors.

The formal measures of decentalization and "functionalization" of the firms can represent a continuum leading from the idealized central and functional firm to the ideal type of decentralized product organization. This continuum serves the limited purpose of a simple ordering between two firms. A firm was considered to be under the state's tutelage or to have adopted a strategy of state support if its product orientation was toward state markets and if it received more than one-third of its funds for R and D from the state. The funding measure was confirmed with an expert source, and the market orientations were evident after a year of following these firms. However, this after-the-fact pairing and the handful of pairs means that the evidence can only be suggestive.

In the three direct matches the firm oriented toward the state was markedly more functional and centralized than its market-oriented counterpart. In the match where one state firm was compared with three market firms, the state firm was more sharply functional and centralized than any of the other three.

The fourth match between two large firms is more complicated. The large size and wide product diversity of the state-oriented firm has meant that some decentralization along product lines was unavoidable, but this decentralization has cost the corporate center its strategic control of the enterprise. The *groupe* is more a federation of operating units than a corporate whole, and its sub-units are nearly out of control. Moreover, there are sharp gaps between hierarchical echelons within the firms, and there is little coordination between functional groups or different product groups. The state-oriented company does appear to be an assemblage of bastions of power, each defending its autonomy at the cost of the well-being of the whole. Nonetheless, while the top management cannot exercise effective continuing control over the operating units, there is a decided tendency to centralize important strategic or even tactical decisions of those operating units. Only in this way, it would seem, can any direction be exercised.

The market firm on the other hand, has successfully established divisions without creating gaps between echelons in the firms. The operating heads of the divisions form what might best be called the corporate council that formulates strategy, and the principle that those who formulate strategy must execute it appears to apply at lower levels of the firm as well. In the one product area shared by the two firms, the division of the market firm appears to have more thoroughly integrated the functions, though neither firm had exactly solved its problems. A closer look at these two firms will be possible in the next section, but the decided impression is that the market-oriented firm had resolved its organizational problems more thoroughly.

Case Studies of Four Firms. The data on the formal structure of the firm can only indirectly suggest the processes at work within it. The four cases presented below are those in which I developed the most thorough understanding of the firm. Significantly, they include two matched pairs of firms: "Genset" and "Norgood" form one set, and "Industrial Electronics" and Thomson-Houston form the second. That more open access developed in these firms, and not in four others, was in part resulted from chance acquaintanceships and in part because two of the firms were obvious candidates for any analysis of high-technology electronics firms in France. An effort has been made to disguise the identity of three of the firms. Since the electronics industry in France is quite small, that has also meant suppressing certain facts that would help illuminate the analysis of the firms. Disguising Thomson-Houston seemed unnecessary and also impossible.

Genset Products. This medium-sized firm has carved out a market segment in a brutally competitive sector of the industry. A high-ranking executive in one of its American competitors remarked that this was the only French operation in that sector that understood both the business and organizational problems of remaining competitive in any part of the market. "Genset" had no choice but to evolve a competitive strategy because the state markets were already held by other firms.

The firm's current organization was developed, according to several sources within the firm, to avoid the blockages in communication that create problems in developing and marketing products. Until the middle 1960s the firm had been organized around functions, but problems in development affected competitiveness and made the firm receptive to new organizational ideas. The firm was not making effective development choices and found it inordinately difficult to stop projects with limited prospects. At the same time products that went into production often had to be redeveloped to permit the use of standard industrial manufacturing equipment. The result was high development costs and late market entry.

The idea for a reorganization around product lines and a lower-level integration of functions was "imported" from the United State by the firm's president, who was impressed by the success of this form of organization in his visits with American firms. "Genset" is now organized around product lines with a product group director responsible for three of the four families of products. The fourth group still reports directly to the president.

This decentralization has given the product manager the resources and authority to act on his own initiative. He controls all aspects of the products in his line: the basic or applied research, the development, the production, the sales, and whatever service might be needed. His control over the group is formally quite broad. He bears the final responsibility for product decisions and has delegated to him the right to hire and fire for the group. He is, however, expected to consult with his president about product choices that represent changes in the strategic emphasis of the firm and about any major capital purchases.

This increase in the product-group director's authority was accompanied by giving him direct responsibility for the performance of his group, and the accounting system was changed to permit this. Before, it had been very difficult to judge the health of the company, the profitability of any product, or the performance of any section of the firm. The new analytic accounting system was designed to permit judgment on products and the individuals responsible for them.

These judgments and the direct investigations they brought about were not perceived as threats by the managers, but were welcomed as a basis for resolving problems in face-to-face exchanges. I did not personally witness any of these "judgment" sessions, but certainly the approach to judgment was sharply different from that described as the French authority dilemma. One manager remarked: "To be judged is an advantage for me, I am not alone. . . . when I am judged there is always a discussion and then we can find the solutions for the problem in the direct exchange of views. . . . I would not accept a judgment if it were to come from above like a flash, but a discussion . . . yes."

Lower-level initiative and responsibility were evident in the description of the firm presented by this manager and other engineers, and were also visible in the strength of its organization. The internal workings were unanimously described as open and flexible in contrast to the other electronics firms where the men had worked. As one manager noted: "The absence of structure is the strength of our company; certainly there is the danger of anarchy, but this system works, if one takes initiative." There was ample evidence of that initiative. Each of the R and D engineers interviewed pointed to products that had been started at his initiative and developed under his guidance. In one case, a young engineer rushed into the office where I was conducting an interview to announce to his colleague that he had negotiated R and D support from a government ministry for a project the two of them had pushed in the company.

Sharp lines did not seem to be drawn between tasks or echelons. One engineer remarked that the "hierarchy simply doesn't touch our work from day to day." Disagreements, he said, had to be worked out at the lower levels, because pushing them up the hierarchy simply didn't resolve them. He explained that responsibility shifted from project to project and since several were always underway at any one time, the lines of authority and dependence were very confused. He insisted that naming his official boss would not reflect either his actual responsibilities nor his interactions in the firm.

Responsibility, moreover, appeared to be broadly defined. That decisions were not taken alone and no one left to work alone was repeatedly cited in the interviews as a strength of the firm. Shared responsibility was seen as necessary to insure coordination, and was not intended to put a collective umbrella over individual responsibilities. One older engineer who had had difficulty adjusting to the firm described how he slowly learned to accept responsibility for all aspects of a project. In the firm where he had worked before coming to "Genset", the development group had been responsible only for meeting certain technical standards with a prototype, after which they washed their hands of the affair, but at Genset he was "responsible for everything." Since he is responsible for seeing that the product works when the client uses it, even though he doesn't have production responsibilities, he has taken up the habit of surveying the production line to spot differences between laboratory and line condition that might influence quality. For him and others, broader responsibilities had meant more direct styles of work, particularly face-to-face resolution of problems: "I put those I work with in front of me and we resolve the problems. You know, this isn't an administration here, we have to work directly with each other."

Putting this new system into operation was not a matter of putting new lines on a paper chart, and there were problems of transition. The system was accepted, it is reported, because it clearly worked better and because there were *fewer* serious personal conflicts. Because all project term members are responsible for a product, have the same boss, and are judged according to the same standard of product profitability, they can work the problems out between them. Before, when there were different bosses with different budgets and different definitions of "success," there had been serious fights over who should do what and who was responsible for what.

The organizational evolution within the firm can be captured by the comments of one product-group manager. He remarked that after two years he had succeeded in eliminating the alibi that someone else is responsible for the particular problem. No one in his group any longer dares to say "I'm not responsible for that" (*C'est pas moi, je ne suis pas responsable"*).

Norgood Electronics. "Norgood" has been one of the instruments of state electronics policy, and although they make products similar to "Genset's", they sell in different sectors of the market and are not direct competitors. "Norgood" consists of two separate divisions that share only a sales force and a general management. Each of them is roughly the size of "Genset" and evolved separately, and it was only recently that they were united in a rationalization of the structure of the parent firm that owned them both.

A. Hudson Division. The Hudson Division has specialized in technologically advanced products, an effort that the state has encouraged and subsidized with the intention of minimizing French dependence on American suppliers and licenses. The division grew under the tutelage of the state, and the Grandes Écoles managers at the head of the firm have always had direct access to the offices of the administration.

Ten years ago operations were sharply divided by the functions, with rigid definitions of responsibility, and little adjustment or coordination inside the firm. Development and production, moreover, were separated by substantial physical distances, which exacerbated already strained relations. The isolation of the laboratory and development teams from the industrial and commercial divisions resulted in serious errors in product choices and made the transfer from development to production a serious problem. The lab's responsibility ended with the demonstration of a working prototype and the submission of their technical data. Products were therefore designed without regard to production problems. The laboratory could afford this indifference because it received substantial funding for much of its research directly from one or another state administration, support which depended only on the creation of a prototype and not on the production of the product.

This independence also allowed the lab to indulge in technological snobbism and to ignore any restraints of commercial necessity. Since the researchers were entirely free to follow the paths they found technologically interesting, they had effective control over the firm's product choices, and often—one director remarked—it was more important to outshine the Americans in the lab than to assure competitive products for the company. Although both current general management and former laboratory officials now recognize the difficulties, it required a true catastrophe to point them up. The lab had achieved interesting results using technique A, but had entirely ignored the possibilities of technique B—even after it appeared on the market. Technique B did not offer important performance advantages, but it profoundly changed the constraints on production, resulting in sharp price drops. Ultimately, the entire industry followed the new route, and both the technological and market position of the firm were seriously and permanently eroded. Even then, the state sheltered the firm from the consequences of its errors.

Although the firm was not allowed to sink, pressure from the state for change became substantial, and this catastrophe, a new president, and important changes in the parent company's general management did produce two reorganizations. Product groups have been created that integrate development and production personnel and have rationalized a previously confused production process. The advanced products group, though, has reproduced a functional division at a lower level, but the divisions are not as deep and are more manageable than before. In all, two levels of hierarchy have been lifted, the distance between the production and development managers has been substantially reduced, and many management functions have been decentralized.

The lower-level managers seemingly welcomed the additional responsibility and noted that work in teams had increased as the multitude of sub-services and sub-divisions were eliminated. The divisions that remained, however, were both obvious and difficult to penetrate, and the engineers report that they still generate problems.

The production-development groups are not responsible for selling their products, for profitability, or for strategy. The sales force is not even responsible to the division head, but reports directly to the president. The chasm that remains between sales and production-development leaves real control of the product groups in the hands of the division head and control of the division in the hands of the president.

The failure to decentralize appears to stem from the firm's relation to the state. Because product choices are, in fact, the result of negotiations by the division head and the company president with state administrators, the sales division serves only to distribute the product. With product choices in this unit sensitive to state requests rather than to market demand, sales need not serve as a weathervane nor be integrated into the product groups. Similarly, since any losses sustained in the market have been covered by the state as part of the price of a technology policy, there is no need to concern the production-development team with profits so long as production costs are restrained and the products of interest to the government are manufactured.

B. The Missouri Division. The Missouri Division was never intimately tied to the state because its products were simply too standard to attract much interest. Although it is profitable, the unit is treated as a poor sister in the company. Like the other division, Missouri had reorganized production and development tasks along product lines, but it does not have an independent sales force and thus cannot achieve the more thoroughgoing decentralization that is undoubtedly necessary for its market-oriented strategy.

Efforts to decentralize on a product-line basis were begun a number of years ago, but were disrupted when the general management of the firm changed. The continuing problems of putting products into successful production prompted another effort, but the exact process by which it was begun and carried out is cloudy. Some managers see it as a continuation of the original effort, whereas others claim that it was a conscious effort to copy a successful reorganization in another firm, but the explanation offered by the present director, who promoted and implemented the current plan is revealing:

> Delegating power is not at all natural to me, but we had serious problems. For me the worst was that all the problems mounted up to me. To resolve the conflicts between services I had to go into the smallest details. Everything came up to me to arbitrate.
>
> I had started taking courses before seeking an answer, but in 19-- I really thought I was going to die. The firm was growing rapidly, there was a crisis in the leadership, and one in the industry as well. I worked from seven in the morning until late at night and I still couldn't finish. I was really afraid I would have a heart attack. *I had to delegate power.*

Now that the system is in place, this director argues strongly in favor of decentralization. He maintains that functional centralism left *"Chaque dans sa coin"* (each in his own corner), while in modern industry the problems fall in the crevices.

His argument that an effective decentralization of production and development responsibilities had taken place would be hard to dispute. Nearly every other interview I had with a chief executive, whether the head of a firm or a factory or a division, was interrupted by secretaries, "essential" telephone calls, and other people within the factory. Yet I met with this gentleman for four hours in the middle of the work week, and our only interruption came while walking to lunch when a subordinate asked the time of a meeting later that day. "This factory," he said, "works without me. Look, the phone doesn't ring, no one needs me. If I weren't so interested in strategy it would be a bit irritating."

The Missouri Division is in fact deeply decentralized, although the director keeps more control than he would perhaps care to acknowledge. There are two distinct product divisions, each headed by product-group directors. The other services in the factory are considered staff functions that are intended to be responsive, if not exactly responsible, to the two product-group managers. Each product-group manager has a development director and two production directors who report to him. Each of the production directors is responsible for a product type, in whatever variety it may appear. He is responsible for seeing that the product is properly designed, just as his development counterparts are responsible for seeing that it works. There is no longer evidence of conflict in the passage of products from development to production, although everyone agreed that in one of the services the solution had required the departure of one manager and a year for the new manager to integrate himself. Once a unit that dragged its feet entering the market, the Missouri Division now conceives of itself as a commando force able to rapidly move to fill holes left by its larger competitors. Since product choice is usually dictated by the actions of its competitors, this choice has also been left to the product-group managers. While the director plays a role, and often a subtle and important one, in product choice, the consensus is that the product-group manager leads the choice process. In fact, one of the product managers initiated on his own the research that led to his entire product line.

"Norgood" had not achieved a decentralization along product lines in any way comparable to that of "Genset". The difference seemed to lie in relations to the state and the market. In fact, at "Norgood", the sharp division between Sales and Production-Development seemed to be more the source of tensions within the organization than an organizational means of resolving personal conflicts. During one interview in the Missouri Division the manager took a telephone call from the sales group. The sales manager wanted to know whether the production manager was certain that a piece of information given by one of his subordinates was accurate. The subordinate was called in and went into a rage, really a tantrum, insisting that the sales people had no right to interfere with or question his work. He had given the figures, and that was all that could be expected from him. When the episode was over, the production manager explained the fight to me, which was certainly the most serious one I observed during my entire period of research in France. Very simply, his explanation was as follows. Separated by organizational lines and several hundred miles, there was only occasional contact between sales and production people. The sales people, dependent on production for delivery to clients, had no way of influencing production schedules, since they were too far apart to be physically present on an informal basis and there was no formal system of adjusting to their demands. The result, he said, was continuous outbursts from his subordinates, who said they could keep production costs down only if they could stick to the original scheduling. Therefore, despite sales pressure for schedule adjustments, they resisted "interference" because they had no incentive to adjust schedules. In the absence of personal contact with sales personnel to temper the fight, they resisted quite vehemently.

This break between sales and development-production had an important strategic consequence. Production was responsible for the production costs at a fixed volume, and sales for volume based on a given production cost. No one was responsible for profit, and without a regular formal connection between sales and production-development in the form of a common boss, or physical proximity, or overlapping or identical responsibility in the form of, perhaps, profit—it was difficult to initiate or pursue the optimal mix between price-sales volume relationships and volume-production costs relationships. Each functional unit apparently took the other unit's estimates as given, because they had no basis for analyzing them as variables. Just how important this was to the firm was impossible to tell, but it was clear that one form of analysis crucial for strategic planning in this industry was made difficult by the firm's organizational structure. Conversely, of course, a different understanding of the business problem the firm faced might have produced a different organization.

3. *Industrial Electric.* Industrial Electric neither sells to the state nor is subsidized by it, but pursues industrial clients for its wide variety of products. It has grown from modest origins to become one of

France's larger firms, although it is a medium-sized operation by American standards. Until recently the firm was functionally organized despite its size and the variety of products it makes, but several years ago the firm was entirely divisionalized. The origins of this decentralization into product divisions came from the difficulties of planning the futures of the myriad and not entirely related products, not from pressures of the technology, and so the process by which this decision was taken was not thoroughly investigated. The reorganization was apparently successful, with the general management delegating tactical choices but retaining strategic control of the company. Without question, the firm corresponded more closely to the American idea of divisional management than any other I encountered in France.

A. Electronic Equipment Division. This unit, built from a single product line that was obtained several years ago by purchasing a small firm already operating in a field, is in fact a small firm growing into a medium-sized one. Until 1970 its organization had been sharply functional and highly centralized with clear lines drawn between research, development, industrialization, and production. There were three organizational hurdles a product had to pass before it was produced, and there was no regular basis for a long-term collaboration between marketing and research. Later a product manager was added, but he had no formal authority; he served only as a kind of intermediary, and also as a kind of lobbyist for a product in each of the functional branches.

Toward the end of the research an important organizational change occurred which aimed at insuring an easier passage of products from development into production. This change united under one man all development and production activities, but stopped short of adding marketing responsibilities to the product manager's job or providing a tie between the marketing and sales branches and long-term research.

The organization has slowly evolved toward decentralization and lower-level integration of functions, but one senses in its operating style some of the difficulties Crozier notes. The director was said to have had formal power, but limited ability to use it; while lower-level made demands for precisely defined responsibilities. It is this combination that Crozier depicts so well. Furthermore, there is clearly a tendency for each functional division to move along in its own direction. To this observer, these features appeared to be the result of the division's history. Part of the department's management had been with the original firm which was absorbed, and its actual power had dwindled. The group's manager had since been unable—for whatever rule of French law or stipulations in the sale agreement—or unwilling to fire the remnants of former management. The holdovers have clearly resisted his authority and attempted to preserve their own independent territory. Unable to clear the air in a single stroke, and without a clear model of how to integrate the functional services for long-term innovation and development, the director's hands have been tied and demands for sharp limits of responsibility have been heard. My experiences in the second unit of this firm make me suspect that an authority dilemma, broadly speaking, was not at the root of the problem, although resistance expressed itself in "typical French" styles.

B. The Development Group. This unit has a special responsibility at Industrial Electric, taking on special development projects for other divisions when requested by either the division or the general management. The unit is divided into a series of product-group managers, each of whom directs one or more teams. A team will consist of a core of people within the unit plus other affected individuals from the department where the product will end up—particularly the sales manager and the production manager. The activity of one product development team was analyzed in depth.

"Industrial Electric's" product "Blurp" was under severe pressure because a competitor had recently bought out a superior product and threatened the firm's market position. A product development team was assigned the broadly defined responsibility of putting a replacement product on the market with a specified budget. It was thus responsible not simply for research, development, a prototype, or a pilot production line, but for handing over to a department a completed operation.

Four men formed the core of the team—a product manager, an administrative expert, an electronics engineer, and a designer—but their group which numbered ten in all also included the production manager, who would later be responsible for the facilities and was deeply involved in their development, and the sales manager, who would be responsible for selling "Blurps." The offices of the four core members were within five yards of one another and the entire group met once a week for an afternoon to coordinate the progress of their efforts.

A sharp focus on profit and on an American management technique called PERT aided the cohesion of the group. Whatever the formal techniques, however, this development group was organized without hierarchical distinction—the product manager was at the center of a circle rather than above a line of subordinates since many of those on the team were his hierarchical equals—and it depended for its work on broad definitions of responsibility and ongoing face-to-face relations between the group members. All those interviewed emphasized that the system required that they resolve the technical problems among themselves, and that this involved broader definitions of responsibility and more face-to-face contacts than they had previously experienced.

This approach, one engineer emphasized, required that one take account of the work requirements of the others, because the regular meeting forced continuing compromises. In the end, it was easier to take account of those requirements in the first place than to fight it out afterwards. One older team member remarked that before joining the team he had always worked in a hierarchical system, and that he found the defined area of responsibility and independence within it very comfortable. However, he said he now recognized the greater effectiveness of the team system and found pleasure in the quality of the work they were able to do. He was responsible for an important design advance, but he emphasized that in a sharply functional organization his innovation would not have been possible.

The reports of the work relationships were confirmed in a product development meeting I attended. The administrative director of the project, responsible for analytic accounting and progress accounting, chaired this meeting and the product manager intervened when he felt it was necessary. The authority was divided from the outset between the product manager and his assistant. Throughout the meeting, the product manager never made a choice alone, but pushed the discussion —although he was not chairman—toward agreements. Many of the problems on the agenda which involved production coordination with the development engineers had already been resolved at the initiative of several of those on the team. Usually an effort was made to explore the implications of those private decisions for everyone else present. The administrative manager was concerned that too many decisions were now being made in the hallways, as he put it, where all the aspects couldn't be examined. Several times one of the engineers would argue that his proposal was the "only way" the problem could be solved, whatever the needs of the others were; but in each case the problem was broken down and compromise solutions were found. Once, interestingly, the older engineer who had lamented his lost independence responded to a demand that he undertake a task somewhat outside his limited responsibility with the remark "It isn't my responsibility," but he was overridden with references to the PERT control system and project needs. In the end he accepted the task with a deadline of two weeks.

Finally, the major issue of the day was tackled. The location of three drill points in production threatened to disturb the electronic performance, and either the layout of the circuitry had to be modified or the production process changed. The possibilities and limits on changes in the circuits and the production techniques were explored to identify a fit between the two. The discussion ended when each engineer decided that the feasibility of each of the several possible solutions had to be explored. The issue was to be discussed again the next week. Although the discussion had been excited, it was clear that the issue would soom be resolved. It was not difficult to imagine what would have happened had the men been separated by an organizational wall with a narrow definition of responsibility. The product easily could have been handed back and forth forever while an essentially trivial problem that was no one's fault or that fell between everyone's realm of responsibility held up the project. Moreover, with separate functional services, each with a separate budget, the problem would arise of whose budget would support the modification. There would be an important incentive to refuse the responsibility so as to preserve budget reserves for dealing with a later crisis. With project budgeting, the budgeting incentive was to work together to reduce the cost of any modification to the whole project. The cost of the modification came from funds reserved for that project, not from the particular unit.

4. *Thomson-Houston-CSF*: (Since the history of this company is so well known in France, disguising the name is impossible. Moreover, since the number of persons interviewed at Thomson was large and varied, none of the confidences have been compromised in this very general discussion.) Thomson-Houston-Hotchkiss-Brandt is the national champion of the electronics industry, and at once a creation and an instrument of state policy. Thomson was created by a fusion of medium-sized firms, nourished by state subsidy and guaranteed markets, and occasionally rocked by the jockeying of the state ministries. Thomson-CSF is the professional division of the *Groupe* (goods made for state or industrial markets are called professional products in France), and although the problem of this critical division and the *groupe* are difficult to separate, the emphasis in this research has been on the professional electronics division, which is a large firm in its own right.

Thomson-CSF, as described in the interviews, displayed many of the characteristics that would be predicted by Crozier's model: centralized authority that lacks the power to implement its will; sharp divisions between strata and among operating units; conservative and cautious management at lower levels that could only be described as an absence of initiative, and formal procedures that are often blamed for the sluggish movement of the firm. The absence of effective sanctions, except for gross and obvious failures, was widely cited as an impediment to effective control of lower management behavior and to risk taking and individual initiative as well. Since inaction was not punished, it was safest to do nothing.

From a business perspective, the firm has neither an evident strategy nor a workable organization, although there are some who argue that both are now emerging. Managed as a group with a confusing melange of subsidiaries, divisions, and joint ventures, the lines of authority and control are at best unclear. There is no long-range planning, and strategy results from the short-run product choices taken by the operating units—often under the direct influence of a state administration. Areas of collaboration between operating units such as CII, the computer subsidiaries, and SESCOSEM, the semi-conductor division, are generally left unexplored. It would be fair to characterize the firm as a collection of units, each hiding in its own protected and relatively independent corner. Thus, as one highly placed government official explained it, "Thomson-CSF, despite forced fusions to expand its size, has neither the massed power of a large firm because it is not coordinated, nor the supple and quick responses of many small ones."

The problems originated in the growth and evolution of the firm. Thomson-Houston-CSF consists of two firms which were joined only in 1968. Thomson-Houston was founded in 1893 with French capital to exploit the electrical patents of two American engineers, and when General Electric bought the American patents of Thomson and Houston the rights to exploit G.E. patents were extended to the French firm. Thus from the beginning, Thomson-Houston depended on American technology and followed the lead of G.E.

CSF, on the other hand, has been described as a research laboratory that was only incidentally a business enterprise. The forceful and charming Maurice Ponte, a Normalien and a member of the Académie Française, molded the character of this company. He managed, according to all accounts, including his own, by having an intuitive grasp of the technologically possible and by having confidence in particular men, eschewing structure and organization. The result was a highly centralized firm dominated by its research personnel. CSF was the darling of the state, and in the negotiated market of the state administration, the efforts of an undoubted technical genius sufficed for many years. In the 1960s serious financial problems, attributed by the management to the conservatism of the banks and by outsiders to the inadequate accounting of R and D expenditures and an impossible centralization of the firm, led to a change in management and finally to fusion with Thomson.

For Thomson, not yet recovered from two other important mergers with companies of approximately its own size, absorbing CSF has proved to be inordinately difficult. The two firms had different approaches to business and management, and had been competing in many market sectors. Now they have had to join forces because neither was large enough simply to swallow the other. Although there was some pruning of management forces, few operations were closed. Therefore there was jockeying and maneuvering for position by managers of the two companies at the division level as well as in the general management. It was not unusual for a division manager to be from one firm and his assistant to be from the other.

Since the state was deeply concerned with the firm's well being, it took an active hand in these struggles. The firm's current president, not an alumni of a Grande École, is being pressured to retire and the fight for succession is also an administrative struggle for position within the firm. Some observers go as far as to argue that the battle over succession is a battle between Grands Corps factions for dominance in the industry. For a period there was even talk of a further fusion with CGE, the large French electrical company, and a spate of resignations have flowed from the infighting.

The absence of strategy or rational management, therefore, simply reflects the uncertain and fragmented power relations within the firm. In these years of uncertainty it is little wonder that each unit attempted to carve out its own domain and protect it. The impact of the confusion in the organization's management on company performance is cushioned by Thomson's dominant position in the state markets and the continuing subsidies of her losses in many sectors. In all fairness, some of the unprofitable sectors could be closed were it not for the continued pressure of the state to maintain them. A closer look at two of the operating units—the research laboratory and a development project—can highlight the influence of technology and protection on organization.

The research laboratory. The research lab is the acknowledged master of its own house, and the transfer of its findings to the industrial divisions is at best spotty. Although a division of the general management, the Général Direction Technique, has formal responsibility for determining the research directions from year to year, it has no power— and little influence is reported—over the allocation of funds within the laboratory itself. It can do little more than proclaim the status quo as policy. Even within the laboratory, policy is more an accumulation of existing positions than a tactic for implementing either a corporate or a research strategy. Unable to change personnel or impose direction on its research, the lab is trapped in its own history and shaped by the past, not the future. Since a major portion of the lab's funds come directly from state agencies, it has been able to live independently from the industrial life of the company.

Life inside the laboratory was consistently described as divided into isolated groups working on their own projects with little knowledge of work in other sections of the laboratory. One American engineer intimately familiar with this lab argued that the laboratory at Corbeville reflected the French misunderstanding of technological development. While science, he said, requires semi-isolated and focused groups concentrating on their own projects, technology demands the constant addition of one technology to another to produce a marketable produce. He suggests, in fact, that very few engineers in the laboratory were familiar enough with the work of their colleagues to draw on it when they needed it, and cited several products in the computer field that could be assembled within six months by an effective team from existing technologies at the central laboratory. Another engineer, not of French origin, who works at the laboratory and attributes the success of his own work to his intimate familiarity with the other technologies in the laboratory that he can call on when he needs to, also insists that the isolation of the projects is an important handicap to effective work. Few individuals, according to him, were familiar with a wide range of the projects in the laboratory, and fewer would ask for assistance even when they had such familiarity. Often, he said, he was asked to act as a catalogue or intermediary, and in one ironic case his aid was sought by an engineer who didn't know that a component of the type he needed had been experimentally produced in the office next door to his own. Three engineers interviewed were familiar with both American laboratories and Corbeville, and all emphasized the greater flow of information, sharing of ideas, product orientation, and time constraints in the American labs.

A development project.[6] The development project was undertaken in a division of the former Thomson-Houston that was at the time functionally organized. It has since reorganized along product lines, but the product groups remain centralized and functionally divided. There has not been a decentralization as much as a recentralization at a lower level.

At the time, Thomson was competing with CSF for military contracts and trying to prove that it possessed a technological capacity not dependent on copying General Electric. Therefore in a contract signed with the ministry of the army, low price and high performance were promised, a trick not unknown in America. The promises were made because the firm had recently stumbled across an advance in the underlying components in an American research laboratory that made the remarkably higher performance a matter of improving an existing prototype, not undertaking a search of a new technology. However, when contract was made with the American laboratory after the contract was signed, the French discovered they had misread the article on which their promises had been based. The performances they had promised the government were in fact ten times those anticipated from even current experimental technology. A major advance was required.

The development group was divided into its technical specialties and proceeded to work on the problem in their existing specialties while still assigned to their previous posts in one or another hierarchical service. After two years of frustration, what would not be called a product team was created, uniting four engineers from different services under a single boss. When the group was working together, they found they had been blocked by a gap in the underlying physics which no one had seen from his isolated perspective.

Before the project was completed, a second major crisis arose that involved what everyone remembers as a very painful battle between the production unit and the laboratory. The responsibility for the development of one device, central to the product, had been assigned to the laboratory, and a classic story began to repeat itself. The device operated by itself in the laboratory, but not when it was installed in the entire apparatus. Because the development had been long and expensive, the question of responsibility became a fighting matter between the director of the team and the laboratory project director. Whoever was responsible would be required to pay for the redevelopment out of his particular budget, which made it very tempting to refuse responsibility. The problem, not unexpectedly, was that the operation of the entire apparatus affected the physics of the vital electronic device. Those responsible for the entire project did not have the detailed knowledge of the device to correct it without redeveloping it, while those who had developed it did not understand the conditions under which it was operating. Finally two engineers ignored the struggle over responsibility between their respective bosses and found the technical problem. One of those two men remarked, "The technical fights can be resolved, but the fights over position and budget are the difficult ones." Divided responsibility, he argued, encouraged conflict.

5

Between the Market and the State: Dilemmas of French Electronics Policy

The dissolution of the Délégation à l'Informatique in the fall of 1974—almost a decade after it was established—marked the end of the Plan Calcul, the program intended to foster a viable French presence in the computer industry. Giscard's new government, faced with the ever-mounting subsidies required to float the plan and the unwillingness of at least one of the industrial partners to increase its capital investments, moved to change the state's commitments and arranged the sale of CII (Compagnie Internationale de l'Informatique) to Honeywell-Bull. That transaction has been attacked politically from each end of the spectrum: from the left, which made nationalization of the electronics sector a part of its electoral program and viewed the sale as a victory for CGE's Ambroise Roux, who wished to rid himself of an albatross; and from the right, which persists in its dreams of French technological glory. The settlement between the companies with major stakes in CII, which will deeply affect their positions in other sectors, was still in dispute in mid-1975 and as a result the final accord has remained unsigned months after its announcement. Furthermore, crucial aspects of the protocol between the government and Honeywell remain secret. Consequently, the strategy intentions of the government remain obscure, and an evaluation of this decision must await the clarification of the arrangement. At any rate, the exit of the Plan Calcul brings down the curtains on an epoch in French policy for electronics, and provides the opportunity to evaluate ten years of a state industrial policy. Thus whereas the previous chapter considered the organization of individual firms in the industry those years, this chapter will consider the effect of state policy on the industry's competitive position.[1]

For a decade, then, the French government pursued a political goal, technological independence, by directly supporting and protecting French electronics firms. Its policies, though, appear to have had the unintended economic consequence of damaging the conduct and performance of the very firms which served as instruments of policy. The French state, accustomed to imposing its will on the marketplace, has been unable either to isolate the French firms or to alter the structure of the international industry. In this setting, forcing the firms to conform to the goals of the state slowly weakened them in the marketplace. The eroding position of the firms in turn threatened the state's ability to pursue its technological goals. However, allowing the firms to conform to the constraints of the market would have required the government to abandon or to redefine many of its policies. The dilemmas to be considered here were provoked by a policy goal of technological independence, which appeared to require that the state change the industry structure rather than urge firms to adapt to the market.

French policy for the electronics industry was set forth in the "era of the technology gap" and inspired by the fear that national independence would be lost and France shoved into the second or perhaps third rank of nations by the rush of technological advance that came from America.[1] The particular wave of electronics technology developed in the 1950s and 1960s was not as disquieting as the more general concern that the magnitudce of American aid, the structure of American industry, and the organization and management of American firms would ultimately bring about a permanent French political and economic dependence on foreign technology and a domination of certain French industries by foreign capital. It appeared, therefore, that the state should intervene to support the development of vital technologies and to modernize the electronics industry, in order to insure that French firms could defend the national position.

There are those, however, who would argue that the fundamental goal of the government was always the modernization of the industry, and that the "technology gap" rhetoric was consciously manipulated to promote this goal.[2] In this interpretation, the Control Data computer temporarily denied France by American policy was not in fact essential to atomic development in France, but was instead an incident that gave force and legitimacy to government demands for change.

Since the government conception of a modern industry called for a few large producers capable of competing in all products, both interpretations lead to the same conclusion—the government should assist the reorganization of the industry and support efforts at research and development. Similarly, whether the fears of a technology gap prompted the policies or legitimated them, an atmosphere of national glory through noble technology emerged in which the engineers had little difficulty engaging government support for technically—not commercially—inspired projects such as SECAM, the French color television system.

The debate faded away, perhaps as Jean-Jacques Saloman argues,[3] because the problem was finally clearly seen and everything remained to be done, only to be revived when, in the face of sudden trade deficits, the Americans began asking whether they had "lost their technological lead."[4] Harvey Brooks and Richard Nelson, among others, have reopened the old debate. Brooks has observed that the pace of technological advance has been slower in the United States than in Europe since World War II and gone on to argue that the recent trade turn-around results from a decline in American surpluses in technologically intensive goods. In its new version, "the technology gap" has exchanged political perspectives and concerns for the economic problems of trade.[5]

Multiple meanings for the term "technology gap" have long clouded our understanding and confused the formulation of policy. The economic reality which inspired the label and the policies that might have been appropriate were markedly different from the political imagery the term evoked. Given the biases of the decision makers and the political mood of the time, perhaps the problem could not have been defined any differently. These perspectives, though, have been institutionalized in current policies and underlie the dilemmas examined here. Articulating the multiple meanings of "technology gap" can point to the origins of the policy dilemmas and perhaps suggest some of the ways out of them.

In the most literal sense, there probably never was a "technology gap" between Europe and America, certainly not a gap of the kind that might characterize the technological relations between Third World and industrial nations. With very few exceptions—one being military products such as certain atomic techniques or integrated circuits in their earliest phase—there were no products which the French *did not have and could not use.* That is, the French had available to them the full range of advanced technologies, and the scientific and industrial infrastructure to use them existed. Differences in productivity levels certainly existed, but differences in the quality of the capital stock reflected dozens of social and economic factors, such as the reluctance of noncompetitive and often family-owned and small firms to adopt new methods and relative factor prices. Under any circumstances, the productivity problem, although of real concern to the French, was hardly at the heart of the debate.

Nor could it be said that the products were not made in France by French nationals. In electronic components, for example, production of each new generation began in France as the market grew large enough to justify manufacture, not import. Similarly, IBM and Honeywell-Bull were manufacturing computers in French plants manned by French engineers and even managed by Frenchmen. Therefore, strictly speaking it was not even true that France lacked the capability to produce these advanced goods.

Although the technology gap implied a genuine difference in technological capacity, it referred in fact to something much more limited and specific. *French firms—that is, firms composed of French capital— could not assure the production of certain products nor initiate technological advance in certain fields.* Thus at its core the "technology gap" was a question of the market position of different national firms. Although technological advance may have affected those market positions, the difficulty more often than not was the inability of French firms to translate technological possibilities into competitive products and defensible market positions. Certainly this was the case in the failure of Machines Bull and COSEM. It was as much a failure of the firm that produced a technology gap as the other way around. In this context, strategies aimed at particular technologies or specific gaps never came to grips with the real problem, and may simply have perpetuated it.

What should be done about the fact that French firms do not produce particular goods depends, of course, on what difference it makes. Apart from a simple defense of the interests of national capital, there are reasons why the French government felt uneasy with foreign firms, particularly foreign electronic firms. First, foreign firms may be less responsive to government policy and less bound by the rules of the business game in France. For example, they may be less willing to assure stable employment and exports, two central elements of French economic policy. In fact, employment in electronics, particularly in foreign firms, is very small, while exports demand a competitive position in some goods which are not necessarily the most advanced. Neither exports nor employment would seem to justify the major programs that were initiated.

Second, early access to certain technologies such as components may affect the competitive position of product firms in a variety of sectors, and therefore a national producer and innovator is essential. Since American manufacturers, the argument runs, tend to produce only standard catalogue items in France, and develop their new-generation products in the United States, there is a need for a national producer. There are, though, many more effective and less expensive solutions than the present floating of a national producer. Some form of implantation in the United States, or a tie between a French group and one of the American components manufacturers, such as the one envisioned between SESCOSEM and Motorola, or that now established between CII and Honeywell, could resolve aspects of the problem.

Finally, it is argued that a dependence on foreign technologies is simply a threat to national independence, in some distant and not clearly defined way, and here we come to the heart of the issue. As Raymond Vernon (1968) writes: "When advanced nations find themselves reliant upon outside sources for the technology essential to their national objectives, a deep sense of insecurity is generated. Whatever the economic analysis may suggest, therefore, nations are likely to feel more at ease if the sources of technology seem to lie within their control than if they are largely external."[6] We might recall the comments of the working group of the Planning Commission that failure to maintain a semi-conductor capacity would mean that France would start down the road to underdevelopment.

Simple insecurity was at the bottom of the technology gap debate, but even acknowledging that European fears are more justified than Vernon suggests, it is not clear that the response needed to be the actual production of particular technologies such as large-scale computers. Admittedly, once the problem has been defined in this way, a logic leads to policies that support national production, but considering the costs and the limited success of national production, a further consideration of the possibilities seems called for. What precisely are the dangers?

Even if the French government were denied the use of a technology controlled by a company with a foreign base exactly at the vulnerable moment when a new generation of products became available, the older products would probably suffice—although they would be less efficient —for a number of years. The time to react and develop a French product would still exist. One policy, therefore, might be to maintain the capacity to develop that product, if it became necessary. Thus, it may not be essential for companies controlled by French capital and sensitive to French policy to produce the most advanced products, but only to maintain the capacity of producing them if necessary. Since the prototype and the industrialization of products represent the bulk of its overall cost of development, the applied and basic research necessary to maintain a defensive position is relatively low. If the firm, moreover, is producing related or more traditional products in the same sector, much of the research cost would be absorbed by other products, reducing the necessary subsidy even further. Actual product competition with the international leaders, on the other hand, would probably demand subsidies orders of magnitude greater than the minimum defensive subsidies.

If the level of subsidy were the only issue the discussion would be academic, since the state would most likely pay a higher subsidy to reduce the uncertainty inevitable in a defensive position, even if it clearly perceived the cost and choice. However, the insistence that particular high-technology goods be produced by French capital, not simply that a defensive reaction capacity be maintained, has generated serious dilemmas in French policy. Producing these goods today may in fact make it increasingly difficult to maintain a defensive position tomorrow. The problem—how to achieve technological independence—is a political one, but the underlying cause is economic. Addressing the political symptoms may simply aggravate the economic problems.

The First Dilemma—The Cost of a Technological Strategy

Debates over the technological options open to Europe have often confused the perspectives of the firm and those of the nation-state. For the firm, the problem is to make a product it can sell at a profit, and except for reasons of corporate strategy, it doesn't matter what that product will be. For the nation-state, however, the problem may be to insure that there are firms making *particular* products that it needs to serve one or another national goal. The problem arises when the products which the government desires are not those which will permit the firms to make their profits. Thus, for the firm the market structure represents a set of constraints to which it must adapt in selecting and making products, while for the government that market structure may be a set of obstacles blocking particular policy objectives. The French electronics firms might be able to prosper both in size and technological capacity, but whether a firm making a particular cluster of products, such as a broadline French semi-conductor or computer producer, can survive and prosper is a very different question. Unless the state can change the structure of the industry, the market constraints of firm strategies represent limits on state policy. By encouraging and often forcing firms to ignore these constraints in order to gain a national supplier of particular technologies, the state endangered the firms and undermined many of its own policies.

The thrust of French policy, at least until very recently (see Chapter 3), has been to insulate French firms from the market's constraints so that they can be responsive to the demands of the state, which have called for a French presence in every important sector of technology. American military and space spending, the small size of French firms, and a limited French home market have indeed put French firms at a competitive disadvantage in those product sectors of greatest interest to the state. But that does not mean they cannot be competitive in other sectors, nor that they cannot maintain a position in many of the important sectors.

The magnitude of American military and space programs did insure that the cutting edge of technological advance came from America, but as the Japanese invasion of many electronic market segments demonstrates, it hardly made American firms invulnerable to competition, particularly in consumer goods. In the active component sector, the government programs helped American firms to take a strong and early position in the market for each component generation, although the impact of government subsidy alone (as distinct from its vast purchases) was quite limited.[7] The ready availability of the technologies under licensing agreements and the vast variety of applications meant that a firm could pick a market sector and defend it even if it was not an innovator. Electronic companies in other European countries have used their product divisions as captive markets to insure the volumes needed for semi-conductor production. The American technological advances did not mean that all others would be pushed out of all markets, although for certain product lines American domination is said to be unbreakable.

For the vast variety of electronic products, the advantages are even more limited. The American government purchased highly sophisticated goods with little popular or industrial use, and the companies producing for military markets had difficulty reaping benefits in civilian sectors. Christopher Freeman analyzed the problem when considering the British position in electronic capital goods: "Most military and space hardware is designed for specific application under severe environmental conditions. A firm which tries to sell an essentially military product on the civil market will usually fail."[8] Firms that first develop a product for the military, moreover, are not likely to sell that product in civilian markets. Phillips of Holland, the several Japanese firms, and the French success in civilian radar demonstrate that the American military and space programs did not simply squeeze the Europeans out of their markets. Although pursuing the Americans in the most advanced technologies of military importance was probably impossible, since American military expenditures are fifteen times those of the French, competitive strategies were possible in civilian sectors.

Similarly, the advantages of firm size have been exaggerated. There do not appear to be economies of scale for research and development.[9] If anything the contrary applies, and thus the larger firms should not be expected to be more innovative and productive than small firms. The problem is that for any given product, there is an absolute level of resources that must be devoted to R and D, regardless of total sales. A firm must be able to keep abreast of the continuing technical changes in components, to introduce new improvements, and to launch an entirely new product if forced to do so by the competition. Scale thus becomes an advantage only for particular products. In fact, the success of small and medium-sized firms had been evident in many sectors of the electronics business. Certainly the classic example is Texas Instruments, a small firm in the 1950s with sales of only $20 million a year in small instruments. It took licenses from Bell Labs for the transistor and built itself into a 832 million dollar firm by 1969.[10] Without the military market this phenomenal growth would not have been possible, but Textronix, a firm set up by two engineers after the Second World War, has built a considerable empire on an industrial product, the oscilloscope. The success of small British and German firms in numerical control of machine tools and knitting machinery indicates that in Europe as well as America a small firm can make its way in electronics.[11] Similarly, the careful strategy of Moulinex in electric consumer goods, admittedly a different problem with lower development costs, allowed this small French firm to grow into an effective, medium-sized firm in the household appliance industry. With its stable technology and mass markets, moreover, the industry favors larger firms. Size alone is crucial, then, only if one is interested in particular products or in establishing a firm capable of competing in all products at once.

Without question both the structure and the small size of the French market creates a serious problem for French firms, probably the most serious handicap they face. French electronic production is only one-thirteenth of the American, although when military expenditures are subtracted the difference is much less.[12] Nonetheless, the ratio of production is less than the population ratio, perhaps because the United States is more highly and more uniformly developed; the declining sectors such as small merchants and peasants are not exactly markets for electronic goods, while large-scale farms and supermarkets are. The larger American market permits the American firm to absorb its development costs over a larger volume of production, argue the French, and this gives them a comparative advantage when they arrive in France. This assumes, of course, that everyone is selling identical goods, which is clearly not true in electronics; that the French are unable to develop products which are more desirable for other reasons; and that economies-of-scale production continue in an unbroken linear progression. For many goods, the French market is certainly large enough for firms to capture available economies of scale in production. Most importantly, the larger total market in America means that potential demand for a new product will reach a point justifying production sooner in America than in France. Until the point at which

French demand justifies a local plant, the product will be imported. When the critical threshold of demand is passed, the American firm may already be in an excellent position to begin production in France. Yet this is probably an advantage only for the most advanced goods, not for all products.[13]

All of this, of course, assumes that the American market is not accessible to the French firms; if it were they could reap the same benefit as American firms. Certainly, the "buy American" policy of our government blocks French access to the U.S. military market unless the French firm produces in America, and the sheer technological advance of American component firms and in specific capital goods areas such as computers cuts French firms off from sectors of the civilian market. Nonetheless, the French conviction that the American market is impenetrable, and an organizational structure in French firms that would make attacking a competitive foreign market a difficult task, may be as important as actual competitive conditions in explaining the absence of a French presence in the American market. In some areas, such as civilian radar, the French do have a competitive edge, and many of these industrial products, while sometimes less advanced or luxurious, are often considerably less expensive. In fact, several French firms, both large and small, are now working out arrangements to enter the American market with a broad range of products, and in certain other cases decisions not to enter are made on grounds of organizational difficulty, not competitive disadvantage. Some industry officials, however, think it is heresy to believe that the American market is open to French attack, and could, in fact, have been years earlier. For example, one highly placed French executive reported that an American adventure launched under his leadership failed because of his own company's inadequate organizational structure. The implication is that organizational difficulty, not a lack of market opportunities, troubled the French.

The American firms, then, have had certain advantages, but primarily in the most advanced and elaborate products. Thus, for example, no French firms are competitive in large central processing units for computers, but several firms are able to compete in the markets for smaller machines and peripherals. The French state has simultaneously ignored and raged against market constraints because its political goal of technological independence has required French firms to compete in the very sectors of the market where they were most handicapped.

Since France is only a medium-sized country with limited resources whose market represents but a fraction of the world electronics industry, the French state could never hope to change this economic reality. Although programs of direct transfer and administrative purchasing have created a small shelter, the firms huddled there still remain deeply vulnerable to the evolution of a competitive world outside. As the industry develops, there is no assurance that marginal positions for favored firms can be maintained except at ever-increasing levels of subsidy and continued dependence on the state. At the same time, effort expended in non-competitive sectors can only distract attention and divert resources from the firm's essential task of choosing competitive products and taking up defensible positions in the world market.

Since the state's purpose in intervening in the electronics industry was political, one cannot judge the success of its programs by the profitability of the firms. Nonetheless, the market position and competitiveness of the firm do affect the cost of achieving any particular goal. The dilemma, then, is that a politically inspired technological policy that requires unprofitable business strategies runs head-on into economic constraints which the state cannot change. Ultimately this endangers the long-run well-being of the firms which must be the agents of that political policy. The effort to close a technology gap by creating a French producer of specific "modern" goods may only have perpetuated a traditional industry, an industry looking to the state and the French market rather than toward its competitive situation in a world industry.

The technological strategy, then, puts firms at a competitive disadvantage for the products they are obliged to produce, and also distracts them from developing more profitable products and product strategies. This is, moreover, an equally serious problem for the state. Confronted with the rapid product evolution of the industry, each firm must develop and market new generations of products. *A subsidized and privileged, but economically marginal, national producer cannot guarantee the state a national source of technology in the future.* As a follower and probably a distant follower, the firm will almost certainly have low profit margins, and few if any advantages to offer clients in competitive markets. In many cases, in fact, the image of being a subsidized and non-competitive firm gives a second-class aura to the products, making them even harder to sell in an unprotected market. In France the small size of the administrative market for many goods prompts a search for other administrative markets in Eastern bloc or Third World countries, but these markets, even if they can be found, will always be vulnerable to the political relations between these countries and America. The growth of American trade with Eastern bloc countries, for example, will permit Control Data and IBM to sell computers in previous French market preserves and will weaken the French position. Whatever protected markets can be created, the basic problems will remain because the major markets are the competitive ones. With low profit margins, a weak competitive position, and limited production, the firm will amost certainly have difficulty mustering a competitive development effort on its own. It may be unable to respond to a sharp product jump, thus finding itself in an ever-weaker position, *without ever assuring a national source of the technology in the future. What has been purchased is the symbol of a current producer, but not the political security of a permanent supplier.* The primary problem remains the weak competitive position of the firms.

Another glance at the Plan Calcul, the French plan to create and nurture a national computer producer, will suggest both the problems of a technological strategy and the alternatives to it. Not only did the plan create a firm, but it specified its first product—a large computer based on a central processing unit of French design. Therefore, from the moment of its birth, CII was in competition with the bread and butter products of its established American competitors—hardly an enviable position for a fledgling firm. It is estimated that in this sector of the computer business, a firm must control a minimum of 5 percent of the *world* market if it is not simply going to be squeezed out by its larger competitors. Even when sold, CII did not control a much higher percentage of the French market, which is itself little larger than 5 percent of the world market. CII's world market share, therefore, was miniscule. The Plan's subsidies of $40 to $50 million dollars a year, which have benefited CII almost exclusively, were originally intended to put the firm on a competitive footing. Now there is little hope that the subsidies can soon be ended. At best the firm is in a marginal and vulnerable position, but SESCOSEM—the semi-conductor subsidiary of Thomson-Houston which was later absorbed as a division of the company—has been the real victim of a technology policy.

Since the central processing unit of a computer is little more than of semi-conductor components, a French computer manufacturer requires a French semi-conductor manufacturer to guarantee national production. However, since SESCOSEM was not a strong firm, CII machines were designed around components of the American firm of Texas Instruments, a world leader. SESCOSEM, though, was obliged to develop and produce the catalogue of Texas Instruments products to insure a French second source, although it is only a fraction of the size of Texas Instruments. In an industry where late entry is fatal, SESCOSEM was relegated by decree to this role and must develop products for which it is not even the primary source. At the same time that the need for an independent French semi-conductor firm was being emphasized by the state, the cost of subsidies continued to mount, and an endless downward spiral ensued. Thus, because SESCOSEM was weak, it could not be guaranteed a market, but because it must guarantee production, it is impossible for it to develop a sound economic position. Reversing the situation now would be difficult at best, and

SESCOSEM, never particularly robust, would still have serious problems. The technological objectives of the state have set the economic trap. Importantly, the current desperate position could have been avoided, perhaps, had more competitive policies with a greater market emphasis been adopted a decade ago.

A similar process has been observed among other producers who use the state's umbrella of preferential purchasing to produce thoroughly uncompetitive goods—often products in which they have a hopeless position. A technology strategy in electronics, then, can create French producers but cannot assure their future. Furthermore, in forcing them to imitate the giant world leaders without their resources or market position, they cannot become aggressive and effective challengers either.

If the state cannot change the market constraints, the alternative is for French firms to select market segments in which they can compete and develop their strength as they grow. Two apparent market constraints on French ambitions and tactics should be described here, but it must be emphasized that neither one of them is compatible with long-term technological independence. First, given the more limited resources of the French state and firms, it appears that initially it would have been desirable to select for major investment those areas where the undeniable French technological capacity could be turned into defensible market positions. Thus, a careful market strategy is a vitally essential complement for any technological hopes. Second, since the cutting edge of electronics technology was coming from America, for clear reasons of market structure and government spending, it was necessary for firms in all other countries to become effective followers in certain sectors—that is, minimize the time it took for new technologies to be absorbed and ideally modified and exported. Product innovation, and even innovation in component applications, remain possible; but it is essential first to acquite the most advanced technologies, by license if necessary, and then to then build on the back of the work the Americans have dome. The French, apparently, either have fought for utter independence of licensing arrangements, as was the policy of CSF, of have accepted relative technological independence. Both strategies force the French firms to follow directly in American tracks. The French have had neither the resources to be leaders nor the quickness and iungenuity in adapting initial breakthroughs to be effective followers.

The Second Dilemma—Organization and Economic Behavior

The state's efforts to modify the structure of the electronics industry, or more exactly, to shelter and support French firms in their pursuit of specific technological goals, not only imposed dubious business strategies but also dampened the pressure for organizational change—change necessary if the firms are ever to be truly competitive on world markets. It is now acknowledged that the organizational and management heritage of a protected past is a serious threat to the long-run well-being of the industry, and that both management and organization must evolve if the firms are to be competitive. The Sixth Plan acknowledged this: "These companies do not yet possess the strength and the profitability necessary to assure their growth in the future. That they have been exclusively oriented toward a small French market for too long, the difficulty they have had establishing corporate strategies, and the inability to take strategic consideration into account in day to day choices explains this situation [the weakness of the French firms]"[14] However, the possibility that government protection and support may impede the organizational adjustment of the firms is never stated publicly, although some officials will privately acknowledge the danger.[15]

The paradox is that efforts to neutralize the market structure, change it, or even simply provide support and subsidy have recreated the negotiated and protected business environment of the French past. In this shelter the legacy of anti-competitive firms with centralized and functional structures drags on. The analysis in Chapter 3 suggested that state support reduced pressure for organizational adjustment and directly provided incentives to maintain traditional organizational structures, an hypothesis supported by the limited evidence available. Gareth Pooley-Dyas' evidence that the competition induced by France's entry into the Common Market provoked important changes in both the strategy and structure of French firms confirms the argument that the state's dampening of competition slows the evolution of competitive business structures in French firms.[16]

The argument and evidence presented here, it should be noted, have not considered the modernization of French management, but have dealt instead only with the organization of the firms. Pooley-Dyas's evidence, however, and the impression gathered during a year of research inside the firms, suggest that the modernization of management is intimately tied up with the evolution of the organization. A separation of strategic and tactical responsibility, for example, is nearly impossible in a centralized organization, and profit analysis by product is extremely difficult, and often of little use, in a functionally divided organization. In one firm discussed here, effective strategic planning was impossible because the appropriate information was simply scattered across the organization, which had no means of assembling it and considering it. It is reasonable to expect that the evolution of management capability follows a pattern similar to the evolution of the organizations.

The presumption here has been that traditional French organization is inappropriate for firms competing in the electronics industry because it would be inefficient or simply ineffective. When competing with more efficiently organized firms, the logic follows, the French firms would be at a disadvantage. Thus whatever its primary purpose, French state support, which has the secondary result of sustaining traditional organizations that are incompatible with modern and competitive industry, subverts its own goals.

The need for a medium-sized country, such as France, to focus limited resources has simply accentuated the problem. Obviously the merger movement, which left only one major French electronics producer in many market segments, has reduced internal competition. Many firms, therefore, do not even have to scramble to find shelter under the government umbrella. Equally serious, the merger, although aimed at amassing and focusing the resources in the industry, almost inevitably created serious internal conflicts, which only multiplied the problems of creating efficient and effective management. In a rapid growth industry such as computers, as Nicolas Jécquier argues, the benefits of a merger will be short-lived if the growth rate of the newly formed firm is even temporarily reduced by its reorganization problems.[17]

There is substantial evidence, moreover, that problems inside the French firms directly contribute to their weakness in international markets. Commenting on the competitive position of European firms, Christopher Freeman has written: "American firms have had significantly shorter lead times [than European firms] in the last ten years at least. That was the opinion of almost all of those firms or individuals who had experience of development work on both sides of the Atlantic."[18] Freeman's conclusions based on work a decade ago were confirmed by the interviews conducted during this research. In his study, part of the transatlantic difference is attributable to the greater resources American firms commit to projects and to earlier access to components and sub-assemblies, but the major part is clearly related to organization and management techniques.

While this may be a general European problem, the French, it appears, have not done as well as their European neighbors. In a study of the speed of the diffusion of semi-conductor technology, Tilton measured the time between the first commercial production of a device in an innovating country and the first production in follower countries.[19] During the fifteen years studied, the French were overall the slowest. While their overall lag time was reduced by 14 percent during the later years of the study, British lead times were reduced 40 percent and Japanese response times 65 percent. Germany's lead times slowed a bit, but since 1960 the French response times were more than 60 percent longer than the British and 110 percent slower than the Japanese. That is, once a new semi-conductor technology was begun, it took the French much longer than their British and Japanese competitors to begin to produce it. One industry source familiar with semi-conductor development in France cites cases of French teams starting from identical points with roughly similar resources taking twice as long as their American counterparts.

Even more revealing is France's trade balance in patents, licenses, and technical assistance in electronics, which suggests that the French export their research and development and import their production know-how in the form of licenses. With the exception of Italy, France has a negative balance of exchange in patents and licenses with each of its major industrial trading partners.[20] The value of patents, the basic underlying knowledge, is only 2 to 3 percent of the value of licensing agreements, often including the specification of a production system; this means that in electronics, France is a heavy importer of other people's production know-how. The enormous deficit with the United States and Holland certainly reflects the operations of the multi-national companies, but the deficit with Belgium, Germany, Great Britain, and Switzerland are not so easily explained. While France is importing production know-how, it is exporting research and development. In research and development work[21] France has a heavily positive trade balance overall, and more importantly a positive balance with each of its trading partners, including the United States[22] This suggests that France tends to export its basic technological capacity in the form of research and development studies, and to import the finished fruits of that labor in the form of products or the licenses to make these products. Research and development activities are not being brought to industrial fruition in France. Most bluntly, the data speaks of a French techological capacity that is not being converted into products and a market position for French firms.

These weaknesses can be seen in the histories of many of the firms as well. Inadequate financial control and the failure of its product development efforts caused the collapse of Machines Bull, the French rival to IBM, in the days before computers were the dominant product of business equipment manufacturers. Importantly, the Machines Bull computer, the Gamma 60, was considered to be extremely sophisticated technologically, but ill-suited for a commercial market. Similarly, CSF, the technological king-pin of French electronics firms in the early 1960s, suffered from important weaknesses in strategy and control that combined with declining government markets to create a crisis. The current weakness of the French electronics industry is as much a result of the failures of French management as it is of the handicaps in the market-place. Therefore, policies aimed only at compensating for disadvantages in the market attacked only half the problem.

Conclusions

In most countries much of government support for R and D projects, as distinct from the funding of pure science, has been for a variety of large-scale systems technologies. Obviously, weapons systems fall in this category, as do such various semi-civilian projects as the American moonshot and the French-English Concorde. These projects undoubtedly involve widespread technological innovation, although how generally applicable these advances may be to non-military or earthbound needs is a subject of lively debate. Certainly, with a few exceptions, most notably semi-conductors, the impact of these large-scale systems on the evolution of particular industries has been limited. Whether the money is well spent, whatever the spin-offs, must ultimately depend on a judgment of the value of the system itself.

Considerably less money is spent directly to promote industrial innovation or the expansion of R and D and innovation-centered industry. In this second case, the particular products are of less importance than the growth and health of the industry, and the value of the expenditures must be judged by the contribution to industrial development. Importantly, the funding strategies that may be appropriate for systems investment may be utterly inappropriate for promoting industrial innovation, at least where the goal is economic expansion in general or the growth of a particular sector. This analysis of French policy in electronics suggests the consequences of confusing these separate goals of government R and D investment.

In France the state attempted to maintain at least one national supplier of each politically important electronic technology. The dilemma was that the protection and support required to produce specific products may, in fact, have weakened the firms that must be the long-term instruments of state policy. Without strong firms, the supply of technologies cannot be assured in the future. The difficulty of fighting the market and the complete absence of any guarantee of success suggest that adapting to the market constraints and first insuring strong and healthy firms may be more effective in the long run and cheaper today. It may be necessary to abandon the symbols of technological indepencence, national producers of particular products, before its reality—strong and innovative firms—can be realized. Nor would the shift require the French to abandon technological security, even temporarily, so long as they preserved their ability to respond if critical products were ever denied them.

Although, as noted earlier, the Honeywell deal is as yet difficult to interpret, it could be read as an effort to reverse French policy along lines suggested in this analysis. CII's medium and large machine activities have been joined with Honeywell-Bull, the French company in a sector where it is more likely to compete profitably. Whether the decision to force the sale rather than prop up this ruling company was an isolated solution to an increasingly costly venture, or a message that the state will no longer support hopelessly uncompetitive ventures simply to maintain a French presence in certain prestige sectors, is not clear. Importantly, a nearly simultaneous decision was taken to enter a crash program to expand telephone service in France, creating a vast new market for the two giants, CGE and Thomson-Houston. The difficulties of disentangling these two partners in their joint CII venture are directly tied to maneuvering for position in the new market, a struggle made all the more fierce because the cooperative accords between the two firms expired with renewal. Most interesting of all, of course, is the American alliance, the decision to promote an Atlantic venture and to break the European Computer Alliance, UNIDATA. Honeywell-Bull will take the place of CII, if the accords are finally signed, as the privileged supplier to the French state, and will in fact receive a substantial increase in guaranteed sales. The question of course remains what the French will receive from the deal —whether they have in fact exchanged a troubled company for substantial influence in IBM's principal world rival. The crucial issue is the importance of the guaranteed French sales in the strategy of the parent company. Equally, agreements as to the disposition of Honeywell-Bull, in the case of corporate difficulty—hardly an unknown occurrence among major computer firms—will also determine the value of the bargain. The issue is, in a sense, whether the French have abandoned their computer position to the benefit of certain computer giants, or whether they have a hold—a handhold, certainly not a stranglehold—on the policies of a foreign multi-national.

Put differently, this analysis suggests the limits on a government's ability to shape the growth of a domestic industry that forms an integral part of an international marketplace. Neither the goals of French policy—technological independence for economic and security reasons— nor the underlying principle of state intervention is questioned by this critique. Some state policy was almost certainly required to consolidate and anchor the French electronics firms in the heavy weather of international competition. The basic questions are whether the chosen policy was in fact the most effective means of achieving the government's objectives, or, given the limits of the French state's ability to influence the electronics industry, whether all the objectives were in fact possible. Chapter 7 will reconsider this problem and try to put the electronics case in a wider perspective.

III

*Industry between
the Market and State:
An Interpretation*

6

Organization, Culture, and Economic Behavior

Until now this essay has been concerned with the structure of relations between business and the state in the French electronics industry, and with the consequences of those relations for organizational and economic behavior. Our analysis has focused rather narrowly on the firm, the institution of production. This chapter, by pulling together several themes that have emerged in the discussion, will interpret and extend our research results. Looking back at the case study, we shall consider what general conclusions can be drawn from it about the organization of an industrial society as a whole.

Our concern will be with three main questions or issues: First, what is the relation between structural change and individual behavior within a single organization; and more particularly, what are the respective roles of culture and technology in shaping the organization of the firm? Second, how does the organization of a dominant institution affect the organization of a subordinate one; and in particular, what is the impact of its organization on the state—or more broadly, on the institutions of political life, on other institutions in the society? Third and finally, how does the organization of the firm affect its own economic behavior? In the interests of clarity, these three issues will be taken up separately, since the substantive content of each problem is different; but theoretically they form a single discussion, beginning with the organizational adaptation of a firm to its environment and ending with the effects of that adaptation at any moment in economic behavior.

Technology, Culture, and Organizational Change
The Problem of Organizational Structure and Behavior

Behind our research has been the assumption that the common problems posed by industrialism, "the imperatives" of technology in this

159

case, constrain the ways in which institutions of advanced societies can be organized, while the particular historical heritage of each country produces variety in the ways their common problems are resolved despite the constraints. Such a perspective poses several questions, such as how restrictive are the constraints in fact, how are they perceived in the affected institutions, and how do existing social arrangements change—or alternatively, how do institutions channel and resist the pressures of technologies. Other efforts to analyze the diverse patterns of power and authority have rested on this notion, namely that the old power arrangements of pre-industrial societies re-express themselves in the manner in which similar problems are resolved as nations industrialize and modernize.* This study has been concerned with the continuing development of existing institutions rather than with the establishment of the basic institutional structures of modern life, but similar questions, nonetheless, are raised.

The element of the French historical heritage considered here was the structure of traditional patterns of authority that typify arrangements of power in France. Authority patterns, as used in this discussion, are the formal arrangements of positions of power and the relations between those positions, and one may thus refer to centralized or decentralized authority patterns or structures. Distinctive national patterns of authority, it should be observed, have survived changes in regime and class control of the state apparatus. Thus the French Revolution, according to Tocqueville, completed an evolution toward centralization that had begun under the old regime. Similarly, the basic authority patterns of Russia and China survived their twentieth-century revolutions. We have not been concerned, furthermore, with which groups control which positions. Both nationalized and private firms in France are centralized, and one might expect, following this logic, to find a similar pattern in a factory controlled by the workers as well. The opposition between these French organizational structures and the production requirements of innovation-centered science-based industry has allowed us to consider the influence of culture, in the form of traditional authority patterns, on organization.

The pattern of organizational change that occurred in the French electronics firms can best be understood by distinguishing between

*For example, Reinhard Bendix has argued that the relative position of classes in the pre-industrial world shapes both the ideological justification of the entrepreneur's role and the very organization of authority in the factory, while the process of early industrialism in turn shapes the managerial ideologies and organization of the large-scale bureaucratic industry that appears later. Reinhard Bendix, *Work and Authority in Industry* (New York: Wiley, 1956).

strategic or *critical decisions and routine* or day-to-day decisions. The predominant concern of organizational theorists with efficient conduct of the routine and with the explanation of day-to-day organizational behavior often tends to hide this distinction and divert attention away from the adjustment of an organization to the important changes in its environment. Promoting efficient organizations was the objective of the Taylor school, as well as of the human-relations approach concerned with the behavior of the group[1] and the functions of the executive.[2] Even Crozier's work began with a consideration of day-to-day life in organizations, although his formulation of the conduct of the routine permitted him to push further, into the relations between critical and routine choice. The works of Woodward, Burns and Stalker, and Lawrence and Lorsch, analyzed in the second chapter, all sought, for example, to identify the appropriate structure of the routine in different technological and economic environments, while Wilson and Simon tried to explain patterns of day-to-day behavior. Considerably less has been said about the exercise of organizational leadership and about the "dynamic adaptation of the total organization to internal strivings and external pressures."[3] In fact, however, it is the critical decisions which define the purposes of organizations and design the structure that will carry them out, thus shaping the context within which routine operations occur.

Clearly, these two processes are overlapping and interrelated. Just as strategic or critical decisions set the ground rules for the conduct of the routine, the ongoing operation of the organization will affect the way strategy is formulated and limit the choices that appear and that are possible to implement. This is not to say that routine is necessarily dysfunctional,[4] only that institutions are simply not neutral.[5] In fact, one might characterize organizations by the relations that exist between critical and routine decision making, as Crozier does when he defines French organizations as systems that alternate between periods of stalemate and crisis. However intertwined critical and routine decisions may be, they do represent distinct processes and must be considered separately here.

In this case, the adaptation of a firm's organization to the imperatives of technology represented part of its strategic adjustment to its economic and institutional environment. The efficient use of technology was required by certain strategies, but the choice of strategy was affected by the actions of other institutions such as the state, the banks, and competing firms. Thus, the leadership of a firm made the critical decisions to adjust the structure of the firm to the technology's requirements when it perceived the current organization as an obstacle to strategic goals. Authority patterns and typical cultural behavior, on the

other hand, are presumably expressed in the *organization of the routine.*
These routines, and the ideological blinders and propensities toward
particular actions that support the typical routines of any culture,
affect the problems that can be perceived and the plans that are
conceived and implemented. Traditional authority patterns in an organization support existing routines and cultural biases because the structure
of authority sets the terms in which problems are presented and provide
the tools for responding to them, not because an individual's current
attitudes so sharply limit the behaviors he can learn that the structure
of an organization is restricted.

Leadership and Critical Decisions. The leaders of an organization
can make critical decisions that shape both the *strategy* and the
structure and thereby constrain the organization of day-to-day life.
In business terms, strategy can be defined as "the determination of the
basic long-term goals and objectives of an enterprise, and the adoption
of a course of action and the allocation of resources necessary for
carrying out these goals."[6] The choice of these goals and objectives,
the definition of the purposes the organization will attempt to accomplish, limit all subsequent choices. Conversely, it must be acknowledged, an accumulation of routine choices may coalesce into a strategy.
Conscious strategic choices, though, can abruptly alter these limits
on daily life. A strategy for a firm, like an ideology for an individual,
identifies what is important and implicitly assigns priorities to the
problems the firm encounters. Thus, for an electronics firm with a
strategy of competition in unprotected international markets, efficient
development of new products may have the highest priority, while
for a firm selling primarily to the state, "efficient" links to the government may be more essential.

Structure, on the other hand, represents the design of the administrative processes of the organization, but decisions about how these
processes will be arranged clearly can be critical choices. For example,
a decision to abandon functional organization and to restructure along
product lines represents a vital moment in the history of a firm.
While strategy and structure decisions are logically separate, and a
given structure can limit the strategy choices possible, the evidence
suggests that shifts in strategy tend to precede and shape the structure
of the organization. This certainly has been the conclusion of this study,
as well as that of the work of Chandler[7] and Bruce Scott[8] in America
and of the multi-national research project carried on at the Harvard
Business School on the divisionalization of business.[9] By defining the
critical problems in the firm's environment, the strategy encourages
structures that will efficiently organize the day-to-day activities to resolve

them. Of course, satisfying the convenience or preference of members may interfere with the organization's ostensible goals. In fact, the decision to give precedence to the organization's goals or to the member's predilections might be considered a strategy choice.

In the case at hand, the organizational imperatives of technology were perceived when the inefficiencies and inadequacies of the traditional system became obstacles to the strategic goals of the firm. Firms following a strategy of competition in unprotected markets perceived organizational problems as sources of inefficiency, measured either in cost or in time, that affected their position in a competitive market. Firms following the strategy of state aid and protection tended to recognize the inefficiencies only when threatened with product or firm failure. Since the traditional centralized structure was an efficient instrument in a political strategy, elements of the old system were often retained by the state-oriented group even after the production problems began to appear. It is significant that in the single case studied here where competition within the state market was an important factor, an effort to preserve that market by meeting quality and time delay objectives also initiated change.

Mounting pressure on the chief executive resulting in intolerable strain was twice cited as a factor initiating a search for a new organizational plan, but this was only mentioned in firms or divisions of firms that were substantially involved in the competitive marketplace. In thoroughly protected firms the working pace could apparently be tailored to the limits of the executives. One might imagine that the day-to-day inconveniences of working in a centralized and rigidly functional organization, when in reality the tasks required decentralized responsibility and continued face-to-face adjustments, would in itself generate demands for organizational change and result in a series of partial adjustments throughout the organization. In fact, unhappiness with existing routines appeared to produce change only when the strategy of the firm forced the top management to pay for the organization's inefficiencies with overwork. One might speculate that in another cultural setting the process of change would have been different.

In the firms where the basic structure remained unchanged, either informal mechanisms emerged to resolve the technological problems or the position of the firm was sufficiently secure that it could ignore the inefficiencies. Again, the degree of adjustment is explained by the firm's strategic problems. In the first case, means of informal horizontal communication were found within a functional organizational structure, while in the second the problems could simply be avoided. Only in smaller firms was it possible to make marginal adjustments within a traditional structure or escape change altogether. In the larger firms, the inefficiencies became sufficiently serious, whatever the strategy, that some formal change was required. In sum, when a firm required increased efficiency in its development and production of new products, then it adapted its organization to the technological imperatives.

The state thus arbitrated the balance that was struck between culture and technology by forming the strategic options open to the firms. By making politics as important as industrial efficiency, pressure on the firms to adapt to their technologies was reduced, while the importance of relations with the administration encouraged them to keep traditional organizations. *Put more broadly, the firm's strategy and thus its structure and the organization of the routine will reflect its institutional and political setting.*

Technology, therefore, did not exert a mechanical and independent influence on organizations; rather, its impact was mediated by the critical decisions about goals and strategies made by the firms. These choices were directly and deeply affected by state policy in this case, but more generally the impact of technology depends on the role it plays in the strategies of organizations or individuals. Interestingly, even the process by which the problems were identified and defined appeared related to the strategy choice, although the evidence was based only on self-reports and was sketchy at best. Firms in the competitive market, though, appeared to have been aware of their competitor's behavior and willing to borrow from them. In the protected firms, on the other hand, the impression was left that changes resulted from their own analysis of the technology and their own evaluation of what should be done.

Routine Behavior and Critical Choice. Critical choices may change an organization's strategy or structure, but the decisions are taken in the framework of existing routines. Whether change comes from new leadership or old, the existing routines of the organization will bias the politics of organizational change by influencing what becomes an issue, which groups are likely to win, the freedom to change past decisions, and the opposition that might rise up against new policy. The exercise of institutional leadership is a political process, and like all of politics is profoundly affected by existing structures, routines, and authority arrangements. At Norgood Products, for example, centralization and the political predominance of the research divisions meant that the needs of the factory, which included greater horizontal contact with the research group and more independence, could never be effectively expressed. The factory, organizationally and physically isolated from the general management, was politically helpless.

Similarly, the leaders' ideological maps, which define what is valuable, permit potential rewards to be perceived, predict what the results of actions will be, and suggest how to act in a situation, will determine how any problem is formulated and the values on which a decision is taken. For example, one former electronics official involved in the government's unsuccessful effort to salvage Machines Bull thought that the appropriate solution would be a market sharing agreement with IBM. His entire perspective had been formed by cartel arrangements, and his attention was diverted from the critical organizational and development problems. Since these critical choices cannot be separated from the existing routines or from the ideas of the elite in the organization in which they are made, an institution's evolution is intimately tied to its cultural context.

In the electronics firms studied here, both the existing routines and the ideas of the managers affected the process by which plans were formulated and implemented, and ultimately they influenced the extent of the change itself. The result of the existing centralization appeared to be that decisions to reorganize were taken at the top without the involvement of lower levels. Furthermore, almost without exception, lower-level executives denied having made demands for change, and most seemed genuinely ignorant of the process of decisions that led to these choices. The changes were imposed on them and often were described as unexpected thunderbolts.[10] Interestingly, where independent product managers or division-managers positions were created, these executives reported participating in subsequent organizational changes, and thus structural change affected the process of further change. The overall impression, it should be noted, was that organizational change was very much a top-down process. Moreover, as change occurred, it came in sharp jumps more often than in slow evolution. Thus, while the changes themselves broke with the French organizational tradition, the process of change often fitted the model of stalemate and crisis depicted by Crozier.

The existing patterns not only affected where decisions to change were taken, but often limited or contained that change as well. Liquidating the past was a war of attrition, not a blitzkrieg. Many people had important stakes in the existing game, stakes which were defended by legally enforceable rules. For example, existing rules prevented wholesale dismissals and blocked the general management from insisting that engineers change their place of employment. This problem slowed the transfer of research activities from a central research operation to the production divisions and tended to maintain outdated lines of research at the lab. Similarly, decentralized authority and broadly based responsibilities were often new experiences for those involved, and learning new ways of operating often took time. One company president, for example, might face the need for decentralization and appoint divisional directors, only to have those directors apply their own previous experience with authority and recentralize responsibility, although at a lower level. When the lower-level manager had profit responsibility, he would face the leadership problem of adjusting his own internal organization to the demands of his technical and economic responsibility and would learn for himself the lessons of delegating authority. Thus, organizational learning continued long after the original critical decisions had been made.

Finally, many behavior patterns characteristic of the culture did appear in the adjustment of the product-development groups to their newly defined responsibilities. It seemed that work partners on the job were seldom companions outside the factory, and thus social relationships could not ease the friction that might emerge at work. Several engineers remarked that they worked most effectively with their counterparts in other divisions who were also personal friends, but that such relations were rare. This did not actually prevent effective work relationships from being established, but longer periods of adjustment were required than would probably be typical of an American firm. However, since these work groups will stay together longer than they would in America, the costs of a longer start-up time can be absorbed without serious loss. These longer start-up times, though, might interfere with sharp change in the product orientation of the firm. Thus, the product development groups might themselves evolve into new bastions of authority. That is, after a basic structural adjustment is made, the pre-existing cultural predispositions may reassert themselves within the new structure.

Cultural Limits on Change in Patterns of Routine Behavior. The features typical of French organizations were produced, according to Crozier's argument (considered earlier), by individuals and groups pursuing their particular goals inside organizations. Yet changes in organizational structure and behavior occurred that broke with French organizational tradition. Why was there no widespread opposition? One might simply conclude that the French authority dilemma and French culture in general had, in fact, no importance in forming organizational structure; but the empirical evidence that the attitudes and patterns described by Crozier are important in France is too substantial to be ignored or denied. Our findings can be explained, though, by considering two complementary accounts of organizational routine.

In Crozier's analysis of power relations in organizations, the members are cast as autonomous political strategists, using whatever power they

command, power created by discretion in applying rules or in performing tasks, to achieve personal and group goals. The resulting bargain
between the groups produces the distinctive structural features of the
organization. Since the culture shapes the goals individuals seek, the
organizational bargains and thus the organizational structures in one
culture should differ from those in another. In an analysis in which
the distinctive structural features of an organization in a particular
cultural setting are identified as the products of personal goals, attitudes, and values, there is an undoubted bias toward a position that
culture is "carried" by the individual and "expressed" in the institutions. Crozier's hypothesis is that the specifically French features of
the bureaucracies he studied had come into being because they resolved
contradictions in French attitudes toward authority.

Certainly, Crozier does analyze how existing organizational rules
will shape the struggle, making one strategy more workable or profitable than another. Thus, for example, because the positions of groups
in the monopoly studied by Crozier were frozen and individuals could
not pass from one group to another, the existence and many of the
privileges of each group were already assured. Furthermore, Crozier
acknowledges that the pattern of French administration itself tends
to perpetuate the dilemma, though this tends to make his argument
circular. In highlighting the individual's active role, Crozier de-
emphasizes the organization's influence on the individual's values and
attitudes. This suffices for the analysis of stable organizations in stable
environments; but when the patterns of behavior do change, a more
complex model of the relations between individual attitudes and organizational structure must be considered.

The neo-rationalist emphasis on the organization's role in limiting
individual choices—or more exactly, in structuring the boundaries of his
decisions—provides a complementary approach to Crozier's. Let us
begin with Clark and Wilson's suggestion that the incentive system
is the principal variable affecting organizational behavior,[11] and envision
an individual enmeshed in a network of incentives and threats.*
These incentives, to use Simon's vocabulary, represent the unexpected
consequences of alternative behaviors open to the individual.[12] In its
simplest form the neo-rationalistic logic states that within the limits

*The same logic of incentives prompting actions can explain the critical
choices of strategy and structure, but our discussion here will be limited to
routine behavior. According to Clark and Wilson, the motivations of the people
in the organizations will determine the forms of incentives that are offered.
An organization, in this logic, will adjust its incentives to the motivations of
members. Later in this chapter, this assumption will be questioned, and it will
be suggested that the reverse is also true—that the structure and character
of incentives can influence the motivations of the individuals.

of his knowledge, his habits, and his skill, the individual will adjust his behavior to maximize his utility in whatever currency the organization deals. *This approach emphasizes the influence of the structure of the organization and its network of incentives on the individual members in their day-to-day behavior.* In caricature, the individual appears here as a passive button-pusher in a box of organizational stimuli, and the organization becomes the sum of those rather passive choices. Of course, this analysis acknowledges the particular characteristics of each individual's choice and acknowledges conflict, bargaining, and internal politics, but the logic of both Clark and Wilson and Simon and March seem locked in by their initial assumptions. For Clark and Wilson, the individual simply responds to the incentives, and there is no analysis of how the incentives are arranged to accord with the motivations of the individuals. Similarly, March and Simon urge that we look to the organizational limits and boundaries on choice, although it is acknowledged that individuals behave according to different value or choice functions, and that these choices might include political actions to change the limits and boundaries.

How groups and individuals might control or influence the structure of the incentives or the boundaries on their actions is not directly considered. Although March and Simon comment on the uniqueness of each individual's choice function, and Clark and Wilson contend that incentives are matched to individual motivation by the organization, the structure of the organization itself emerges as a powerful independent influence on behavior.

The two approaches clearly suggest different explanations of cultural differences in organizations. Crozier would focus on the "attitudes" and goals of the individuals. The neo-rationalist perspective would examine the different costs and benefits of particular behaviors, or the potential rewards of specific games, in different settings. For example, Americans are said to be readier to take risks than Frenchmen. That may be so because they are better able to tolerate risk or because they value high returns more than their French counterparts, but it may also be so because the rewards for success are higher in America and the penalties for failure are greater in France. The career of a graduate of France's elite technical school, Polytechnique, is nearly assured. He will enter one or another of government ministries, at the top, with his status assured, and after years of service he can move to the general management of a private company and make his fortune —*unless, of course, he makes a serious and compromising error.* Striking out on his own, on the other hand, does not necessarily promise status or financial rewards greater than those he is already promised. With the stock market as weak as it is, starting one's

own business does not, in the short run, assure the enormous rewards
of quick capital gains. Ironically, any capital gains must ultimately
be reaped by selling the firm to a larger company or group, of which
the graduate could be a high-ranking officer if he chose. At the same
time, his social status and power as a functionary or as the executive
of a large business will be greater than it would probably be as the
founder of a dynamic young enterprise.

In America, by contrast, an MIT engineering graduate simply wins
the right to enter another round of competition, be it in a company
or a graduate school. His previous success assures him nothing, though
he may have a privileged position in the new competition. Breaking
out on his own entails different risks than following well-beaten paths,
but in either case there are substantial risks. For him, starting his
own business might mean substantial and often quick financial rewards,
and his social status will be none the less—perhaps even greater—
for having made it on his own.

Similarly, the costs of failure are different for the two men because
the routes to success in America are much more diverse than they
are in France. If the American fails in business he can return to
graduate school if he likes, or still go on to join a large company,
or with the diverse capital markets available, start a new company
again. The Frenchman, however, may have permanently lost some of
his privileges. The difference in risks is doubly true inside an organization, where the Frenchman's schooling may set both the bottom and
the top levels of his career horizon, while the American will face an
endless competition. It is not so mysterious that the Frenchman is
averse to risking what he has won while the American is eager to
reach out for further successes. For the two men to behave in a similar
fashion, each in his own country, the Frenchman would have to set a
much higher value (or the American a much lower value) on quick
success or independence, because in France the probability of success
in an independent venture is less, the rewards of success itself probably
lower, and the costs of failure higher. *Thus, culturally distinct patterns
of behavior can be "carried" in the organization's rules, rewards,
and arrangements.*

Structure and Accommodation. These two approaches have complementary strengths; the one highlighting the individual's active manipulation of the structure to achieve his goals, and the other underlining
the influence of organization on behavior. They suggest that an organization might be conceived as an assemblage of formal roles in which
a variety of official and unofficial games are played.[13] Possession of a
formal role, one might say, is the basic ante price for all the games,

although some games require specific roles. The different roles initially provide the players with resources such as the power and authority with which to play, although the individual brings some of the resources to the role with him. The rules are partly officially established and partly informally evolved among the players. The rule-changing game is one of the central attractions, in fact, and both official and unofficial rules are the subject of politics and bargaining. Similarly, the strategies are partly the creation of the individual and partly dictated by the group of which he is a part, and in any case they have evolved as a response to the existing rules and rewards. *Yesterday's fights, institutionalized in the rules, shape today's strategies, and the outcomes of current struggles will in turn influence tomorrow's strategies.* Since many of the conflicts inside an organization will be settled in the political arena outside, and the rules imposed on the organization by the state, *the institutionalization of the political struggles of the past, the establishment of particular values in the forms of rules and procedures in organizations, can contribute to the formation of the typical behaviors of a culture.* Thus, routine behavior in an organization can be seen in part as political process outside the organization as well as inside it, and thus it may be considered both as a product of the members' active manipulation of their environment and a result of their passive accommodation to it.

At the same time, however, the patterns of routine behavior will result from the progressive evolution of the organization's strategy and structure, so let us pursue our analysis further. Different rewards are held out to the participants in the games, and one might distinguish between the official incentives of the organization and the unofficial rewards offered by the other games. In some of the games, individuals may be relatively passive participants responding somewhat mechanically to the rewards, while in others they may be active strategists attempting to influence the game and its rules. Because each game requires a specific strategy and behavior, one vital decision the individual must make is which game he is playing. Thus, for example, the promotion game may demand that he satisfy his superiors, while the good-companion game may demand that he satisfy his peers. If the individual switches games, even if his strategy for each of the games remains the same, his day-to-day behavior may be deeply affected. Moreover, if he must play a new game, he may be able to learn new strategic approaches, although he will undoubtedly try to use his old strategies in the new game. Thus, for example, a member of the research group in an electronics firm may have to choose between the product-development game and the group-power or scientific-research game. He may be hesitant to abandon an old game in which his rewards are well understood for a new game he can't envision, but if he does switch games, he may then adopt new ways of playing.

This allows us to imagine how the critical decisions made by the organization's leadership can be translated into changes in routine behavior. Critical decisions altering the organization's structure and rules will affect the rules and rewards of all games, making some games more attractive than others and raising or lowering the costs of different actions. Equally important, it may make old strategies obsolete, and require that new ones be learned. It is evident that strategies learned in the past will shape behavior in the future. The critical questions, though, are these: how sharply will existing behavior limit the types of organizational change that can occur, and what kind of change in the basic strategies or attitudes is possible? The wider either of these limits is, the less resistance one would expect from organizations or individuals to demands and pressures for change. In fact, it is clear that the *same men* can create a *variety of organizations*.

In the French electronics firms, to return to our case study, engineers and executives did learn new ways of behaving when the critical decisions to reorganize the firms were made. The rewards for different games were changed, and whether or not the individual's attitudes remained the same, organizational innovation occurred and the individuals acted differently. For example, one engineer mentioned that in the new system broad responsibilities and face-to-face work relations meant that the resulting products were better, and he took great pride in the contribution he was able to make to an important design innovation as a result of the new system. He lamented his lost independence but favored the new system and style of work. The increased rewards of the new product-development game, in terms of job satisfaction, outweighed the costs of losing his independence. Similarly, several engineers cited reduced tension and less conflict as one of the rewards of the new system that emphasized horizontal relationships. They found it difficult and unpleasant to fight for the independence of the group in a work environment which continually pressed for interaction and integration, but an insistence on limited responsibilities and independence was the traditional way of dealing with outside pressure. Furthermore, the budgeting system in many cases left open little room for compromise between the groups. Instances were cited where the engineers on their own worked out arrangements that permitted them to resolve the technological problems, but nothing suggested that these private arrangements would ever have accumulated to produce permanent changes.

In the sampled firms, it seemed that the institutionalization of new procedures required a fiat from above, although there is no reason to believe that this would be necessary in another culture. The members of many of these French firms, then, were able to sustain face-to-face conflict and accept interdependent work relationships, styles that were supposedly incompatible with their cultural heritage. Learning the new organizational game appeared to be a conscious and intellectual process in which new rules and predictions about the rewards for different strategies were evolved. While changes in organizational structure and individual behavior did occur, no data was collected which could suggest whether the underlying attitudes or predispositions of the individuals were altered or whether, in fact, a wide variety of behaviors can be supported by any particular collection of attitudes. At any rate, no psychological explanation of the observed change in behavior is required for this discussion.

The strategic choices of the firm, then, determined how highly efficiency was valued, and thus how tightly the requirements of the technology were permitted to constrain the organization of the firm. For firms which chose to seek government protection and support, maintaining effective political relations with the state was a critical organizational problem that was often resolved by maintaining aspects of their traditional functional and centralized organizations, while the importance of efficiency was reduced by subsidy. While the technological imperatives made themselves felt through the firms' strategic choices, the ongoing routines of the firm that expressed the traditional culture patterns of organization and authority affected how the problems came to be perceived, where the initiatives for change emerged, and how deeply and quickly the organization was reshaped to fit the imperatives of the technology. However, once the critical decisions were made, the individuals were able to break out of the traditional mold of organization and authority and work effectively in a more decentralized organization. Individual attitudes toward authority did not sharply limit the changes that were possible in the behavior of the organization and of the individuals.

Organizational behavior, then, is shaped not only by its internal dynamics but also by its relations with other institutions and by shifts in the tasks it must perform. Critical choices made in response to such developments can provoke changes in patterns of routine. Differences proposed here with Crozier's interpretation of French organization may turn on this issue. He considers organizations in isolation, while the effort here has been to see them in continuous adjustment to their environment.

Dominant and Subordinate Organizations:
The Problem of the State's Influence on Cultural Behavior

In France the state had a powerful, direct effect on the organization of firms which sought its protection as part of their basic business strategy. (See Chapter 3.) Not only did state aid reduce pressure for change, but firms tended to parallel the state structure in order to negotiate for resources more successfully. This suggests two questions: first, the impact of dominant organizations on subordinate organizations as a general problem, and second, the impact of the state (the single most important institution in a modern society) on the organizational structure or other institutions in the society and thus on the patterns or routine behavior identified here as culture.

Dominant and Subordinate Organizations. In one sector of the electronics market, the state clearly dominated the firms, and the firms in turn adapted their organizational structures to allow effective communication with the state, in fact giving the appearance that they consciously mimicked the state structure. To explain these results, one might argue that the organizational structure of a dominant organization shapes that of a subordinate organization. Some organizations quite evidently are independent of each other: a workers' council in a Yugoslav factory and a PTA group in Scottsbluff, Nebraska, have no contacts, no indirect influences, and probably are not aware of each other's existence. On the other hand, the University of Paris is quite clearly dependent on the French state, even if it manages to preserve some measure of autonomy in the conduct of its own affairs. The notion of domination and subordination, however, can still be used to discuss the relationship of two organizations, even when no pure dependency relationship exists between them. To argue this as a general proposition, though, one must identify those aspects of the relationship between two organizations that allow one to be called dominant and the other subordinate, and then specify the channels through which the structure of one can influence the structure of the other.

In the broadest sense, one organization dominates if it has the power to affect the well-being of the other organization in critical ways—or, more loosely, if it controls vital elements in the environment of the subordinate organization that affect the way it can behave. One of a variety of forms of control may establish domination, and the organizational consequences may be determined by the particular form of control. One organization may *command the resources required* by another organization, or at least access to those resources. Thus, for example, if a firm is desperately short of capital, it may be dependent on a bank which will supply the funds. One organization may *determine what tasks* another institution will perform. A small manufacturer in Turin plays the part in automobile manufacture left to it by Fiat, for example; or alternatively, a secondary school's educational task, to provide college preparatory material or manual training, may be specified by the school board. One organization may *lay out the procedures and rules* that another organization must follow in performing its tasks. Federal regulatory agencies or cartel organizations spell out for particular firms the way in which they must carry out their business activities.

How, though, will the organization of the dominant institution affect that of the subordinate one? The critical assumption is that the dominant institution controls something of vital importance to the dependent unit; it may allocate resources, define tasks, establish rules or procedures. Consequently, the subordinate organization must try to influence the choices of the dominant institution. *How it can do so is determined by the structure of the organization of the dominant institution—that is, the routes of influence are spelled out by organizational structure.* The activities of the dependent organization must then be organized to have access to the dominant organization, which in fact may mean imitating the structure of the dominant organization to allow effective communication; and even if the subordinate organization does not plan that as a concrete strategy, the accumulation of particular choices will produce this result. This is not to say, clearly, that a subordinate organization cannot decide to try to force changes in the structure of the dominant organization; only that it will be easier to adapt than to fight, and that a fight over structure will be chosen only as a last resort. Thus, in many ways the structure of a dominant organization limits the choice and marks off the playing field for a dependent organization in the same way that the structure limits the options of a group within an organization.

Similarly, the dominant organization may in fact develop organizational units to deal with the subordinate organization if the tasks that the subordinate organization performs are sufficiently vital. Then, we might expect to find a case of a mutual dependence in which the structures of each organization affect the other. In the situation of mutual dependence, absolute size differences may contribute to dependency relationships, because the adjustment a large organization may make to a smaller unit will affect only a part of the operation of the larger organization. One must ask whether formal control of one organization by another suffices to establish the dominance of the organizational structure of the one institution. That is, even if decision-making within the state is ultimately controlled by business through forms of political pressure and even outright bribery, the formal control of rule-making by the state, for example, forces the firms to adapt their organization to the state to achieve communication and influence. If the state's structure creates serious political problems of control, then an effort would be made to alter the structure to make control of decision-making easier. This would imply, though, the capture of power within the state to alter structure. The intent would be to make the state favor one group more than another, or to change existing choices. In that case, efforts to restructure the state would be opposed by those who would lose, and the final structure would reflect precisely a new institutionalization of a general political fight.

The question remains of how profoundly and in what ways the structure of a dominant organization will affect that of a subordinate organization. One organization may, in fact, be dependent on another, but the two may interact so seldom that special arrangements will be made on those few occasions, leaving their separate structures and routines otherwise intact.[14] One critical issue is certainly how continuous and widespread the interchanges are. If the interchanges are continuous, then some permanent arrangements for contact must certainly be made, involving, for example, a government liaison office or a corporate service division. However, if the contacts are narrow and limited, then a single office might be the only point of contact between the two organizations. For example, government purchase of pants for uniforms need really involve only two contacts. The order must be put out for bidding by manufacturers, and payment must be made after the pants are received by the purchasing department. Thus, the interactions can be cut off from all the other operations of the two institutions.

The development of a weapons system, however, is an altogether different problem. The planning group of the military must be in continuous contact with the development group throughout the creation of the system. Every small technical change must have performance consequences, and it is for the user, not the manufacturer, to decide which mix of characteristics is most appropriate. Moreover, the process of ongoing surveillance will involve interactions at all levels of the organization between financial control personnel, engineers, strategists, and the like. The borderline between the two groups may, in fact, blur. The second issue, of course, is whether the dependent organization can end its relationship with the dominant one without serious costs to itself. If, in fact, the dominant organization has a monopoly control of resources, rule-making, or task definition, then the dependent organization has nowhere to turn to and must work doubly hard to insure adequate communication. Finally, one might examine whether there is a link between the form of control, which made one organization dominant, and the adaptations made by dependent organizations. Does control of rule-making by a regulatory agency have different consequences than control of task definition by a general contractor, for example?

Evidence other than this case demonstrates the impact of dominant organizations on the structure of dependent organizations. A considerable literature suggests that organization provokes organization, implying an ever-widening bureaucratization of modern society. Organization of one interest, it has been noted, encourages the organization of competing groups. Similarly, organization of private groups may prompt government organizations and, conversely, government regulation may produce groupings of the organizations being regulated.[15] Evidence of this kind, though, does not directly engage the argument put forth here, which requires a demonstration of the structural impact of one organization on another. Here, the literature seems more scattered. In a study of American industrial relations, Richard Lester has observed that "Centralization in the industrial relations policies of management generates a corresponding tendency within the union dealing with that management, and similarly management tends to react in the same direction to union-centralizing developments."[16] In this case, the two organizations are interdependent, and thus match changes in the other's structures. Studies of federal funding on the operation and organization of local agencies also provide evidence for an argument of this kind. Most recently, this shift from the program-specific funding of the sixties to the revenue-sharing procedures of the middle seventies is said by some to have produced changes both in the organization of local dealings with the federal government and of the local organization of particular programs.[17]

The thrust of this argument, then, is that the structure of a dominant organization affects the structure of a dependent organization, forcing the dependent organization to accommodate its structure to that of the dominant organization. Since in the previous section it was argued that structure sets the context in which routine behavior can emerge—in fact, particular structures tend to generate particular kinds of routine behavior—then this argument suggests that by "transmitting" organizational structure, patterns of routine behavior are transmitted as well. *This would suggest that common patterns of routine behavior, labeled here as culture, will emerge among organizations that are sufficiently interdependent, and that in particular a dominant organization may transmit its pattern of routine to a subordinate organization.* What are the implications, though, that in this case study the dominant organization was the state? That is the next question.

The State's Influence on Cultural Behavior. Moving beyond a purely abstract discussion of "dominant" and "dependent" organizations, let us now speculate on the impact of the structure of the state (the central organization of a modern nation) on the patterns of routine authority behavior (one element of culture) in the society at large. There is some supporting evidence for the discussion which follows, and one can postulate the problem as a testable hypothesis, but, nonetheless, the argument is exploratory and speculative. The argument is that the structure of the state, and the politics surrounding the creation of the state, directly contribute to the patterns of routine behavior that we call culture. The evidence and argument presented thus far suggest such a speculation. Concretely, we have observed how the state has, in fact, served to maintain culturally traditional authority patterns in those firms that are dependent on it. More abstractly, we have argued that organizational structure establishes the framework within which routine behaviors emerge, and that organizational structure and the routine behaviors associated with that structure can be "transmitted" from a dominant to a subordinate organization.

The state, the permanent structures and institutions of government, is at least formally the central institution in a nation—the one institution which bears at least a possible relationship with all others. In fact, this is a fundamental characteristic of the modern state: it is the only organization with which at least potentially all members of the nation will interact, and thus it provides the one common experience with authority in the society. Thus, the state is the single organization most likely to put its imprint on the structure of other organizations in the society, and the individuals that compose the society.

The structures of any organization, it was argued earlier, represent the institutionalization of the political fights in the organization's history, while the results of current struggles will shape tomorrow's strategies and structures. In the case of any state it is quite clear that the political struggles surrounding its creation contribute directly to its current structure. Thus, *national patterns of authority behavior can be understood as the residue of the political struggles that create the state.* In this analysis, the state stands as an intermediary between political struggle and one aspect of cultural behavior, patterns of authority. Such an impact of the state may be particularly evident in France precisely because the presence of the state is felt in so many aspects of social life. In fact, one might argue that the more widespread the role of the state is in the community, the more closely patterns of authority behavior in the community as a whole will match those within the state itself. It is also important that the basic outline of the French state was laid down in the feudal years. Thus, when modern politics emerged, mass participation and parties, for example, adapted themselves to the structure of the French state. Conversely, in the case of Italy, when a state apparatus was created during the process of political modernization, that state structure reflected the organization of the party system. Thus, for example, the patron-client relationships of the Italian state have their roots in the organization of political power by the dominant political party, the Christian Democrats. This argument in no way implies that the French state stands in some way outside and above the rest of society, imposing on the community a pattern of authority relationships; it says rather that the structure of the state institutionalizes a particular pattern of authority relationships which already exists in the culture. Again, to understand that distinctive national pattern, one must look to the politics surrounding the establishment of the state.

Michel Crozier, interestingly, comes very close to developing such a position in his work *The Bureaucratic Phenomena.* In support of his contention that distinctive French patterns of authority do exist, he turns to Tocqueville for historical evidence that the struggle between the central government and local communities in the eighteenth and nineteenth centuries displayed many of the same characteristics as today's struggles within the factories he studied. The implication is that the same "dilemma in the attitudes of Frenchmen toward authority" was at work in both periods. The political struggles that Tocqueville describes, however, are those of a king attempting to establish the control of his central government over the provinces once ruled by nobles and often of different ethnic sources. The local strategies for dealing with this all-powerful central authority were responses and reaction to the king's strategy for establishing administrative control over the territory he claimed. Ultimately, to maintain that French patterns of authority originally had psychological roots, one would have to demonstrate that the strategy the French king followed reflected his own attitudes toward authority. But even if one had the records of some imaginary psychoanalyst of Louis XIV, it would be much easier to contend that the strategy he adopted—a strategy for bringing the nobles under his control, centralizing power in Paris, and establishing a bureaucracy in principle loyal to the crown—emerged from the political options open to him, rather than from his psychological propensities. If the political sources of the structure of the French state are acknowledged, then the historical data supports the argument that the particular national process of state building in France produced structures that fostered distinctive patterns of authority behavior in that country.

Kenneth Jowitt has argued along very similar lines to account for the distinctive features of political culture in Marxist-Leninist countries.[18]

> The relationship of political culture and political structure may be compared to the relationship that exists between the formal

and informal organization of a factory. . . . It is the informal organization of the state that we shall refer to as political culture. More precisely, *political culture refers to the set of informal adaptive postures—behavioral and attitudinal—that emerge in response to and interact with the set of formal definitions—ideological, policy and institutional—that characterize a given level of society.*[19] [Jowitt's italics.]

Jowitt is arguing, in essence, that political culture should be defined as an informal adaptation to political structure. One can hypothesize that distinctive political cultures result from particular structures, not from some psychologically rooted notion of national character. Jowitt notes, for example, that an analysis of Chinese authority patterns will identify "unique" elements of political culture, such as "ambivalence toward authority and tendency to avoid conflict," which are, according to Crozier, "distinctive and basic features of contemporary French political culture." The implicit conclusion of this reasoning is that the common structural features of the two bureaucratic states—formal centralization with local units attempting to defend their autonomy against the all-powerful center—have common behavioral and attitudinal consequences. Interestingly enough, Theda Skocpol concludes that these common structural features of the French and Chinese bureaucracies made them vulnerable to successful class-based revolutions. Jowitt contends that East European Marxist-Leninist regimes all have common cultural features because they share structural features imposed by the Soviets, although specific national characteristics affect the response in any particular country.

One might put this argument somewhat differently and maintain that the establishment of particular political institutions, other than the state alone, is what shapes patterns of routine behavior. This argument was advanced earlier, when the patterns of behavior inside a particular organization were discussed. "The institutionalization of the political struggles of the past, the establishment of particular values in the forms of rules and procedures in organizations, can contribute to the formation of the typical behaviors of a culture." Cynthia McClintock, in her work on peasant organization in Latin America, presents evidence that political structure precedes and shapes political attitudes by demonstrating how new structures of peasant life produce sharply different attitudes and behaviors.[20] Similarly, Suzanne Berger has shown how the political behavior of two Breton political regions, identical on every social and economic measure of political life, including the directly observable and measurable standard of voting behavior, differ as a direct result of differences in the organization of politics.[21] That divergence can be traced to the period following the First World War when the prewar political apparatus had been destroyed. In each of the two regions, the same two groups were competing to organize politics.

The victory in each case was contingent on particular events, and depended more than anything else on which group got its organizing drive launched first. The divergence may have been contingent, but the differences that resulted have endured, suggesting powerfully both the importance of political institutions for explaining political behavior and the idea that more than one form of organization and behavior can be sustained on the same socioeconomic soil. The fundamental problem in both French departments was to organize so as to influence state behavior or protect themselves from it. The particular local institutions operated in a political space articulated by the state; their organizational options were, in fact, limited by the organization of national politics. All this suggests that explanations for differing political cultures or routine behaviors of a culture may be found in the political struggles that established the structure of the institutions.

Organization and Economic Behavior

Finally, we come to consider the impact of organizational structures, and the cultural and political bias expressed by those structures, on economic behavior. As argued in Chapter 5, French electronics firms were seriously handicapped by having organizational structures which weakened them in international competition. A serious policy dilemma therefore arose, because state policies which were intended to support the firms in the market tended also to reinforce the organizational inefficiencies. French interest in assessing the influence of industrial policies on the vigor and efficiency of the firm is now growing; but in the 1960s the French were hardly predisposed to consider the question. Had the problem attracted their curiosity, however, they would quickly have stumbled into a theoretical void. One simple assumption of neo-classical economic theory—that whatever its internal functioning, the firm will approximate a fully informed maximizer of profit, arranging the factors of production in the most efficient way—would have led to the conclusion that the structure of the market determines the conduct and performance of the firm. While such simplifying assumptions may often be useful, and are particularly reasonable in the American cultural context, the clear anti-competition ethic and the gross inefficiency of many firms in France calls them into question here, and the evident effects that these organizations have on economic behavior urges that such considerations find a place in theory. If the organization of the firm varied randomly, or was simply a reflection of the market, then there would be reason to exclude it as a variable from the analysis of industrial organization. If, however—as we assume here—firm organization in different cultures systematically differs from the ideal type of a profit-maximizing, efficient operation, then its influence on the market must be included in the analysis.

Put more generally, the organization of the firm is not simply a product of its economic task, but of its political and social environment as well. The consequence is that if organization affects economic behavior in any systematic way, then the examination of micro-economic behavior cannot be entirely separated from the analysis of political and social behavior. In fact, for these purposes, one might consider the organization and internal behavior of the firm to be a factor of production that affects the efficient use of all other factors, and thus affects the firm's conduct and performance in any particular market context. The implication is that *the conduct and performance of the firm will vary with changes in the organization of the firm in any given market context.*

Several problems suggest the importance of considering the influence of the organization of the firm on its economic behavior. First, when the organization of a set of firms is grossly inefficient, as is the case in the historically and culturally rooted centralization and hierarchy of French firms, or when there are cultural restraints on the firm's conduct, then conventional logic and traditional assumptions may lead to grossly erroneous predictions about performance. Second, if the organization of a firm or a set of firms is undergoing radical change, as has been the case with the movement toward divisionalization in France the last twenty years, then the conduct of those firms—given the same structure of the market—can be expected to change. Both cases represent situations which refute the arguments that the intuitive sense of businessmen or the corrective benefits of competition will produce "profit maximizing behavior," because in both cases the bias is systematic among a whole set of firms. Finally, arguments about the behavior of the modern corporation engaged in between Galbraith and Scott, for example, circle around the role that corporate structure plays in the firm's behavior. Let us use the French problems as an opportunity to suggest both how economic analysis can hide the influence of the organizational variable and how this variable could be introduced. In fact, showing how it can be introduced is to suggest how it is hidden.

The classic analysis of industrial market structure and business behavior argues that the *performance* in particular industries depends on the *conduct* of the firms, which in turn depends on the *structure* of the industry. At its extreme, as in the influential work of Joe Bain, the intermediary variable of conduct is suppressed, assuming that conduct will mechanically follow structure, and a direct empirical link is observed between market structure and economic performance.[22] The structure of the market—its concentration, the barriers to entry, and so on—exert external constraints on the behavior of the firm.

The problem, as Marc Roberts has pointed out, is that "instead of asking how or why organizations choose as they do, it is generally assumed in the traditional analysis of structure-performance relationships that participants can adequately define and generally pursue profit-maximizing behavior."[23]

Scherer's more recent treatment of the problem reintroduces the notion of conduct, contending that the link between structure and perform-ance is a two-step process: structure constraints conduct, and conduct in its turn is linked to performance.[24] Scherer acknowledges that organiza-tion can influence conduct in a given market structure, but stops short of pushing the implications of his insight to their logical conclusion. His comments about the influence of organizational structure and of values other than profit maximization on the conduct of the firm disperse themselves, because he does not suggest a systematic way of integrating them into a theory of business behavior and industrial evolution. This last step does not appear necessary since in the end he holds closely to the notion that the only divergences from the ideal come in monopoly conditions. Scherer, nonetheless, provides us with the tools to take the last step by hinting that all is not determined, but that market structures are the result of constrained probability processes.

Market structure, then, constrains the choices of the firm, or limits the set of choices possible. Even if it is profit-maximizing and perfectly informed, the firm must still make a judgment about what wishes to take in what period of time. Thus, we must speak not of the firm's choice, but of the probability distribution of a set of choices. Carried further, we might say that each particular organizational structure or value set represents a different probability distribution of a set of choices. Thus, Firm A and Firm B, confronted with choices 1 through 10, all of which are limited by the market structure, will have different probabilities of making any of these choices. (See Figure 1.) If the biases

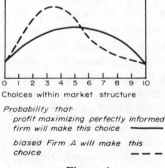

Choices within market structure

Probability that:
profit maximizing perfectly informed
firm will make this choice   ————

biased Firm A will make this
choice   — — —

Figure 1

or limits on Firm B push it outside the acceptable choice set, it will either fail or retreat into the acceptable set, presuming that the other firms are perfectly informed profit-maximizers and the restraints remain the same.

The firm's implication of this argument, then is that organization affects the probability that a firm will make a particular choice, and therefore influences the conduct and the performance of the firm in any market situation. The key defense of economists against this implication is that any firm going outside the market limits will be forced to exit from the market, and that therefore organizational behavior doesn't matter.

Let us take the next crucial step and speak not of Firm A and Firm B, but of Set A, and Set B, and Set PM, each representing identical industries composed of identical firms. Let us assume that the choices of all the firms in each set are similarly biased, but that the bias is different for each set, perhaps as a result of different social values or different political rules. Set A and Set B are biased away from the perfectly informed profit-maximizing probability distribution, while the managers of the firms in Set PM were so well socialized by their economics professors that they conform exactly to the profit-maximizing model. Then, one can expect that although the market structures are initially the same, the choices of the firms in Set A will differ from the choices of the firms in Set B, and that Sets A and B will differ from Set PM. After all firms have implemented their choices, the set of possibilities facing the firms in this second round (at time A 1)—in other words, *the structure of the market*—will also change. However, only the firms in Set PM will be penalized for not conforming to the perfect market ideal. Firms in Sets A and B will not be forced back into the straight and narrow path of profit maximization. The implication is that the systematic organizational biases will promote a market evolution in different directions for each set. (see Figure 2.)

Two conclusions can be drawn from this exercise. First, commonly held organizational constraints or biases among firms in an industry will influence the evolution of the market structure by influencing the choices the firms make at time B. Second, and critically, *the influence of organizational variables on the behavior of the firms and on the evolution of the market is suppressed from view.* Since at any moment the firms are making choices within the constraints of the existing market structure, they never violate the rule that market structure in a large sense determines the conduct and performance of the firm.

Setting aside the possibility of finding an industry that evolved from an identical point in two countries, or of comparing an actual evolution to a model of evolution under a different set of assumptions,

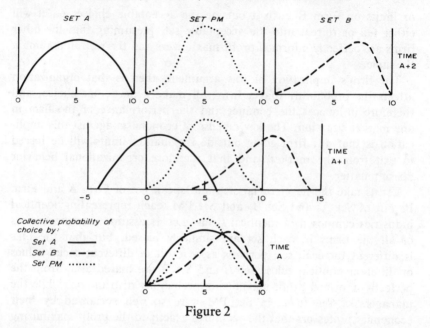

Figure 2

the influence of organization can be seen only if some event thrusts the sets of Firms A and B into the same market, which was more or less the case in the postwar French electronics industry. Then, competing in the same market, the different conduct of the firms and their different performances can be observed. One might expect the firms with the less competitive organizations—either in structure or in values —to perform less well and to be prompted to copy their competitors. The rapidity and completeness with which the less competitive firms adjust will be quite important in determining the structure of the joint market over time, particularly the relative position of the firms from each set. The adjustment of a firm's organization to its new external environment is not instant, and that lag may have important consequences for market structure and for the relative performance of the two sets of firms. Thus, as one American electronics president said of his French competitors, "They made the worst of a difficult situation."

If the government of the least competitive set of firms wishes to promote their position, it can act to alter the market structure to encourage their performance, or it can press them for organizational change. Theoretically, a serious dilemma will be posed if the policies that create a more favorable market structure also damage the organizational structure of the firms. The approach outlined above makes it possible, at least, to pose the problem, even though it does not suggest how to solve it. My bias clearly is that the French electronics industry would be in a stronger position today if more attention had been paid to the structure of the firms and less to the structure of the market.

The evidence in this case study has suggested the argument that a systematic decision-making bias of all members of a set of firms means that none must pursue a strategy of profit maximization to survive; or, put differently, that culturally distinct patterns of economic behavior in a nation's firms, and that consequently growth in any particular industry will differ from that which would be predicted by an analysis that assumed profit maximization. The analysis that links microeconomic behavior to political and social variables through the mediation of organization structure can be made in a less orthodox fashion and carried several steps further, however.*

Let us consider whether for a *particular* firm, one member of the set, variation in economic behavior can be linked to variation in organizational structure. To argue that organizational structure can affect behavior, one must first establish that the institution has discretion in the choices it makes. Economists disregard structure precisely because they contend that market structure so sharply constrains the choices a firm can make without penalty—in the form of lower profits and ultimately exit from the market—that variation can be disregarded. Firms either learn or will disappear.

In fact, however, it is the accepted characteristic of one category of firms, monopolies and oligopolies, that they are not so strictly coerced by the marketplace. Galbraith carries the argument even further and contends that they dominate and plan their environments, and that the goals they pursue are a function of their structure. Interestingly, as noted, even some of Galbraith's critics, such as Bruce Scott, agree that corporate structure does affect behavior; they disagree instead about what the structure of the modern corporation really is and what consequences follow from it. In fact, even apart from the world of the Fortune 500, which does indeed produce a substantial portion of the national industrial product, we may observe a variety of local monopolies such as utilities companies, which extend the size of the productive sector that is not directly constrained by the market. Clearly, the greater the portion of the economy controlled by firms with discretion, and the more extensive their discretion in the market, the greater is the significance of arguments about organizational influences

---

*This argument has been presented within the orthodox formulation of industrial behavior expressed by the classic three-step model: structure determines performance which determines behavior. All that has been done is that structure has been broadly defined as in the Introduction and broader environmental influence on economic choice (performance) has been introduced.

on choices made by firms. In fact, as Roberts notes, analyses suggest that managers do pursue a number of objectives other than growth, but these goals are often disregarded because the managers' insights are difficult to integrate into theory in any systematic way. Roberts writes: "Since all decisions are imperfect and all consequences depend on uncertain processes, outcomes typically turn out differently than anticipated. Thus determining the pattern of corporate values implicit in outcomes raises difficult problems of inference—especially because, as Solow has argued, different objectives may imply qualitatively quite similar behavior."[25] One may evade the problem of inferring values by considering whether particular organizational structures are linked to particular outcomes.

Marc Roberts has considered the relation between the organizational structure of six utility companies, three public and three private, and their behavior on environmental issues.[26] He suggests that organizational variables were directly linked to the choices the different companies made; or in other words, that differences in their external environment—the market setting if you will—could not account for differences in their behavior. It was divergence in organizational strategy, control and incentive systems, and personnel that accounted for the differences in their behavior. He concludes that:

> The structures and behavior patterns included under the terms "public" and "private" are so broad, and so overlapping, that for many purposes that distinction has little or no information value.
>
> In organizations which are structured and controlled so that the consequences to an individual member of various actions are quite different, the perspectives of top management have a relatively greater impact on organizational choices. In situations where members face similar outcomes for various decisions, the ideology and commitments of the membership have more impact on what choices are made.
>
> Members of various functional and technical specializations are often characterized by different perspectives. The size of a functional group and the seniority of its top leadership partially determines how much impact that group's perspective has on organizational choices.
>
> For both public and private companies, survival threats tend to increase internal efficiency and improve performance. For both the ultimate guarantee of their continued operation is their acceptability to the political system within which they function. However, differences in the structure of that system vary the costs outside pressure groups face in changing the organization's behavior and hence the extent to which they do so.

Such an approach, it should be quite clear, blurs the distinction between what might loosely be called economic analysis and political or social analysis.

Let us put this argument in somewhat different language. Let us hypothesize that a firm makes its choices based on some "decision rule," in which case profit maximization represents one potential decision rule, but hardly the only possible one. The decision rules of a firm, the procedures that guide routine behavior and set the terms in which crisis is conceived and resolved, depend, we can argue, on the organizational structure of the firm. In fact, the firm does not have a single rule, but rather a whole variety of rules for various problems and situations, internal and external. Moreover, for any particular problem different groups within the firm will have different decision rules which they would apply if they could. The divergence between rules amongst groups within the firm will be a function of two factors—the incentives that the control system within a particular structure of tasks offers, and the perspectives that various groups, recruited with different training and values, bring to the job. The organizational structure, the distribution of tasks and responsibilities, will determine which rule is, in fact, applied to a particular problem. Thus the firm's choices are made according to a decision rule created and selected, as it were, by the internal organization. Economic outcomes, then, result from the application of the decision rule in particular situations.

We have, it should be noted, inserted the "decision rule" as an intermediary between internal organizational structure and economic outcome. This, it should be underscored, is a logical exercise, and no suggestion is made here that we should infer "decision rules" from any set of outcomes. Roberts warns against such a move, on the grounds that it is difficult to infer from outcomes the basis of the choice—that is, the decision rule used. Why, then, add additional complexity to an analysis which seemed already to establish the principle that organizational structure, dependent as it is on political and social development, stands as a critical intermediary between an economic situation and economic behaviors and outcomes?

Nelson and Winter at Yale University have constructed models of economic behavior that depend on the specification of a firm's decision rules rather than the classical notion of a production function. "The behavioral theory asserts that a firm at any time operates largely according to a set of decision rules that link a domain of environmental stimuli to a range of responses on the part of the firm. While neo-classical theory would attempt to deduce these decision rules from maximization on the part of the firm, the behavioral theory simply takes them as given and observable."[27] Using this model to analyze macro-economic growth, Nelson and Winter generated data that were difficult to distinguish from those generated using the best available neo-classical model. They purport that the great advantage of their approach lies at the micro-economic level—that is, in considering the behavior of the individual firms that underlies any micro-economic data. Their analysis, as they point out, approximates that of Schumpeter,* and as was the case with Schumpeter, the dynamics of technological innovation and competition are easier to conceptualize in their analyses than in the neo-classical formulation. Whether these advantages in economic analysis are significant, and what price must be paid for them, is not a judgment for this economic laymen to hazard. (It must be admitted that it is not entirely clear exactly how these decision rules are generated, for example.)

The importance of their theoretical model to this discussion is the very substitution of a "decision rule" for a production function. The production function specifies a set of possible combinations of the factors of production with the particular combination chosen by the profit-maximizing firm under conditions of perfect competition—the conditions that most efficiently combine these factors at particular price levels and output levels. The very apparatus of the production function and the assumption of profit maximization directly excludes considerations of organization structure from the analysis.

But the decision rule, as has been argued, can be analyzed as the function of organizational, political, and social influence, not simply of economic factors. Thus, economic behavior becomes reintegrated

---

*More generally, the evolutionary theory differs sharply from the neo-classical theory in its image of the role of firms in the growth process. In the neo-classical theory, firms are viewed as possessing the capabilities to operate the technologies of interest to the theory, and also as being competent to choose from that set the technique and level of its use that is most profitable. They are viewed as technicians and managers. This is not only in the positive theory, but in the normative theory. For Lange, and the welfare economics tradition that has followed him, firms were "clerks" undertaking the work of society and following certain decision rules which guide what they do. In the evolutionary theory, as in Schumpeter, firms retain this clerk role, but there are always opportunities to improve upon existing technologies and practices. Thus, firms have the role of searching for improvements, of screening and selecting new departures.

Substitution of the "Search and selection" metaphor for the maximization metaphor, plus the assumption of the basic improvability of procedures, blurs the notion of a production function. In the particular model that we developed, there was no production function—only a set of physically possible activities. The production function did not emerge from that set because there was no presumption made that firms used the "most efficient" of the activities. Relatedly, there is no sharp distinction in an evolutionary theory between "moving along" a production function and "shifting to a new one," as there is in the neo-classical case.

into social analysis, as a very particular but not separable set of choices and decisions. Seen in this way, the exclusion of these factors from neo-classical analysis is by no means the inevitable consequence of parsimony and elegance, but rather the arbitrary result of the particular nature of that theory. Whether neo-classical theory provides tools more useful for economic analysis or not, this argument holds. Greater usefulness in neo-classical theory, if indeed it is more useful, may result from inherent advantages in the theory or greater investment in developing the apparatus of an inherently less fruitful approach.

The neo-classical exclusion of these other factors, as the several analyses presented here suggest, is not neutral technical choice without analytic consequences, rather it blinds analysts to often very critical questions. The firm can only be easily examined as responding to a limited range of elements which actually influence its behavior—the structure of the market and the static conditions of production. Whenever the economic or political situation allows discretion, and if there are systematic biases away from profit maximization in the set of firms in the market, analysis based on the assumption of profit maximization can prove deceiving. Certainly, when considering problems such as political control, the reality of politics must be introduced as an addendum to the consideration of economic incentives. In a traditional framework, the impact of the direct interaction of firm and state cannot be considered, for example.

We have thus come full circle. We started the chapter with an analysis of change in a single organization as a response to shifting conditions in the economic, technological, and political environment, with the substantive focus being the firm. Now we have concluded by considering the impact the organization of these firms has on their purely economic behavior.

7
The State
at Home and Abroad

The electronics industry, seen by the French as a matter of vital concern, is very much part of an international marketplace, and earlier chapters have examined the evident difficulties of reorganizing and nurturing the industry in the face of intense international competitive pressure. (See Chapters 3 and 5.) It is now time to ask what general conclusions can be drawn from this case study about business-state relationships in France and the French position in the international economy, particularly since government economic intervention since the war must be judged quite successful on balance. It seems clear, for example, that the state provided the spark which transformed postwar reconstruction into unprecedented expansion and then supported and defended a policy of rapid industrialization.[1] Moreover, in vital sectors such as oil and steel, government policy established and maintained an industry structure of its own definition without being thwarted by political opposition or economic constraint.[2] Set against this record, it would be misleading or flatly incorrect to conclude that this case study simply suggests the inability of the nation-state to defend the interests of a domestic industry in an increasingly international economy, or that it demonstrates the economic distortions produced by political tampering with the market. On the other hand, the electronics case is not simply an anomaly to be dismissed when examining the postwar French economy, and must be given a place in any interpretation.

This chapter will argue that one can systematically account for the difficulties in electronics and the success in other sectors by examining the strategies and options favored by the structure of relationships between business and the state, including the organization of the state bureaucracy itself. This structure produces essential continuities in the domestic and international economic policies of the French state, whatever government is in power and often without seeming regard for the problem at hand. The institutional structure of the economy[3] can thus be taken as a mediating variable that patterns government responses to both domestic and international economic pressures. Moreover, since that structure is a product of the particular national route from feudalism to the industrial society,[4] as has been argued at length here, a nation's international economic policy must be seen as a function of the structure of its domestic economy. Certainly the pattern of international economic life produces pressures and episodes that a nation must cope with, but the responses are conditioned by domestic institutional arrangements. Whether in the domestic or the international arena, whenever the capacities of the French state have matched the requirements of the problems at hand, policy has been successful. Like any organization in a structured environment, the French state can do some things better than others, and it is more successful when the task at hand can in fact be handled effectively by what it does best.

The electronics case is distinguished from oil and steel by the problems that must be resolved, and, hence, by the domestic and international tasks the state must perform, rather than by the state's policy approaches. The approach has been, for the most part, the same in the three instances. This case, then, suggests the limits of the French state's ability to determine the structure and conduct of a domestic industry and its place in the international economy; put somewhat differently, it suggests the distinctive strengths and weaknesses of the French system.

Institutional Structure and Domestic Policy

The capacity of any state to implement particular policies and achieve domestic economic goals, then, is systematically influenced by the patterned set of institutional relationships in the national economy, the structured institutional setting in which it attempts to act. In the following discussion, we shall focus on two elements in this institutional network: first, the organization of the state, both the formal arrangement of power within the bureaucracy and the relation of the bureaucracy to the legislature and the executive, including its accessibility to the political community; and second, the relationships between the financial systems, the business community, and the state bureaucracy. Two examples may serve to indicate the influence of these factors.

In Britain, as in France, the government supported a merger drive in the 1960s that resulted in increased industrial concentration. In France the state often acted in alliance with the *banques d'affaires,* institutions experienced with the initiation and sponsorship of industrial reorganization, and the nationalized deposit banks that provide the bulk of available investment capital. The banques d'affaires, though, are a distinctive product of continental industrial development with no real counterpart in England, and the Ministry of Finance in France has a power of disposition over investment capital not possessed by the English treasury. The financial community in England, by contrast, grew by servicing English trade and commerce, not government or industry, and, during the years that Sterling served as an international reserve currency, it even acted as the institutional support for world commerce. The country's financial institutions, concentrated in London's "City" district reflect this history and are more embroiled, it often seems, in international commerce than in domestic industry. Consequently, when an effort was made to reorganize British industry, a government agency had to be created to provide an instrument that could affect the financial organization of industrial capital. The Industrial Reorganization Corporation, established as part of the Labour government's drive to modernize British industry, was composed of bankers and businessmen who could draw on state resources to support favored merger efforts even against the opposition of other segments of the banking and business community.[5] In a sense, then, this government agency was created to substitute for the banking-state business complex that was born naturally of industrialization in France. In a reversal of the Gerschenkron logic, the industrial first-born is found imitating the institutional arrangements of the latecomers in order to cope with the difficulties of managing the organization and reorganization of large-scale capital, problems that did not exist when England first industrialized but which were nevertheless issues on the continent from the beginning.[6]

In a different vein, the character of the Italian state bureaucracy paralyzes government efforts to implement macro-economic policy. As La Palombara argues, the bureaucracy is not organized to make or implement general policy, but only to give or deny concessions, authorizations, or tax exceptions.[7] This bureaucracy, as is often noted, is the product of the electoral base of the grab-all Christian Democratic Party that has ruled Italy since the war. That party harvests votes through patron-client relationships in which political support is exchanged for specific favors, a tradition particularly widespread in the South, where political elites mediate between peasants and the political system. The consequence, as many economists note, is that fiscal

policy, resting as it does on the even-handed and rational administration of tax and expenditure policies, is ineffective in Italy. Efforts
to achieve macro-economic stability thus rests almost exclusively on
monetary manipulation, a mighty weight to be borne by any single
policy instrument.

The initial concern of this essay was with the organizational response
of the business firm to an environment that included the state, while
our concern here (as in Chapter 5) is with the ability of the state—
operating in a specific structured setting—to manage the activities of
other institutions in the society and thus to achieve particular economic
outcomes. The organizational arrangements within the state bureaucracy, it is argued here, systematically affect the success of such efforts.
The state, though, is not simply one organization like the others;
it is a public body, at least in principle the formal expression of the
political community. It is thus the one bureaucracy whose ends and
purposes are tied to the society as a whole, at once an executive
instrument and a political prize. Its behavior, then, must be understood
as a product of its organizational character and its ties to the society.

But can one even speak of the state as a coordinated and directed
institution, as if it were set apart from the social groups that attempt
to use it, the agencies that are its instrumentalities, or the political
executive that seeks to direct the bureaucracy? Competing models or
paradigms of the state, often serving different analytical purposes,
suggest quite different answers. For example, liberal theory, evolved
to consider the internal arrangements within a society, clearly views
the state as the mirror of the community, the reflection of power
within the society. The government—it is hard even to speak of an
autonomous state in this theory—serves as a neutral scale weighing
inputs from competing groups, rendering some judgment on their
relative power by action or inaction. For the Marxists the state reflects the
social power relations, relations expressed in class terms. However, in the
theory of international politics concerned with the relations between
nations, the "state" is often treated as a directed agent, a single-point decision maker somewhat like the firm in economics, that can serve as the
focus of analysis. Indeed, the nation-state was in part created by the conflict between bureaucracies that claimed control of specified territories.
Differences in the theory of the state and society, however, can also
be seen to reflect national differences in the origins of the state
as much as in the different uses to which the theory is put. In fact,
the appropriate notion of the state for the analyst depends on the links
between state structures and the society in particular countries.

The distinctive features of the French state, both its internal structure
and its relations to the community, can be clarified when it is contrasted

in textbook simplicity, with the structure of the American government. To consider the economic consequences of a strong state, this contrast will emphasize the French state's insulation from the political community in the Fifth Republic. In the United States the fragmentation of political authority by a federal political structure and a formal division of powers in the national government has permitted specialized elites attempting to influence particular decisions to capture elements of the government as their virtual fiefdoms. Therefore, in this country one cannot truly speak of a single state policy in domestic affairs, but rather of the positions of competing agencies which often reflect the views of competing social groups. This phenomenon has been depicted in the national community by Grant McConnell[8] among others, and in local political life by Robert Dahl, who demonstrated that no single power elite exists in New Haven.[9] Thus, in an important sense the nation-state structure in the United States is merely a framework within which groups compete, although it is clear the organization of the structure mediates the conflict and thus affects both its character and often the ultimate victors. An initial victory by one elite or portion of an elite, which for some narrow band of issues then becomes a part of the state, can be used to handicap competition and thus to freeze economic or social structures. Critically, though, the movement of initiative, power, and control is from the society to the state, from private actors entering or influencing the government. In France, by contrast, one does, in fact, speak of the state (*l'état*) as a powerful, independent force in political life, and the almost metaphysical notion of *l'état* as the unified authority of the society has a powerful symbolic value in French politics. The state bureaucracy was created by the kings in their efforts to control the provincial nobles and administer the society without aristocratic intermediation through agents directly loyal to the throne. Thus from the beginning the state was an instrument of centralizing power, created apart from the society, almost in opposition to it, and thus at least partially autonomous. Mass political movements in France therefore had to adapt to existing government structures, while in the United States the structures were created in an epoch of democratic mass-politics. As noted in Chapter 3, the French state often seems to reach out to capture private allies for its own purposes, and certainly in many economic affairs the initiative lies with the state. A fuller and more nuanced picture would consider the channels of pressure group influence, but the outline would remain the same. Even the ministerial cabinet is staffed heavily from the Grands Corps and the crucial budgetary posts will be filled exclusively from Grands Corps ranks. The argument, it must be understood, is not that private groups never infiltrate, capture, or use the French government, or that there is no public leadership in American society—both notions would be foolish—but rather that the balance of public and private leadership and initiative is very different in the two countries.

This analysis does not suggest how one manages to forge a state policy in France, but only indicates what tools can be used to implement that policy. The initiative in each of these three cases (oil, steel, and electronics) appears to have come from different places, although in each instance the same ministries were involved: the Planning Commission, the Ministry of Industry, and the Ministry of Finance. Thus, the issue of the ties between the state and the society stands somewhat apart from the question of *whose* interests in the society are served, though differing arrangements may allow victory to different groups or coalitions and thereby affect the goals that the victorious can ultimately achieve.

Centralization of the state bureaucracy and at least partial insulation from outside interference, at any rate, are critical features of the French system. The argument here will be that the centralization of the French state provides the possibility of unified and concerted government action, while its partial autonomy allows it to initiate policy and direct events, rather than simply react to domestic pressure. Organizational behavior, however, cannot be inferred simply from organizational structure. One might properly add here that formal centralization, to consider the first of these features, does not necessarily mean capacity for action, let alone unified action. In fact, the popular image of the French state and of French bureaucracy in general is of a giant paralyzed by hierarchical and functional barriers between tasks, formally centralized but informally incapacitated, a paralysis often claimed to contribute to a general inability of the French government to respond to social problems without crisis.[10] Indeed, it is obviously difficult to reform the state's service delivery bureaucracies, such as the Ministry of Education or the PTT.

Although continuing reforms that might avoid crisis are difficult to implement, commentators on French bureaucracy suggest that crisis, when it comes, is met by a powerful, unified, and centralized response, which is tolerated in the face of chaos and collapse.[11] Less dramatically, mechanisms do exist to coordinate the decisions of the highest echelons of the state bureaucracy, and if those decisions can be implemented, then the unified weight of a centralized state can be massed for particular purposes. While ongoing reform at lower-level initiative may be difficult, coordination of strategy on critical issues is not precluded. As during a period of crisis, such coordination may require the arbitration and intervention of the high executive authority. In fact, once a choice is made, strategic coordination led by the chief executive may be simplified in a centralized state because the number of individuals that are involved in the choice and whose active cooperation is required is substantially reduced. Furthermore, as a practical matter, the sharp formal differentiation of responsibility within the bureaucracy is blurred at the top by the system of Grandes Écoles and Grands Corps.[12] School ties and attachments to the Grands Corps cut across the bureaucracy, opening channels of communication and influence at the top of the state bureaucracy, just as they provide informal ties between state and business. This increases the capacity to coordinate high-level decision making. Importantly, perhaps the easiest thing to coordinate in such a system is the allocation of capital, either for private investment or for public infrastructure development, because such decisions do not require the reorganization or agreement of the lower-level bureaucracies.

The Grands Corps system serves in addition to insulate the state bureaucracy from the society because the mechanism of recruitment severely restricts access to high positions within the bureaucracy. Only the minister and junior minister for less prestigious assignments (*secretaires d'état*) are direct political appointments. By contrast, in the American system political appointments extend down through the position of assistant secretary, some three or four echelons deeper in the government structure. Clearly, in France the minister has some control over which of the top civil servants will staff his administration,[13] but he can select only from among those on certain career tracks and proposed by the Corps controlling the position. Since particular Corps have virtual monopolies on particular responsibilities and jobs within the state system, they can autonomously organize the careers of their members, and a decade in advance one can identify the handful of potential candidates for crucial posts.[14] The Corps, as discussed earlier, recruit only from the top graduates of particular schools, and those graduates are almost exclusively of upper-middle-class Parisian background. In fact, one might argue that the recruitment system insures that the state will be directed by the social and economic elites and will not be unkind to their interests. In fact, the entrance exams have, on occasion, openly reflected the purposes of the politically victorious.

From positions in the state, many of the graduates of the Grandes Écoles and members of the Grands Corps leave for high positions in the private business community, dominating many crucial firms and even whole sectors of industry. Since top civil service positions are available only to graduates of the Grandes Écoles, the flow is almost exclusively from the state toward the business community. The top members of the state bureaucracy, holding positions of enormous political importance, represent a socially and even politically coherent and enduring body within French life whose personal careers within the state and in the business community, if they choose to leave public service, rest ultimately on maintaining and extending state power.

The autonomous state bureaucracy was created to serve the kings and reinforced to serve Napoleon, but while such a system creates the potential for state initiative, it in no way implies that such initiative will be taken or suggests that ends will be pursued. In the Third Republic, as Hoffmann argues, the state served to arbitrate conflict within the society and to maintain social balance and political calm, but after the Second World War, when the political decision was made to alter the structure of the French economy, this bureaucracy was once again used as an instrument of executive power. The structure of the Fifth Republic, which insulates the political executive from interest-group influence, and the Gaullist party system, which provides ambitious civil servants with routes to political position, have reinforced the autonomy of the state bureaucracy. Some, indeed, simply view the bureaucracy in the Fifth Republic as an instrument of the Gaullist party:

> The Gaullist and now the Giscardian parties, through purges, attrition, and the creation of "parallel hierarchies" of bureaucrats in the politicized ministerial staffs, have come to control and manipulate the civil machinery of the state in their own interest. The administration is not some strange, monolithic idol squatting immovably in the midst of French society, but at its top, at least, it is a highly political and sensitive group of men and institutions who are therefore quite vulnerable to a sharp change in the political climate. (Witness how openly committed to the right were many high ranking civil servants in last year's presidential election.)[15]

Thus, the state is open to influence only through narrowly defined channels that are controlled by one political group. This does not mean that the state in the Fifth Republic stands as an impregnable fortress in the midst of a society unaffected by traditional political groups. Nonetheless, the channels of influence are sufficiently narrowed so that many groups now feel themselves powerless to exert any political pressure within the state bureaucracy. Without parliament as an intermediary, dealings with the state favor those groups that are able to negotiate on a technical basis and offer something in return for state cooperation. For many, protest seems to remain the only instrument of influence.[16] The bureaucracy, partially insulated from political pressure and staffed by an enduring and coherent group of bureaucrats, can develop an interpretation of the public interest that is more than the sum of particular pressures.

The strategy of economic growth that has so deeply altered French life was developed in the bureaucracy and ran against the interests of much of the government's electoral coalition. Government policy never accords precisely with the wishes and intentions of the groups that compose its constituency, but the discretion open to the French bureaucracy and to the government in the Fifth Republic has been most remarkable on some issues.

One must not exaggerate, however. Much of the day-to-day activity of any government consists of responding to immediate pressures, and in many domains such as social security, the short-run considerations have dominated recent policy-making. Nonetheless, the potential for longer-term action certainly exists, and that potential is perhaps nowhere greater than in the realm of industrial policy discussed here. Cohen and Goldfinger put the issues well:

> When you restructure an industry, you need only the managers of that industry, the State (to organize, to provide the goodies, and sometimes to prod), and then you need merely the passive acquiescence of the trade unions. Nothing else, and crucially, no one else, is needed. Indeed broader participation could only endanger things. The nature of their direct objectives (industrial modernization) permitted the State-big business partnership to concentrate on the supply side (and there only in certain areas), and the nature of their political power (strong in just those areas, weak in direct confrontations with broad based political movements) kept them far away from the active concerns of the major political groups and even further from the machinery of day to day broad participation politics. The big-business technocrats partnership which is the Plan in its day to day operations, is essentially a device to keep the state actively involved in the management of the industrial core of the economy while keeping broad participation politics out.
>
> Thus despite their enormous power in one vital area, the big-business technocrat partnership has never been able to control such vital direct concerns of traditional politics as short term, demand side policy, agricultural subsidies, and social security benefits. The absence of a strong government (prior to 1958) further increased the tendency for industrial policy to have a certain independence. It left almost all long term policy (especially on the supply side) to the stewardship of the technocrats.[17]

Cohen and Goldfinger are arguing, essentially, that the technocrat-business alliance was able to capture, or better yet to create, a domain of policy-making that affected the organization of production in the nation's crucial industries without involving it in broad electoral politics. Thus, short-term policy, particularly affecting demand, remained the domain of traditional politics. Industrial policy, moreover, has many nuances. It is not simply a long-term strategy to renovate and rebuild, but remains in some sectors a social policy to preserve. Recent work on the French textile industry, for example, shows how policies of reorganization and modernization of industries were used as "vehicles for politically willed survival of the non-competitive, traditional industrial sectors. . . . What was originally designed to renew has in fact preserved. . . . Not only were the traditional sectors preserved but the modern sectors' development was controlled by the political strategy of the natural fiber sectors."[18]

One might argue that in traditional industries composed of many small firms, the difficulty of controlling the social impact of industrial change and the necessity of acting through the trade associations make it possible for existing firms to manipulate industrial policy to serve their particular interests of survival. As discussed in Chapter 3 the state continues to play the roles of both social arbitrator and industrial entrepreneur, and although in recent years the balance has swung toward entrepreneurial intervention in some sectors, both traditions remain, each embedded in distinctive organizational arrangements. (See Chapter 3.) The French state, then, has the structural potential for autonomous action, but structure does not determine how or whether that potential is used. A political explanation will always be required to explain the direction of state activity.

When the government chooses to alter the organizational structure of a particular industrial sector, the character of the financial system, the second factor in this analysis, provides it in most instances with a powerful policy instrument. Through the nationalized banks, the Banque de France and state institutions such as Crédit National, the government can exercise selective control over the allocation of credit to industry, or it can make special investment credit at subsidized interest rates available from public funds to particular industrial projects. These are policy tools which the British government simply does not command.[19] In fact, some sources estimate that 80 percent of all private investment in France passes through public or semi-public hands.[20]

The enduring tradition of private bank involvement in the initiation and management of business enterprise is as important as the capacity of the Ministry of Finance to influence conditions directly in particular sectors. The banks are not vital intermediaries between the state and industry, whether they followed or led the creation of industrial enterprise in the second half of the nineteenth century. In particular, the banques d'affaires—which made their profits from the creation, growth, and reorganization of industries rather than by enlisting widespread private deposits to be lent to service the financial needs of companies—are experienced at the task of the financial reorganization of industry that is often required to rationalize production. The role of the Banque de Paris et des Pays-bas, for example, in the affairs of oil and electronics has already been discussed (Chapter 3). Importantly, many of the deposit banks also play the role of industrial intermediary, although after the Second World War their right to hold industrial shares was severely restricted, perhaps to limit the impact of government nationalization of these banks on the rest of industry. However, the firms in many industries, it must be recalled, are predominantly family-owned, and thus quite resistant to bank influence.

The power of the banks in French industry is thus uneven. It is not the pervasive influence encountered in Germany, and, consequently, the state does not have an instrument that is uniformly effective in all sectors. In the more modern and capital-intensive industries of greatest concern to the state, the influence of banks is extensive (although a number of dominant firms such as the Michelin Tire Company are family held), whereas bank voices are less often heard in traditional industries such as textiles. For the most part, firms do not have effective access to medium- and long-term loan funds, however, unless they are involved with the banks, and once tied in with the banks, a firm becomes part of the network of criss-crossed financial holdings among the large "groups." This network often served, it should be remembered, to regulate and control competition among firms in the same sector, making it quite difficult for new comers to penetrate the market. Thus, while the structure of the banking system facilitates the reorganization of existing holdings, it makes the support of newly launched companies quite difficult.

The distinctive capabilities of the French state in the industrial arena have a dual source: the centralization and autonomy of the bureaucracy, and the often intimate relationships between banks and business. Thus on the one hand, the centralization of the state structure allows the allocation of public funds and publicly influenced funds for capital investment to be coordinated and directed toward particular ends; while on the other, the character of the banking system and its intimate dependence on the state make it possible to manipulate the ownership patterns of an industry in order to obtain specific changes in its production capacity and technology. In a business environment long characterized by restrictive business strategies, the capacity of the state to initiate and force investments and reorganizations that will permit growth is an invaluable asset. The uses of state power and the balance between public and private power, it must be emphasized again, are continually shifting. Immediately after the war the emphasis was on increasing production and managing domestic demand, but the challenge of an open economy has laid emphasis on the creation of internationally competitive firms. Reconstruction for production and reorganization for competition pushed the firms into the arms of the state, but now business, fully competitive in an international marketplace, may in fact find the leverage to establish distance from the state. Importantly, as the state's policy goals have evolved its tactics have also changed, moving somewhat away from direction and closer to seduction.

When an industry's problems can actually be remedied by massive, directed investment and when the appropriate strategy can be selected by a centralized organization, as was the case in the oil and steel industries, the initiatives of the French state can be expected to be effective. Both oil and steel are capital-intensive basic industries which produce relatively homogeneous goods, the product of one firm being little different from the products of another; this makes price the only basis of competition and eases the problems of managing the market, a task that falls to the state in the oil sector and to the trade association in the steel sector. If adequate natural resources are available, then the critical problem is to assure sufficient and appropriate production facilities. In these industries production technologies are relatively stable, both because fundamental technical changes are not an everyday occurrence and because the heavy capital investment inevitably locks the firms into long-term choices. The massive investment required to implement basic technical change requires high-level choices to be made within an organization at any rate, and because the technical evolutions are slow, the central management can reasonably acquaint itself with the choices. Essentially, centralized decision making is appropriate in industries such as these. As Lawrence and Lorsch point out, a stable technical and market environment calls for centralized decision-making structures.[21]

The task in steel was to force a structure of ownership that could accommodate the most modern technologies, and then to insure the public and private investment to create them. Massive, new seaside facilities made the existing mélange of small firms wildly inappropriate, while financial difficulties in the industry, caused by the conjuncture of declining demand and strict price controls, allowed the state (acting through the trade association in this instance) to restructure the industry. The new production facilities are being built by the coordination of public capital improvements investment and long-term, low-interest loans provided by the state. The problem in oil was to create French oil companies where none existed, and here, once again, the state initiated and guaranteed the existence of two wholly French firms, one a semi-public company created in alliance with a banque d'affaire and the other an entirely nationalized firm. In both instances, the capacity to direct capital investment was critical.

The vital tasks in electronics are quite different. Success in this industry depends on rapid technological innovation which can be continuously adapted to shifting market possibilities. This is not a capital-intensive industry, and, in fact many of the dominant international firms have been built by rapid expansion rather than by mergers.[22] Mergers that disrupt company organization and interfere with ongoing product development can ultimately be self-defeating. Thus, a capacity to direct massive capital investment and initiate and promote mergers that bring together public and private efforts is of limited value. The rapid pace of technological and market evolution, furthermore, makes it extremely difficult for a central executive within a firm, let alone in the state, to make appropriate product and process decisions. Similarly, it is quite difficult to cartelize such an industry. Interestingly, even in America direct government efforts in electronics to push technological evolution along particular tracks have not been successful, even though these choices were made by technical administrations involved in the use of the technologies. American government aid was important in promoting technological evolution because different agencies were effective in picking up and supporting *privately* initiated efforts. This was possible in part because the fragmentation of responsibility, particularly the division between the military and NASA, created a variety of independent funding sources. Equally, the ready availability of venture capital in the 1960s was an important factor in allowing a multitude of private efforts to push ahead. The diffusion of American efforts was critical to the success of the American electronics industry. The centralization of the French state and the pressure felt by a smaller state to coordinate limited resources pushed in exactly the opposite direction—toward state-initiated mergers, involvement in technological strategies, and concentration of public and private efforts.

The same organizational structures which meant distinctive competence when the state intervened in oil and steel were distinctive handicaps in electronics. In all three cases, as argued in Chapter 3, the state pursued the same strategy, creating operating companies, channelling capital flows, and establishing guaranteed markets by wielding state power and manipulating the web of school and social ties between the top echelon of businessmen and government officials. This strategy was successful in technically stable, heavy investment, production-oriented industries, but it generated problems in a technically unstable and market-oriented industry. Centralized organizational structure is appropriate for a firm in the oil or steel industry—indeed, in many senses it is essential—while a decentralized structure is appropriate in electronics.

The lesson, then, is perhaps that when the government attempts to initiate or manage industrial activity, the structure of the state bureaucracy must correspond to the structure of an efficient firm in the industry, or the state will generate the same problems that an improperly organized industrial management would generate. Thus, for example, the Soviets, who have a highly centralized bureaucracy, have had their greatest success managing heavy industry and have had serious difficulties in electronics. In contrast, America has had major success in electronics, but now finds it inordinately difficult to formulate or implement a coordinated energy policy, a task that would be well-suited to French competences. The problem, of course, is for the state to compensate for its handicaps in industries where its structure may be inappropriate, since unlike a business it cannot simply reorganize for industrial tasks.

The French government, one would predict, would be most effective supporting basic product-oriented supply industries or oligopolistic consumer goods industries with basically stable products, such as automobiles, and less effective in market-oriented industries. It remains a matter of debate, incidentally, whether the state could exert its power on less concentrated industries if it chose. Pointing to the policy instruments at its disposal, some observers conclude that the state could exert influence in diffused industries if it chose to do so. The work of McArthur and Scott, however, clearly concludes that despite the state's concerns in less concentrated, more market-oriented industreies such as machine tools, it was not successful in shaping the industry to its liking. The issue is not formal power, but the ability to focus and direct influence. Here we should recall Stoleru's belief that a few firms should dominate critical industries to facilitate the exercise of state power. Certainly many sectors besides oil and steel meet these characteristics—diverse industries such as electrical generating equipment, rail transport, or nuclear power, to name only a few. From another perspective, one might expect the French to be effective in areas of reconstruction or in adjustment to new technological resource conditions.

In a sense, then, the French possess a capacity to manipulate the industrial infrastructure of their economy—the industries supplying energy, material, and transport. Manipulation of these industries, one might argue, can create the conditions for expansion, transformation, and growth in the rest of the economy. According to *L'Express* (April 28 through May 4, 1975) in 1974 five industries received the bulk of state investment funds: steel (530 million francs), oil (216 million francs), electronics (375 million francs), naval construction (626 million francs), and aeronautics (1,368 million francs). An evaluation of state policy, then, would rest on the selection of priority industries and the strategies adopted for or with the firms in them. Part of recent public investment in industry (whether by loan or subsidy) has served to preserve existing jobs, and part has served to advance the economic infrastructure; but, importantly, a significant amount of the money in aeronautics (the Concorde) and electronics (the Plan Calcul) has served only symbolic purposes. The end of the Plan Calcul and the expansion of investment in telephones are among the signs that suggest a reorientation of public investment on economic criteria.

National Industrial Policy in an International Economy

Extraordinary international competitive pressure as much as any mistaken tactics of state intervention produced the difficulties of the French electronics industry and therefore the focus of our discussion must now move from the domestic to the international arena. The French, unable to control the international development of this industry or to insulate their firms from it, were unwilling to adjust to the constraints of the market. In fact, one might argue that the critical difference between the electronics case and that of oil and steel was not the specifics of sectoral policy, but rather the ability of the French state to mediate the access of foreigners to the national marketplace. Seen in this light, traditional French tactics of industrial intervention might be said to work when the French state can act as gatekeeper to the French economy. It might be argued, however, that the problems of international economic interdependence no longer permit the nation-state to play this gatekeeper role, interposing itself between domestic industry and the international economy. Taken alone, the electronics case could indeed suggest such a position; but the French state, working in an active fashion that simply extends its domestic strategies to the international scene, has in fact been able to establish generally acceptable terms of economic interdependence in industries such as oil and steel, terms that certainly could be considered better than anything that would have been achieved by the private sector without state intervention.

In France, the centralized and semi-autonomous state pursuing a politically defined and generally unified policy has been the central force in foreign economic initiatives, just as it was the initiator of postwar reconstruction and expansion. Moreover, French foreign economic policy ought to be seen as an extension of its domestic industrial strategies to the international scene.[23]

The basic intent of French economic policy, both at home and abroad, has been to insure acceptable economic and social outcomes by political means if necessary, suppressing or restructuring the market when required. During the Third Republic, essentially from the end of the war of 1870 until the Second World War, protectionist policies sought to insulate France from the international economy so that economic life could be arranged among national groups, with the state arbitrating differences. After the war, increasing economic interdependence—produced by the establishment of an open, liberal world economy and by the explosion of transportation and communication technology—and a French commitment to rapid industrialization made simple protectionist policies inappropriate and inadequate. The state was therefore forced into an activist role abroad as well as at home, and successive governments, using the extensive powers of the French state, sought to arrange and secure France's position in the international economy.

The French strategy, then, has been to specify particular economic outcomes and to attempt to dictate them by political tactics, not simply to create conditions that favor French firms. The particular tactics of foreign economic policy reflect this basic policy stance. Most obviously, the fundamental political deals which created the institutions of European integration, the European Coal and Steel Community and then the European Economic Community itself (EEC), secured subsidies for the French peasantry and the access of French steel to adequate iron ore. The story of the Common Market has been a continuing effort to advance the interests of French agriculture—the rest of the EEC providing a subsidy to French farmers, through the Common Agricultural Policy, that relieved pressure on the French government. Equally important, bilateral state trading agreements and manipulation of the Franc Zone financial structures have created guaranteed markets for French exports that have been directly linked to domestic industrial strategies,[24] a trading tactic widely used in electronics policy. Such direct arrangements were reinforced by direct and indirect export subsidies: exemption from some taxes and domestic price controls that made foreign markets seem attractive, for example. Finally, the state has managed to mediate access to the French market, despite the elimination of internal tariffs in Europe and a common external tariff. In oil and in some segments of the electronics industry, for example, the state simply assigns market shares to particular firms. (See Chapter 3.) The continuing capacity to act as an intermediary between the domestic and international market—to mediate selectively if not entirely control the external pressures—gives the French state considerable power to affect domestic activity, thus, in fact, increasing its influence with French industry. In turn, the ability to affect directly the organization and behavior of domestic industry makes the state a more effective intermediary.

Under what conditions, though, are these strategies and tactics workable, or, more exactly, what are the limits on the nation's ability to protect or direct a domestic industry in an international economy? Put somewhat differently, under what conditions has the French state been able to mediate access to the national marketplace? In the case of oil, the French were able to wrench back control of their domestic market from foreign companies, but in the case of electronics they were unable to maintain an acceptable degree of control. In each instance, critically, the problem was not simply defending against a post-World War Two wave of foreign penetration; rather, it was a matter of reversing a pattern of control and production that had been established for the most part between the wars, when oil and electronics suddenly appeared to be crucial industries requiring national control. Multinational oil companies had long supplied the bulk of the French market; at one time before the CFP (the oil company created with state support) was set up in the 1920s (see Chapter 3), they supplied virtually all of it. The decision made in 1959 to use oil as a transitional energy source in the shift from coal to nuclear power seemed to require even greater direct French influence. Similarly in electronics, IBM had long held an important share of the business equipment market in France, although in this instance the collapse of Machines Bull during the transition of office machines from electro-mechanical to electronic equipment and the intense competition of other U.S. firms expanded the American market share. It was the actual and mythical importance of the computer industry, however, as much as the expansion of American market shares, that focused attention on the industry. The concern over the interpenetration of national economies is raised as much by increased demands for national control, resulting from increased pressures for political control of domestic economic events, as by fundamental changes in the pattern of international economic activity.[25]

Let us, then, reexamine the three cases, focusing on the state's capacity to mediate between domestic industry and the international economy. In the petroleum industry, the French state was able to assure an adequate supply of crude oil and to control the distribution of refined products to provide guaranteed markets for companies of its choice. Crude oil supplies are, as we have discovered recently, ultimately in the hands of the government controlling the territory where they are produced. Thus, successive French governments were able to negotiate for oil supplies on a state-to-state basis, tying oil purchases to a package of relationships between govenments. Whether private companies could have made better bargains during those years is a moot point; what is important is that the French could and did operate on a bilateral political basis. Since the import of massive quantities of oil requires special facilities, the government can easily monitor the import of refined products and the origin of crude supplies, requiring companies to build facilities in France if they wish access to the French market. Those refineries, in turn, provide a second monitoring point, and, in fact, control over the number and ownership of these facilities amounts to control of the final products market. The characteristics of final products, moreover, are relatively stable and can be affected only by altering the technology of refining, a slow process at best. Finally, within a very wide range, product costs are not critical, assuming that balance-of-payment problems are not generated by paying for the crude supplies. These costs can be passed on to consumers without serious distortion of the economy.

By contrast, in electronics, the state could not itself assure a supply of the critical electronics products, components, or final goods. It had to depend on private companies to develop and manufacture a constantly evolving range of goods at a pace set in the international market-place. (See Chapter 5 for a detailed analysis of the policy dilemma in this industry.) The capacity of the firms to respond, finally, depended on their ability to compete in international markets, because the state was unable to insulate them from its pressure and powerless to restruc-ture the international industry. Over the years adequate *supplies* could only be assured by healthy firms, but competition was the greatest in the products of greatest immediate interest to the state. The tech-nological goals of the state weakened the competitive position of the firms, while erosion of the firms' market positions diminished the capacity of the state to pursue its technological goals. Nor could the state assure *markets* to the firms for the bulk of their production. Most of the product purchase decisions were in private hands as well. The state could have only a limited impact on these choices, in part because the decision-makers were diffused and partly because price and quality of products could not be equated at a single point—such as at the refinery in the case of oil. French firms and their foreign competitors were not selling identical products, and price and quality differences in these goods mattered to the purchasers. Unable to assure supply or control markets, the state was essentially helpless.

Steel is somewhat more confusing. The state could assure an adequate, domestically produced supply and it could control its price. International and particularly inter-European trade in steel did increase after the war, but such trade was never so extensive that it threatened the existence or well-being of the French industry. The international steel market appears to be a competitive, often high-cost supplement to domestic production during periods of upswing, not a threat to national producers' control of their domestic market. Several explanations are possible. The simplest would be that of location advantages, assuming that reasonably parallel production costs are of such advantage that traditional sales patterns will be disrupted only by massive shifts in supply or costs. This would imply that the state need only assure reasonably efficient production, and the market will act to preserve national patterns of production. Extensive international trade in steel, and particularly Japanese success in this area, however, suggest that location does not firmly fix market patterns.

The question remains whether the French did act directly to assure and protect national steel markets, despite the elimination of inter-European tariffs. State influence is enormous in major steel consuming industries such as aircraft, naval construction, automobiles, and the like, and market patterns may be sustained, therefore, by pressure on purchasers. Alternatively, pressure might be brought on foreign producers or governments to prevent an invasion of the French market. There is no direct evidence of such efforts, and probably they did not seem necessary. Any temptation a more efficient foreign producer may have had to invade the French market, assuming that transport costs did not eat too deeply into his product advantage, would be dampened by the obvious willingness of the French to protect the well-being of their firms. A real invasion of the French market, a replacement of French producers in their own market, would require the expansion of production facilities, which would be a costly and potentially dangerous undertaking. Also, the French could respond by subsidizing domestic production, whatever the restrictions of the Rome Treaty, or by subsidizing exports to the invading country. Such a potential would discourage taking the massive risk of expanding plant capacity.

The European steel industry, in essence, is a stable oligopoly supported by national policy, and unless one element withers, leaving a vacuum, no one would seem to have much to gain from a destabilizing of the present arrangements. Furthermore, the dependence of the other European steel companies on their national governments means that a rival would in essence have to approve, if not finance, an invasion of the French market—a serious political provocation. Thus, in some ways, the oligopolistic structure of European steel companies dependent on national governments creates a situation in which power never need be directly exerted in order to keep out foreign production.

The essence of this analysis, then, is that the state can stand as intermediary between a national industry and the international market—cut off the national economy from the world economy, as it were—when by its own actions it can assure a stable supply of the product and control the market in which the product is sold. Such an intermediary role depends, it would seem, on an autonomous capacity for leadership in domestic industry, and on the ability to coordinate and direct diverse state powers in support of politically defined economic outcomes. This is easiest for stable products sold to a handful of consumers who are open to influence from the state, and it is most difficult for rapidly evolving products sold to a diverse and diffuse consuming public. This analysis, as noted earlier, should not imply that only goods such as oil and steel, which are inputs to other products, meet these standards. Civilian radar, electrical generating equipment, and even television systems all evolve at steady but not blinding paces and can be sold only to governmental or semi-governmental bodies. Even in an interdependent world, then, a nation-state may be able to influence the terms of trade in a wide variety of essential industries.

Whether or not the French strategy of engaging in state intermediation, if not direct trading, to affect the terms of international exchange is successful,* it certainly runs against the grain of the present structure of the international economic system, a liberal system in which the states establish and guarantee the rules of the game, while leaving the actual play to private firms. In fact, with the partial exception of the period between the two World Wars, an open and liberal system has characterized international exchange since the early part of the nineteenth century. England in the earlier period served as an open clearinghouse for commodities and goods from the whole world, an exchange financed by a gold-based Sterling pound and defended by the British navy. As E. H. Carr writes, "The primary foundation of the nineteenth-century economic system was the provision [by England] of a single wide-open and apparently insatiable market for all consumable commodities. It was the existence of this national market which made the so-called international system work. The international system, simple in its conception but infinitely complex in its technique, called into being a delicate and powerful financial machine whose seat was in the city of London."[26] Britain was economically but not politically dominant, and was able to play this economic role because it was tolerated by her political rivals. Economics and politics became divorced, either because trade was so essential to all powers that none would interfere with it (Polanyi's explanation),[27] or because the continental balance of power and the supremacy of the British navy meant no one could interfere (Carr's interpretation).[28] At any rate, English industrialization

---

*Any effort at a precise, overall evaluation of the impact of French foreign economic policy on the well-being of domestic society would, in fact, be virtually impossible. One would have to compare the development of each industry under different assumptions about government activity, a difficult task in itself, and allow in the calculus of benefit and cost varied judgments of the social and economic value of political objectives such as energy independence or limiting political agitation. Moreover, in an important sense, once an interventionist policy was chosen, a strategy of state leadership was most likely to emerge. In that case, a meaningful critique of policy can really focus on the state's choice of industries and the tactics in employed in dealing with those chosen few.

was led by a merchant class turned manufacturers, and its economic empire was built on trade. The flood of trade created by rapid English industrial growth and by imperial expansion, however, threatened industrial interests on the continent, while a flood of cheap grain from the United States and Eastern Europe in the later part of the nineteenth century upset agricultural groups. International trade itself allowed liberal rules, but individual countries could insulate portions of their economy from the fortunes of trade and economic development abroad. Only England kept both agricultural and industrial tariffs low, while Germany and France in particular established uniformly high trade walls, a political task which reinforced parliamentary democracy in France and laid the foundations for Fascism in Germany.[29] Thus, in the nineteenth as well as the twentieth century, the changing character of international economic interdependence profoundly affected domestic politics, in some cases producing radical political adjustments.

The neo-liberal character of the postwar Western international economy had its roots in the political activities of the American government dating from the last years of the war, as Fred Block and Calleo and Rowland have convincingly argued.[30] America vigorously sought to establish an international economic order in which the private firm—not the state, the business association, or cartel—was the primary agent of exchange. That system was constructed on two principles: an automatically adjusting international monetary system built on the dollar (at least until August 1971) that replaced the British Sterling system; and open access for private American companies to the economies of non-Communist countries. Open access, in particular, distinguishes this current liberal period dominated by America from that constructed by the British in the nineteenth century. The American economic empire was built, in essence, on an open door policy, not on direct colonial control. This empire required permission for "transnational organizations," controlled by Americans but operating throughout the world, to perform their specific technical and business tasks (or functions); it did not require control of the politics or administration of the various host governments. Samuel Huntington puts it succinctly when he writes, "Transnationalism is the American mode of expansion." America, he argues, could become expansionist but not colonialist, and evolved a polity designed to assure "access not acquisition."[31] Once such a political system was in place, the evolution of transportation and communication technology in an expansionary economic setting produced a vast expansion of American multinational business and the creation, in response, of European multinational firms.

Whether the sources of the current Western industrial structure are political or technological, it would be more difficult to close the currently open system than it would have been, perhaps, to have prevented it from opening in the first place. At any rate, in both the periods of British and American preeminence, the structure of the international economic system, the rules of trade and exchange, and the institutions that defended those rules reflected the structure of the domestic economy of the dominant country—in each case, a country with liberal structures emphasizing private, not state, power. In both eras, the French used state power to protect their interests, erecting tariffs to cut themselves off from the international economy during the British empire in the nineteenth century and negotiating a place for her industries during the more recent years of American hegemony. Such an interpretation, of course, accounts for French oil dealings in terms other than simple pique with Washington. Their bilateral, state-to-state dealings are simply a continuation of oil policies pursued for years before 1973.

Thus, to observe that the basic statist strategy of French foreign economic policy, rooted in the structures of domestic society, runs against the prevailing international winds is really to argue that France is engaged in economic competition according to rules that tend to favor the domestic structure of a stronger power, the United States. One might therefore ask whether the French are handicapped in this competition. It is not at all clear, in fact, that a statist strategy in a liberal economy is a problem at all. The national evolution of American firms prepared them well for multi-national operation, giving them both the capacity to operate over extensive geographic distances (a basic strategy of competition, not cartelization) and the habit of acting independently of government, though enlisting its support when possible. American firms, then, could enter distant markets, unconcerned in a sense with government attitudes short of outright hostility, and ready to engage national firms in a fight for their local business.[32] The heritage of French firms made them ill-fitted for such a life, and when they engaged in such a direct competition, one could argue, French industries did not hold their own. In all fairness, some observers point to the apparently successful adjustments made by French firms during the brief era of free trade under Napoleon III as evidence that such a transition actually could have been made. Nonetheless, England suggests to some the fate of one open, liberal economy competing with another stronger one, the United States—an argument with some merit, though the German example clearly indicates that American power did not dictate British decline.

What's critical, at any rate, is that a state-led economic strategy permitted the French to mobilize national power to defend against private American multinationals. *The French in essence, thought they would be able, and often were able, to match a state formulated political strategy against a privately formulated economic strategy, hoping in a sense to create selective power mismatches that favored them.* Such a strategy, one might guess, is more likely to be successful when the French are the only or predominant political actor. When an economic issue is politicized for everyone, bringing other states into the game, then one might expect that the French, simply one medium-sized power, would lose much of their advantage. Such a strategy, evidently, could not be successful in all circumstances, and we have just suggested those in which a state-led strategy would be most appropriate; but then the American formula has certainly not been appropriate in all instances either, even in a liberal setting. The point here is that the mismatch between the liberal character of the international economy and the state-dominated character of French society did not in any simple fashion penalize the French.

It is the thrust of this argument, then, that the French capacity to achieve specific economic goals is limited as much by the relative power of the French state and society in the international community as it is by the constraints of interdependence. It is crucial, therefore, to separate analytically American hegemony from the dynamics of economic interdependence, lest the effects of the one be attributed to the other.[33] France is a medium-sized nation with limited resources, by comparison with America, attempting to exert the influence of a major power. In the 1960s, for example, the international monetary system was organized around the dollar as a reserve currency, which provided America with leeway in international political and economic affairs and favored the free movement of capital across national boundaries by private corporations. The French inability to reorganize the system along lines which would allow greater state control and French influence reflected the political and economic domination of America and the relative weakness of the French, not the autonomous power of a transnational monetary system.

Importantly, it was the private Euro-currency market which facilitated the flow of funds from one currency to another outside political control, and thus increased the vulnerability of politically determined monetary arrangements to purely private economic responses. That market, however, emerged not as a product of irresistible economic forces, but as part of a Bank of England policy to maintain England as an international financial center despite the decline of Sterling as an international currency. Such a policy required that London-based banks be free to conduct their international operations in the new international money, dollars.[34]

Whether a Euro-currency system or some surrogate would have emerged elsewhere is open to debate. Certainly, there were depositors who wanted to place funds in an international market for political reasons, or because of the higher interest this unregulated market offered, and there were borrowers who wished access to these funds and to the flexibility the network provided. Others, for political reasons, did not want to borrow in a particular national capital market. Apart from their economic services the international money markets, now referred to loosely as the Euro-markets, often served to filter out politics from finance by inserting an international consortium between borrower and lender. A clientele for the market existed, but if London had not been the site what would have been? London, a broad and deep financial market, is able to spread risks widely and permit individual positions to be disposed of without disruption. Offshore banking in the Caribbean could provide access to such a system, but on its own could never have been the base. New York was ruled out because of government regulation, which in part provoked the placement of funds in the Euro-markets in the first place, though those regulations are now gone and New York has a substantial share of the business. Switzerland could have been an alternate site, but bankers are divided as to whether such a system could have emerged there. Such a market favored London as a financial capital and certainly served the purposes of many multinational companies, but the emergence of this market might well have been politically restrained. Transnational monetary arrangements had power within a particular international political setting.

The French simply did not have the power to impose a system more to their liking. In the electronics case that has been the center of our discussion, the preponderant weight of the American market and government purchases forced the French to adapt to the international marketplace that was created in large part by the Americans. The French had to adapt precisely because they did not have the power to resist this market structure.

The question now, of course, is the impact of declining American hegemony on the international economic system. Huntington recognizes this problem when he writes:

> The principal legacy of American expansion about the world is a network of transnational institutions knitting the world together in ways that never existed in the past. The question for the future is whether and how the contraction of the world brought about by the expansion of the American role will survive the contraction

of that role. Once the political conditions which gave it birth disappear, how much transnationalism will remain?[35]

In fact, a less automatically adjusting, more negotiated international economy seems the likely outcome of the decline of the dollar as an unchallenged reserve currency and the emerging power of the oil cartel over a resource vital to all industrial economies. An increasingly politicized world, where power and politics are less clearly divorced from economic arrangements, would seem to be an environment well-suited to the French capacity for concerted strategic action; yet, if economic conflict becomes overt political conflict, the limited resources of a middle-range power may become more of a constraint on French policy goals than the seeming independence of private actors was in a more open period. The triumph of the French assertion that economics *is* politics, then, may prove a handicap, not an advantage. In such an event, however, the foreign economic strategy of France would most certainly cease to appear anachronistic, and would even emerge as a model for others to follow.

Notes

Chapter 1. Industrial Politics and Economic Activity

1. Charles Kindleberger, *Economic Growth in Britain and France* (New York: Simon and Schuster, 1964).

2. *Ibid.*, p. 34. See also A. O. Hirschman, *Strategy of Economic Development* (New Haven; Yale University Press, 1958).

3. Edward Mead Earle, ed., *Modern France: Problems of the Third and Fourth Republic* (New York: Russell and Russell, 1964).

4. Merrick Brian Garland, "Industrial Reorganization in Britain" (Honors Thesis, Harvard College, 1974).

5. Reference to these practices is made in unpublished work by Suzanne Berger. Other practices similar in kind occurring at early periods are cited by Henry Ehrman, *Organized Business in France* (Princeton University Press, 1957), and in an unpublished paper by Heinrich August Winkler, "From Social Protectionism to National Socialism," presented at the Harvard Conference on Twentieth Century Capitalism, September 1974.

6. David Granick, *Managerial Comparisons of Four Developed Countries* (M.I.T. Press, 1972).

7. An interesting exception is the French steel cartel, which was effective at least in part because only the cartel could approach the banks. Control over investment meant control over the market. In later years when the state could control prices, thus forcing firms to go to the bank, and also controlled the banks, this process gave the state great power in the industry's rationalization.

8. Eugene Golob, *The Meline Tariff* (New York: Colombia University Press, 1944).

9. Stanley Hoffmann, "Paradoxes of the French Political Community," in Hoffmann, ed., *In Search of France* (New York: Harper Torch Books, 1967).

10. *Ibid.*, p. 6.

11. Carré, Jean Jacques; Malivaud, Paul; Dubois, Edmond *La Croissance francaise* (Paris: Seuil, 1972).

12. Charles Kindleberger, "The Post-war Resurgence of the French Economy," in Hoffmann, ed., *In Search of France.*

13. *Ibid.*

14. See Stephen Cohen, *Modern Capitalist Planning* (Cambridge: Harvard University Press, 1969).

15. Stanley Hoffmann, "The State: For What Society?" in Hoffmann, *Decline or Renewal? France Since the 1930s* (New York: Viking Press, 1974).

16. *Ibid.*, p. 450.

17. Jean Charlot, *Le phénomène Gaulliste* (Paris: Fayard, 1970).

18. A variety of works, including those of Calleo and Rowland and Fred Block, point to this conclusion.

19. Kindleberger, *"Europe's Post-war Growth: The Role of Labor Supply* (Cambridge: Harvard University Press, 1967).

20. Suzanne Berger, lectures and conversations.

21. H. Aujac, BIPE (Bureau d'Information et Prevision Economique), unpublished article.

22. Jack Hayward, "Steel," in Raymond Vernon, *Big Business and the State* (Cambridge: Harvard University Press, 1974).

23. See Alexander Gerschenkron, *Economic Development in Historical Perspective* (Cambridge: Harvard University Press, 1962); and David Landes, *Unbound Prometheus* (London: Cambridge University Press, 1969).

24. Maurice Levy-Leboyer, *Les Banques Européenes et L'Industrialisation Internationale dans la première moitié du XIXe Siècle* (Paris: Presses Universitaires Paris de France, 1964).

25. One could argue that micro-economic analysis details one set of constraints and their predicted impact on the behavior of one or several firms. Clearly, the behavior of economic institutions and their exercise of power over economic choices cannot be understood apart from the political setting.

26. The lines of political cleavage represented by the conflicts amongst these primary economic actors might variously be described as interest-group politics, elite politics, or class conflict, depending not merely on one's theoretical and political views, but also on the issues and settings.

Chapter 2. Technological Evolution and French Organization

1. This example was pointed out to me by Richard Gordon.

2. David S. Landes, *The Unbound Prometheus* (London: Cambridge University Press, 1972), pp. 188-190.

3. Alexander Gerschenkron, *Bread and Democracy in Germany* (New York: H. Fertig, 1966).

4. Joan Woodward, *Industrial Organization, Theory, and Practice* (London: Oxford University Press, 1965). Hereafter cited as Woodward (1965).

5. William Zwerman, *New Perspectives on Organization Theory* (Minneapolis: Greenwood Press, 1970).

6. Paul Lawrence and Jay Lorsch, *Organization and Environment* (Cambridge: Harvard University Press, 1967).

7. Joan Woodward, *Industrial Organization, Behavior, and Control* (London: Oxford University Press, 1969), p. 4.

8. Christopher Layton, *Ten Innovations* (London: George Allen & Unwin, 1972).

9. Woodward (1965), p. 38. (See note 4.)

10. The five structural relations are: (a) as complexity increased *the number of levels of authority* in the hierarchy also increased from a median of three levels among unit firms to five in batch production and six in process production; (b) *the span of control of the chief* executive, the number of people reporting to him, and in that sense a measure of centralization, also grew; (c) in contrast, *the span of control of middle managers* was very low among firms at the extremes of the scale (unit and process production), while it was quite broad in the middle. The reason appears to be that at the extremes, work is broken into small primary groups, while in the middle range it is not; (d) *the ratio of supervisory to non-supervisory* personnel declined steadily from a ratio of one supervisor for every 23 workers in unit production to one for every eight in process production; (3) finally, increasing technical complexity required

greater capital investment with a resulting reduction in the ratio of labor costs to production costs. *Ibid.*, Chapter 4. (All figures in the paragraph are from this chapter.)

11. Woodward (1965), p. 32.

12. *Ibid.*, Chapter 4.

13. Tom Burns, *The Management of Innovation* (London: Travistock, 1961). In this study of the Scottish electronics industry Burns suggested the distinction between organic and mechanic management. He argued that "organic" management would be required by the new science-based industries such as electronics.

14. Woodward (1965), p.23.

15. *Ibid.*, p. 24.

16. Zwerman, *New Perspectives*, p. 52.

17. Woodward (1965), p. 64. Woodward fails to explain the similarity between the management systems of unit and process production, technologies that differ from each other in so many other ways. Simply combining them under a single heading without further comment is not satisfactory, because the differences are distinctive as well.

The basic similarity is that work in unit and process production is broken into small primary groups, where individuals must know each other. Work organized through a social group doesn't explain informality, since many social groups have formal and authoritarian characters. The source of informality, perhaps the basic characteristic of organic management, may in fact be quite different in each case.

In unit production, the continual change in products makes the exact operations of the organization uncertain. As a result, continual day-to-day operational relationships between unpredictable combinations of task functions are essential, and thus encourage horizontal communication. In process production, we are often told that work swings between monotony and crisis. Routine work revolves around the monitoring of the machine, and the individual's contribution to production is indirect. This has two important consequences. First, since the machine sets the pace of production, close supervision of the man who monitors the machine will not affect the rate of production. Second, the machine itself is a mechanical control system; its operations define the specific tasks of the individual and determine when they must be performed. Moreover, monitoring work can be controlled from written records. Thus, routine work in process production finds men in small groups performing tasks which do not require close personal supervision. Crisis, on the other hand, puts speed of communication at a premium and informality has real benefits. It is also possible that mechanical control of the work in process production allows the social groups to arrange themselves freely, and those groups might be arranged differently in different cultures. One might observe that the informality in process-control industry may in fact be rooted in American and British culture, not in technology.

18. *Ibid.*, p. 69.

19. *Ibid.*, p. 71.

20. *Ibid.*, p. 72.

21. Lawrence and Lorsch, *Organization and Environment*.

22. Woodward (1965), p. 17.

23. The well-argued and controversial piece, "What Bosses Do," by Professor Stephen Marglin of Harvard's Economics Department, carries the political argument even further. He contends that hierarchies in production organization and technologies, such as factories, which make hierarchy necessary, developed not because they were more efficient, but because they permitted the entrepreneur to control the work process and thus the profit associated with it. The argument suggests that technological efficiency is at its root a political, not simply an economic, fact; and that the most efficient production method can be defined only *after* assuming the relations of social power

within a society. Once technological evoluton within particular class relationships began and technological development along that route was underway, alternative forms of production could no longer compete. Whether Marglin is correct or not does not affect the argument presented here; the course of technological evolution had been underway for centuries in the West, and thus economic and technological efficiency do coincide, and a revolution would be required to undo the hierarchical structures built up. For those interested in the history of technology, the original dynamics of the industrial revolution, and the technical limits on the organization of industrial society, the article makes compelling reading. See Stephen Marglin, "What Bosses Do," *The Review of Radical Political Economics,* Vol. 6, No. 2 (Summer 1974).

24. Lawrence and Lorsch, *Organization and Environment.*

25. James Thompson, *Organization in Action* (Pittsburgh: University of Pittsburgh Press, 1966).

26. Sherwin Chalmers and Raymond Isanson, "Project Hindsight," *Science,* June 23, 1970, p. 571.

27. Don Marquiss and Thomas Allen, "Communications Patterns in Applied Technology," *American Psychologist,* November 11, 1966.

28. This discussion is based on a paper written by Jay Galbraith for MIT's Sloan School of Management, "Organization Design: An Information Processing View," Working Paper, MIT, 1968, p. 12.

29. *Ibid.,* p. 2.

30. Thomas Allen, "Meeting the Technical Information Needs of Research and Development Projects," Sloan School Working Paper, MIT, November 1969.

31. Jay Galbraith, "Organization Design: An Information Processing View," MIT Working Paper, No. 425-69, October 1969.

32. *Ibid.*

33. There is evidence suggesting that the success of the Japanese electronics firms, particularly Sony, was in part a result of effective strategic choices, not only of products but also of lines of development. This, though, required that the director have an intimate knowledge of the reality of his firm.

34. Jay Galbraith, "Boeing Research Project," MIT Working Paper, No. 325-68, October 1968.

35. Jay Lorsch, *Product Innovation and Organizational Structure* (New York: MacMillan Company, 1965).

36. Lawrence and Lorsch, *Organization and Environment.*

37. See Andre Ruldi, "Organization in Two Cultures," in Paul Lawrence and Jay Lorsch, *Studies in Organizational Design* (Homewood: Irwin, 1970).

38. Ruby Bjarne, "Product Innovation in Organization," unpublished paper.

39. Jack A. Morton, "The Innovation Process," *Bell Telephone Magazine,* Fall 1966, pp. 2-15.

40. Michel Crozier, *The Bureaucratic Phenomenon* (Chicago: University of Chicago Press, 1964), Chapter 8.

41. Schonfeld says, for example, "Virtually all recent general studies of France which mention authority . . . take Crozier's analysis as a factual given." See William R. Schonfeld, "Authority in France, A Model of Political Behavior Drawn from Case Studies in Education" (Ph.D. thesis, Princeton, N.J.: Center of International Studies, 1970), p. vi.

42. *Ibid.,* p. 225.

43. *Ibid.,* p. 190.

44. *Ibid.*

45. *Ibid.,* pp. 204 and 208.
46. *Ibid.,* pp. 187-189.
47. *Ibid.,* p. 226.
48. *Ibid.*
49. *Ibid.,* p. 222.
50. *Ibid.*
51. David Granick, *Managerial Comparisons of Four Developed Countries* (Cambridge: MIT Press, 1972).
52. *Ibid.,* p. 80.
53. *Ibid.,* p. 251.
54. *Ibid.,* p. 60.
55. Charles Sabel, *"Mitbestimmung:* German Alternative to the Class Struggle," unpublished paper.
56. Thomas J. Allen, Arthur Gerstenfeld, and Peter Gerstberger, "The Problem of Internal Consulting in R and D Organizations," MIT Sloan School Working Paper, July 1965.
57. *Ibid.*
58. See Stanley Hoffmann *et al, In Search of France* (New York: Harper & Row, 1963).
59. Michel Crozier, *La Sociéte bloquée,* (Paris: Éditions du Seuil, 1970).

Chapter 3. A Competitive Industry in a Protective Tradition

1. Erhard Friedberg, "Promoting Structural Change in the Industrial Sector—a New Role for the French State?" Paper presented at the Harvard Conference on Government Industry Relations in Western Europe, Harvard, October 14-16, 1971, p. 4. The distinction between paternalistic and entrepreneurial roles for the state is in part drawn from his work.
2. Karl Polanyi, *The Great Transformation* (Boston: Beacon Press, 1957), p. 57.
3. Tom Kemp, *Economic Forces in French History* (London: Denis Dobson, 1971), Chapter 1; Barrington Moore, Jr., *Social Origins of Dictatorship and Democracy* (Boston: Beacon Press, 1966), Chapter 2.
4. Pierre Goubert, *The Ancien Regime, French Society, 1600-1750* (New York: Harper Torchbooks, 1974), English translation by Steve Cox; Kemp, *Economic Forces,* Chapter 1.
5. See Kemp, *Economic Forces,* and Goubert, *The Ancien Regime.*
6. See John U. Neff, *Industry and Government in France and England, 1540-1640* (Philadelphia: American Philosophical Society, Independence Square, 1940).
7. Herbert Luethy, *France Against Herself* (New York: Meridian Books, 1957), p. 25.
8. Kemp, *Economic Forces,* pp. 41, 109, 131.
9. *Ibid.,* p. 111.
10. Alexander Gerschenkron, *Economic Backwardness in Historical Perspective* (Cambridge: Harvard University Press, 1962), p. 44.
11. David S. Landes, *The Unbound Prometheus* (London: Cambridge University Press, 1972), pp. 118-119.
12. See Jean Bouvier, "The Banking Mechanism in France in the Late 19th Century," in Rondo Cameron, *Essays in French Economic History* (published by Richard Irwin for the American Economic Association, 1970); David S. Landes in Fr. Crouzet *et al.,* eds., *Essays in European Economic History* (New York: St. Martins Press, 1969).

13. Gerschenkron, *Economic Backwardness.*

14. Landes, *The Unbound Prometheus.*

15. *Ibid.*

16. Luethy, *France Against Herself,* p. 25.

17. Kemp, *Economic Forces,* p. 110.

18. *Ibid.,* p. 45.

19. *Ibid.,* p. 173.

20. *Ibid.,* p. 130.

21. *Ibid.,* p. 132.

22. See Eugene Owen Golob, *The Meline Tariff: French Agricultural and Nationalist Economic Policy* (New York: Columbia University Press, 1944).

23. Henry W. Ehrmann, *Organized Business in France* (Princeton, N.J.: Princeton University Press, 1957), p. 370.

24. John H. McArthur and Bruce R. Scott, *Industrial Planning in France* (Boston: Harvard University Division of Research, Graduate School of Business Administration, 1969), p. 196.

25. Ehrmann, *Organized Business,* p. 377.

26. McArthur and Scott, *Industrial Planning,* p. 195.

27. Friedberg, "Promoting Structural Change" (conference paper), pp. 4-7. *op. cit.*

28. Kemp, *Economic Forces,* p. 32.

29. *Ibid.,* p. 37.

30. Friedberg, "Promoting Structural Change," p. 8.

31. Jean-Claude Thoenig, *L'ère des technocrates* (Paris: Les Éditions d'Organisation, 1973), p. 233.

32. McArthur and Scott, *Industrial Planning.* This evidence does not contradict that of Nicole Delefortrie Soubeynoux, "Les Dirigeants de l'industrie française" (Librairie Armand Colin, 1961). Delefortrie is concerned with upper-level management, which is recruited from a number of schools, not with the "ruling" positions within a company.

33. Gareth Pooley-Dyas, *The Strategy and Structure of French Industrial Enterprise.* DBA thesis, Harvard, 1972, p. 77. The expanded competition in French markets is suggested by the growth of imports into France at a pace much faster than the GNP increased.

	1920	*1929*	*1939*	*1949*	*1954*	*1959*	*1964*	*1969*
Total Imports	113	124	100	100	126	170	324	546
GNP	70	119	107	109	140	170	234	304

Using 1954 as a base, imports increased 430 percent to a GNP growth of 210 percent, while using 1959 as a base the rates are 320 and 180 percent, respectively. (Figures from Pooley-Dyas, pp. 77-78.)

34. McArthur and Scott, *Industrial Planning,* pp. 208, 215.

35. See Raymond Vernon, *Big Business and the State* (Cambridge: Harvard University Press, 1974), Chapter 1.

36. Friedberg, "Promoting Structural Change," p. 7.

37. Lionel Stoleru, *L'impératif industriel* (Paris: Seuil, 1969), p. 218.

38. Friedberg, "Promoting Structural Change."

39. Private conversation.

40. McArthur and Scott, *Industrial Planning,* Chapter 9.

41. *Ibid.,* p. 311.

42. See Richard F. Kuisel, *Ernest Mercier, French Technocrat* (Berkeley: University of California Press, 1967); Pierre l'Espagnol de la Tramerye, *The World Struggle for Oil* (New York: Knopf, 1924), translated by C. Leonard Leese.

43. J. E. Hartshorn, *Politics and World Oil Economics* (New York: Praeger, 1962), pp. 262-266.

44. See *Ibid.*; M. A. Adelman, *The World Petroleum Market* (Baltimore: Johns Hopkins University Press, 1972).

45. Kuisel, *Ernest Mercier.*

46. See Hartshorn, *Politics and World Oil Economics.*

47. See "L'UGP Pivot de la nouvelle politique pétrolière française" (Paris: Enterprise, No. 536, December 18, 1965).

48. See Louis Lister, *Europe's Coal and Steel Community* (New York: Twentieth Century Fund, 1960).

49. See Bruno Le Cour Grandmaison, "The European Coal and Steel Community; The French Industry." M.A. thesis, University of California, Berkeley, Department of Economics.

50. *Ibid.*

51. Stephen Cohen, *Modern Capitalist Planning: The French Experience* (Cambridge, Mass.: Harvard University Press, 1969).

52. Lister, *Coal and Steel Community,* p. 132.

53. McArthur and Scott, *Industrial Planning,* Chapter 10.

54. *Ibid.*

55. *Ibid.,* p. 371.

56. Jack Hayward, "Steel," in Raymond Vernon, ed., *Big Business and the State* (Cambridge: Harvard University Press, 1974).

57. Personal interviews with steel industry bureaucrats.

58. Lister, *Coal and Steel Community,* p. 59.

59. Personal interviews.

60. Hayward, "Steel."

61. Pierre Mondeserat, "Bilan de la Convention État-Siderurgie du 29 juillet 1966." Mémoire à l'Institut des Études Politiques de Paris, 1970.

62. For example, McArthur and Scott, *Industrial Planning,* pp. 359-363.

63. Rapport du Groupe du Travail Électronique, 5th Plan, March 1966, p. 13.

64. The best chronology of the events leading to the Plan Calcul can be found in a dissertation at the Harvard Business School by Pierre Gardoneix, "The Case of the Plan Calcul." Much of this chronology is drawn from that material. That dissertation was submitted in 1975.

65. De Gaulle was certainly involved in the final choice, according to all reports available, but who actually made the decisions and the precise criteria and reasoning at that moment, as distinct from the criteria and reasoning of the proposals, remains obscure to me.

66. *Électronique Actualités,* July 2, 1971.

67. *Ibid.*

68. *Ibid.,* March 24, 1972.

69. "Note sur l'assouplissement de la gestion des crédits du fonds de développement de la Recherche Scientifique et Technique DGRST" (J/D Dardel, Paris, July 10, 1962).

70. John E. Tilton, *International Diffusion of Technology: The Case of Semi-Conductors* (Washington, D.C.: Brookings Institution, 1971), p. 85.

71. *Ibid.,* p. 14.

72. Data taken from the documents of the Sixth Plan.

73. *Ibid.*

74. Inter-European trade figures do not reveal the relative strengths of national producers because the implantation of multinational firms in European countries and the resulting division of production responsibility for the European market on a product basis promotes inter-European exchange, but the resulting data hides the position of

national firms. For example, Phillips, a Dutch firm, produces magnetophones in France and exports them to all of Europe, but all of their electrophones sold in France are imported. Because American firms seldom ship back the United States goods produced in Europe, and Third World countries have not (until the recent semiconductor crisis moved production of many American firms to the Far East) been sources of electronics goods, the American-European trade data are useful.

75. Speech by Paul Richard, President of Thomson-CSF, published in *Électronique Actualités*, February 4, 1972, p. 1.

76. See *Les Industries Électroniques*, a publication of the BIPE, Paris, 1965.

77. Pierre Rey, "L'Industrie de l'électronique en France." Thèse pour le Doctorat Sciences Économiques, Université de Paris, Faculté de Droit, 1975.

78. This discussion has been deeply influenced by Albert Hirschman's insightful work, *Exit, Voice, and Loyalty* (Cambridge: Harvard University Press, 1970).

79. See Alfred Chandler, *Strategy and Structure* (Cambridge: MIT Press, 1962).

80. Hirschman, *Exit, Voice, and Loyalty*.

81. A similar conclusion that involvement with the state had negative impact on R and D organization was reached in a study of American R and D effort: "The Effect of Goverment Funding on Commercial R and D," by Guy Black, in *Factors in the Transfer of Technology*, ed. William H. Gruber and Donald G. Marquiss (Cambridge: M.I.T. Press, 1969), p. 209: "The emerging picture [of the government impact] is one of a less flexible private R and D organization, with more organized and formalized procedures, finding it harder to change schedules, taking a longer time to get company work started, and experiencing more difficulty with emergency technical assistance."

82. The sections on military, telecommunications, and DGRST administrative procedures are based on interviews with the officials involved.

83. Based on a review of the meeting notes of the DGRST committee meetings.

84. My thanks to Jacques Cremer for this insight.

Chapter 4. Organizational Tradition and Change in the French Electronics Industry

1. Gareth Pooley-Dyas, "The Strategy and Structure of French Industrial Enterprise," Harvard Business School Dissertation, 1972.

2. George Trepo, "The Introduction of Management by Objective in France: Reality or Ritual." Unpublished dissertation, Harvard Business School, Boston, 1972.

3. Pooley-Dyas, "Strategy and Structure."

4. *Ibid.*

5. Trepo, "Management by Objective in France."

6. This project was completed a number of years ago, but all of the principal actors were easily accessible. Though their interactions at work could not be observed, the technological and organizational history is revealing.

Chapter 5. Between the Market and the State: Dilemmas of French Electronics Policy

1. See Robert Gilpin, *France in the Age of the Scientific State* (Princeton: Princeton University Press, 1968).

2. Private conversations throughout the research.

3. Jean-Jacques Salomon, "Europe and the Technology Gap," *International Studies Quarterly*, October-November 1970, pp. 5-31.

4. Among the published material see, for example, Lawrence Lessing, "Why the U.S. Lags in Technology," *Fortune*, April 1972, and Harvey Brooks' article in *Harvard Business Review*, Fall 1972. Several unpublished government studies put the problem in even stronger terms.

5. See Richard Nelson, "World Leadership, the 'Technological Gap,' and National Policy," *Minerva*, July 1971.

6. Quoted in Salomon, "Europe and the Technology Gap," p. 19.

7. Herbert Kleiman, "The Integrated Circuit" (DBA *Thesis*, The George Washington University, 1966), Chapter 6.

8. Christopher Freeman, "Research and Development in Electronic Capital Goods," *National Institute Economic Review* (London), No. 34, November 1965, p. 71.

9. Frederic Scherer, *Industrial Market Structure and Economic Performance* (New York: Rand McNally, 1970), Chapter 11.

10. Christopher Layton, *Ten Innovations* (London: Allen and Unwin, 1972), PP. 96-97.

11. *Ibid.*, Chapters 5, 10, and 12.

12. *La Construction électrique et électronique française* (Paris: Center d'Étude des Revenus et des Coûts, 1970), Chapter 5.

13. John E. Tilton, *International Diffusion of Technology: The Case of Semi-Conductors* (Brookings Institution, 1971), Chapter 5.

14. VIe *plan: rapport général du comité électronique. informatique et industries des télécommunications*, February 1971, p. 1.

15. It could be argued that at the outset of the Fifth Plan in the middle 1960s the first priority was to encourage a merger movement in the industry, and therefore the internal effectiveness of the firm was a secondary problem. Such an approach, as argued before, excludes the strategy of fostering large firms by supporting the growth of the most aggressive and profitable businesses. With the merger movement running its course, effective management of the firms becomes a more important consideration. There are some signs, such as the PIT's threat to alter quotas in favor of the more effective firms, which suggests that the government is becoming aware of the issue.

16. Gareth Pooley-Dyas, "The Strategy and Structure of French Industrial Enterprise," DBA Thesis, Harvard Business School, 1972.

17. Nicolas Jécquier, "Computers," in Raymond Vernon, ed., *Big Business and the State* (Cambridge, Mass.: Harvard University Press, 1974).

18. Freeman, "R and D in Electronic Capital goods."

19. Tilton, *International Diffusion of Technology*, Chapter 3.

20. M. Castagne, G. Bussac, D. Courtalon, and G. Gilbert, "Les Problèmes des transfers technologiques—les industries électronique et électrotechnique européene" (Fondation Nationale des Sciences Politiques Service d'Étude de l'Activité Économique, 1970), p. 19.

21. The actual category is entitled "Frais d'études et d'assistance technique." Clearly this includes research or development activities undertaken on contract or the results of studies sold abroad, but at the same time it might include "know-how" associated with production. Certainly in France's trade with the Third World, this "know-how" would form a large part of this category, but this would not be so in trade with the developed countries. Two considerations suggest this. First, know-how is sold to support licensing agreements, and it is extremely unlikely to flow in the opposite direction. Second, I know of many cases of French sales of "R and D" to developed trading partners and many cases of French sales of know-how to the Third World, but only isolated examples of French know-how sold to the developed countries. What was really contained in each category was finally ascertained by interviews with those responsible for trade data.

22. Castagne, Bussac, Courtalon, and Gilbert, "Les Problemes," p. 19.

Chapter 6. Organization, Culture, and Economic Behavior

1. The Interactionist school of Kurt Lewin.

2. See Chester A. Barnard, *The Functions of the Executive* (Cambridge: Harvard University Press, 1950).

3. Phillip Selznick, *Leadership in Administration* (New York: Harper and Row, 1957), p. 31.

4. The word is used here in the sense of Crozier, *Bureaucratic Phenomena.*

5. Suzanne Berger, Peter Gourevitch, Patrice Higonnet, and Karl Kaiser, "The Problem of Reform in France: The political ideas of Logical Elites." *Political Science Quarterly,* September 1969.

6. Alfred Chandler, Jr., *Strategy and Structure* (Cambridge: MIT Press, 1962), p. 383.

7. *Ibid.*

8. Unpublished papers of Bruce Scott, Harvard Business School.

9. This includes work of Gareth Pooley-Dyas and Heinz Tannenbaum under the direction of Bruce Scott.

10. Chandler, *Strategy and Structure.*

11. Peter B. Clark and James Q. Wilson, "Incentive Systems—A Theory of Organizations," *Administrative Science Quarterly,* September 1961, pp. 129-167.

12. Herbert Simon, *Administrative Behavior* (New York: MacMillan Company, 1955), Chapter 4.

13. This analysis owes a deep debt to Thomas Szasz, *The Myth of Mental Illness* (New York: Harper and Row, 1961), particular Part III, and to Erving Goffman, *Behavior in Public Places* (Glencoe, Ill.: The Free Press, 1963).

14. Harold Guetzkow, for example, has written that "Other things being equal, it would seem that the greater the frequency of interaction, the greater will be the degree of institutionalization among organizations" ("Relations Among Organizations," in Raymond Bowers, ed., *Studies on Behavior in Organization,* University of Georgia Press 1966).

15. Both examples are taken from Harold Guetzkow's article, "Relations Among Organizations." The first example refers to David Truman, *The Governmental Process: Political Interests and Public Opinion* (Alfred Knopf, 1951), and the second to Reinhard Bendix, "Bureaucracy and the Problem of Power," *Public Administration Review* (Summer 1945), pp. 194-209.

16. Richard Lester, *As Unions Mature; An Analysis of the Evolution of American Unionism* (Princeton: Princeton University Press, 1958), p. 116. The quote is taken from Guetzkow, "Relations Among Organizations."

17. Work conducted at the Parkman Center for Urban Affairs in Boston suggests this. The evidence is drawn from conversations with the director.

18. Although Jowitt and I have discussed these issues, and his work has been published in the *American Political Science Review,* we reached this conclusion independently.

19. Kenneth Jowitt, "An Organizational Approach to the Study of Political Culture in Marxist Leninist Systems," *American Political Science Review,* September 1974, p. 1173.

20. Cynthia McClintock. This material is taken from drafts of chapters of an MIT political science dissertation still in progress.

21. Berger, *Peasants Against Politics* (Cambridge: Harvard University Press, 1972), particularly Chapter 5, "Rural Organization in Brittany, 1911-1967."

22. Joe Bain, *Industrial Organization* (New York: Wiley, 1969).

23. Marc Roberts, "A Framework for Explaining the Behavior of Resource Allocating Organization," unpublished paper, Harvard University, Department of Economics, 1972.

24. Fredric Scherer, *Industrial Market Structure and Economic Performance* (New York: Rand McNally, 1970), Chapter 1.

25. See, for example, Nelson and Winter, *Neoclassical vs. Evolutionary Theories of Economic Growth: Critique and Perspectus* (Institute of Public Policies Studies, Discussion Paper No. 46, April 1973) (Yale University, New Haven).

26. Such an argument is extensively developed in a recent study by Marc Roberts at Harvard, and this analysis draws on that discussion. (Marc Roberts, "A Framework for Explaining the Behavior of Resource Allocating Organization," unpublished paper, Harvard University, Department of Economics, 1972.) The logic underlying Roberts' analysis is quite similar to the logic in the analysis developed in this chapter and presented in my dissertation. I also appreciate Roberts' permission to read a preliminary draft of his book on public and private utilities; the quotations that follow in the text are from an early manuscript of that book.

27. Nelson, p. 16.

Chapter 7. The State at Home and Abroad

1. See Chapter 1.

2. See Chapter 3.

3. See Chapter 1.

4. *Ibid.*

5. Merrick Garland, "Industrial Reorganization in Britain," Harvard University Honors Thesis, 1974.

6. See Alexander Gerschenkron, *Economic Backwardness in Historical Perspective* (Cambridge: Harvard University Press, 1962).

7. See Joseph G. La Palombara, *Interest Groups in Italian Politics* (Princeton: Princeton University Press, 1964), and *Italy: The Politics of Planning* (New York: Syracuse University Press, 1966).

8. See Grant McConnell, *Private Power and American Democracy* (New York: Knopf, 1966).

9. See Robert Dahl, *Who Governs? Democracy and Power in an American City* (New Haven: Yale University Press, 1961).

10. See, for example, Stanley Hoffmann, *Decline or Renewal? France Since the 1930's* (New York: Viking Press, 1974); Michel Crozier, *The Bureaucratic Phenomena* (Chicago: University of Chicago Press, 1964). See also Chapter 2 here.

11. *Ibid.*

12. See, for example, Ezra N. Suleiman, *Politics, Power, and Bureaucracy in France; The Administrative Elite* (Princeton: Princeton University Press, 1974).

13. *Ibid.*

14. *Ibid.*

15. Steven Englund, "The French Disease," *New York Review of Books,* May 15, 1975, p. 33.

16. See Hoffmann, *Decline or Renewal.*

17. See Stephen Cohen and Charles Goldfinger, *From Permacrisis to Real Crisis in French Social Security; An Essay on the Limits to Normal Politics* (Berkeley: University of California, Institute of Urban and Regional Development, March 1975).

18. Robert Berrier, MIT, notes from dissertation prospectus.

19. Raymond Vernon, *Big Business and the State* (Cambridge: Harvard University Press, 1974), chapter on France.

20. *Ibid.*

21. Lawrence and Lorsch, *Organization and Environment: Managing Differentiation and Integration* (Boston: Division of Research, Graduate School of Business Administration, Harvard University, 1967).

22. See Vernon, *Big Business and the State.*

23. Peter Katzenstein has independently developed a similar argument in considering a somewhat different problem, the impact of transnational relations on foreign economic policy. Considering the case of the United States and France, he concludes that the foreign economic policy of the two countries reflects differences in domestic structures, particularly the relation of the state to society. The thrust of his analysis supports both the logic and conclusions developed here. His paper, "Transnational Relations and Domestic Structures; Foreign Economic Policies of Advanced Industrial States. . . .," will be pubslished in *International Organization* in January 1976. We reached similar conclusions, interestingly, by looking at similar problems and materials.

24. See Susan Strange, *Sterling and British Policy: A Political Study of an International Currency Decline* (New York: Oxford University Press, 1971).

25. See Asa Briggs, "The World Economy: Interdependence and Planning," from *The Shifting Balance of World Forces, 1898-1945,* C. L. Mowat, ed., Vol. 12, *The New Cambridge History,* 2nd ed. (Cambridge: Cambridge University Press, 1968).

26. See E. H. Carr, *Nationalism and After* (London: Macmillan & Co., 1945).

27. See Karl Polanyi, *The Great Transformation* (Boston: Beacon Press, 1971).

28. See Carr, *Nationalism and After.*

29. See Peter Alexis Gourevitch, *International Trade, Domestic Coalitions, and Liberty: Comparative Response to the Great Depression of 1837-1896* (Working Paper, November 9, 1972).

30. See Fred Block, "The Political Economy of U.S. International Monetary Policy, 1941-1971, (dissertation, University of California, Berkeley, Department of Sociology, December 1974); and David P. Calleo and Benjamin M. Rowland, *United States and World Political Economy: Atlantic Dreams and National Realities* (Bloomington: Indiana University Press, 1973).

31. See Samuel Huntington, "Transnational Organizations in World Politics," *World Politics,* April 1973, Vol. XXV, No. 3.

32. See François Hetman, *Les Secrets des Giants Americains* (Paris: Seuil, 1969).

33. This confusion, for example, appears in Edward Morse's treatment of Gaullist France, *Foreign Policy and Interdependence in Gaullist France* (Princeton: Princeton University Press, 1973).

34. See Strange, *Sterling and British Policy.*

35. See Huntington, "Transnational Organizations."

Index

Agriculture, 52
Allen, Thomas, 37, 44
Aujac, H., 8
Authority patterns: and organizational structure, 38-41, 104-106, 166-167; in France, 41-48, 160; in the United States, 43-45, 168-169; in the Soviet Union, 43, 44; state influence on, 177-180
Automobile industry, 16, 20

Bain, Joe, 181
Banks and banking, 4-5, 89; and steel industry, 11, 71; in French economy, 12-13, 54-55, 192, 199-201; in German economy, 12, 54, 200; and oil industry, 67-68; and electronics industry, 86-87
Banque de France, 199
Banque de Paris et des Pays-Bas, 67, 86, 199-200
Bell Telephone Laboratories, 40, 80-81, 146
Bendix, Reinhard, 160n
Berger, Suzanne, 179
Block, Fred, 210
Boeing Aircraft Company, 16, 40
Bouvier, Jean, 55
Brooks, Harvey, 141
Bull affair. See Machines Bull
Bureaucracy: independence of, 7; characteristics of, 41-42, 44, 191-197; change in, 45-46, economic role of, 52-53. See also State, The
Burns, Tom, 22, 161
Business-state relations: history of, 51-55; paternalistic pattern of, 55-58, 63, 199; entrepreneurial pattern of, 58-65, 199-204; and leadership contacts, 59-60, 63. See also names of specific industries

Calleo, David P., 210
Carr, E. H., 209
Cartel des Dix, 67
Cartels, 6, 57-58; in steel industry, 69-70; in electronics industry, 85-86
Centre National d'Études des Télécommunications (CNET), 95-96

CFP. See Compagnie Française des Pétroles
CGE. See Compagnie Générale d'Electricité
Chandler, Alfred, 90, 162
CII. See Compagnie Internationale de l'Informatique
Clark, Peter B., 167-168
CNET. See Centre National d'Études des Télécommunications
Coal industry, 4, 68-69
Cohen, Stephen, 7, 198
Colbert, Jean Baptiste, 58
Commercial Treaty (1860), 56, 57
Commissariat Général du Plan. See Planning Commission
Common Market. See European Economic Community
Compagnie Française des Pétroles (CFP), 67-68, 206
Compagnie Générale d'Electricité (CGE), 79, 84, 86, 96, 136, 139, 155
Compagnie Internationale de l'Informatique (CII), 77, 83, 92, 108, 135; formation of, 76, 79, 149; sale to Honeywell-Bull, 139, 143, 154-155
Component industry: technological development in, 80-82; product competition in, 82-83; American dominance in, 83
Computer industry: French policy for, 74-80, 149, 206; American dominance in, 77, 83
Concorde SST, 14, 154, 204
Control Data Corporation, 74, 76, 83, 140, 148
Control systems, 23-24
COPEP (Permanent Planning Group for Electronics), 74-75, 143
Corps des Ponts et Chaussées, 59, 60
Crédit Mobilier, 54
Crédit National, 97, 199
Crozier, Michel, 34, 41-48, 104, 105, 131, 134, 161, 165, 166-168, 172, 178, 179
CSF, 79, 86, 97, 98, 134-138, 150, 153; merger with Thomson-Houston, 84, 87

Dahl, Robert, 194
Dassault Aircraft Company, 16

227

[